"*Saigon Kids* is a vivid, beautifully written coming-of-age memoir set in Saigon during the tumultuous year that led to full-scale fighting by U.S. troops. It's also a hilarious white-knuckle tour of misadventures that, had they any idea, would have done in Les Arbuckle's parents."

—Laurel Delp — Writer, Editor, and Saigon Kid

"I was totally enthralled with *Saigon Kids* and found it to be a wonderful account of Southeast Asia. It is a timely, warm, and at times, humorous account of two completely at-odds cultures. You won't be disappointed. Les cleverly captures the sights, sounds, language and smells of Saigon during a unique period of turmoil for both the South Vietnamese and in-country Americans. I highly recommend this read for an enjoyable and fascinating journey. *Saigon Kids* is an accurate overview of what it was like to live in this Vietnamese City. I know because I was there."

—Lee Hansen — AFRS Saigon Radio Disc-jockey, 1963-65

SAIGON KIDS

An American Military Brat
Comes of Age in 1960's Vietnam

by

LES ARBUCKLE

TURNER
PUBLISHING COMPANY

Turner Publishing Company
Nashville, Tennessee
www.turnerpublishing.com

Saigon Kids: An American Military Brat Comes of Age in 1960's Vietnam

Cover Design: Georgiana Goodwin
Layout & Design: Roberto Núñez

Library of Congress Catalog number 2017950545.
ISBN: (paperback) 978-1-63353-633-3, (ebook) 978-1-63353-634-0
BISAC category code HIS027070 HISTORY / Military / Viet Nam War

Printed in the United States of America

Dedication

This memoir is dedicated to Sister Kenneth Regan, who taught me to read and write, and my parents, Bryant Joseph Arbuckle and Margaret Mooreen Arbuckle, who gave me something to write about.

Preface

People have often asked me what it was like to live in Saigon during this volatile period in history, so to them I now say, "This is what it was like." I began writing *Saigon Kids* forty years after leaving Vietnam. I wanted to create a gritty and realistic account of what I experienced in Saigon, so be prepared for rough and crude language, unusual sexual situations, violence, suffering, inter-species animal rape, and much self-deprecating humor.

My brothers, Lynn and Lowell, helped a lot with their memories of our family life, but the memories of my social life are necessarily mine alone. Where my memory is hazy, details and dialogue have been gently recreated or reimagined. Some of the dialogue, especially some of the more ordinary conversation, is composed of phrases I remember very well for reasons I'll never understand. The more mundane aspects of my everyday life in Saigon are sometimes stark and clear in my mind, while the circumstances surrounding the life-changing events reside in fog. I'm sure I've gotten a lot wrong, but memory is a fickle friend.

In order to protect the guilty, I have changed most of the names in the book except for the people in my immediate family. Also, Sister Kenneth Regan, Mrs. Elizabeth Tyson, David Phu, and Mrs. Jacqueline Shaffer and her son, Harrison, and his band, The Esquires, are known here by their real names.

Beverly Whealton (not her real name) is a combination of two girls I had eyes for as a teenager (the other was one Bonnie G.), both of whom scorned my clumsy advances in equally clumsy ways. I have combined the events surrounding my failed attempts at romance with these two girls (and Bonnie's best friend), which also includes a fair amount of actual dialogue, dredged from the depths of my memory of those angst-ridden moments.

—Les Arbuckle, September 2017

Acknowledgments

Let me begin at the beginning. This book would not have been possible except for the help of a lot of people, and to them I say "thank you," from the bottom of my heart:

To my brothers, Lynn Arbuckle, Lowell Arbuckle, and Leland Arbuckle, who shared their memories, photos, and stories.

To Zachary Klein, my first mentor and an excellent mystery writer, who first set me on the path to publication with his kind words and selfless encouragement.

To Anne Mini, also an excellent writer and editor, who took great pains to educate me about the ins and outs of the Memoir genre and all things literary.

To Therese DeAngelis, a wonderful editor, patient, kind, and precise.

To my friends in the Encinitas Library Writing group, and the Walpole Writer's Group: Ed, Dave, Ray, Joe, Glenda, Alex, Jennifer, Gail, Frank, Gunther, Harry, Pam, Donna, Maureen, and George, who gave me their concise and insightful opinions, and suggestions, week after week.

Many thanks are also owed to Brenda Knight and all the fine people at Mango Publishing, who saw the value in *Saigon Kids* and brought it to market.

If not for the relentless efforts of my wonderful agent, Roger S. Williams of the Roger Williams Agency, this memoir may not have seen the light of day. Roger believed in my story and remained optimistic during my darkest hours, and for that I owe him eternal gratitude.

My love and appreciation goes out to my wife Joyce Lucia, and my daughter, Emily Rose Arbuckle, for their encouragement and support over the long road to publication, and for putting up with my obsession(s).

And to the all of the *Saigon Kids* who made life interesting for me, I say, "Thanks for the memories!"

Table of Contents

Chapter One

Coup: November, 1963

S aigon is boiling hot. Next to me, dozens of spinning wheels and the metallic grinding of tank treads have set *Le Qui Don* Street sizzling with energy. A half-track belches a black cloud of fumes, so I grab a clean breath and slice through the diesel haze with one hand covering my nose. A juggernaut of Vietnamese military vehicles rumbles noisily down the street, stretching for a half-dozen blocks as the army approaches the palace of Ngo Dinh Diem, the president of the Republic of South Viet Nam. The autumn air is dead still, thick with heat and sweat and the promise of violence.

My father's warning—to get off the street if tanks are rolling—rings in my head like a fire alarm, so I pick up my pace, rushing to get home before the shooting starts. Right now, the streets of Saigon are no place for a fourteen-year-old American boy. I'm the only person in sight who isn't armed.

On the corner a half a block ahead, a Vietnamese officer squawks orders at a squad of ARVN (Vietnamese Army) soldiers hustling to assemble a .50-caliber machine gun behind a pile of sandbags. In the back of covered transport trucks, Vietnamese troops sit quietly in the shadows, hunched over their loaded weapons, staring silently into space. The soldiers look scared, knowing, as they surely must, that today some of them will die.

At the intersection with *Ngo Thoi Nhiem* Street, a tank wedges into a space in the column and a soldier's head pokes out of the manhole of the turret, his face grim beneath his steel helmet. I wave, but he ignores me, concentrating instead on the slow, relentless thrust of the line ahead, clearly afraid for his life.

The sound of the convoy has smothered the usual manic chirping of the birds, and a torrid, dreamy stillness has settled over the neighborhood. Translucent razor-sharp spears of light slant through gaps in the canopy of tall elm trees above, churned-up dust sparkling in the rays like glitter in a fireworks show. I hurry past elegant colonial-era villas: haunted mansions secure behind locked gates and shuttered windows, their occupants as invisible as ghosts. The squeal of tank wheels and the inescapable drone of engines charges the atmosphere as the rebel forces push their way toward the presidential palace, only two blocks from my home.

Then I hear a pop and a high whistle, and the whole world explodes. Near the palace, a tank jettisons a massive blast, and the shock wave hammers my chest like a medicine ball. Machine guns leap to life, punching out a staccato *thukka-thukka-thukka* as another mortar whips into the air. The ground quakes. I hear excited shouts next to me, then the tailgate of a troop-carrier truck bangs open. Soldiers scramble out, dashing toward the palace with their weapons ready.

I panic and bolt for home, my heart pounding so hard it feels like the buttons on my shirt are going to pop off. I fly around the corner onto *Phan Dinh Phung* Street, skitter past our front gate, and throw open the screen door. I see my parents squatting under the dining room table and my father, Doc, begins waving wildly, yelling, "Down! Get down!" I lurch frantically through the living room, drop to the floor, and slide across the tile on my chest, coming to a stop under the table. The next tank-blast shakes the entire house, and the table legs chatter against the floor like castanets. The malignant odor of cordite drifts through our open windows.

I glance towards the front of the living room where my youngest brother, Lowell, only nine years old, cringes wide-eyed under the coffee table next to the couch. He looks like he's going to make a run for the cover of our table until Doc holds his hand up and shouts, "Stay there!"

Our dog, Irving, is a blur of black and brown fur, running wildly between the door and table as each nerve-wracking explosion triggers a fresh round of nerve-wracking barking and whining. Finally, Doc eases out from under the table crouching low, grabs Irving by his collar and shuttles him out to the rear courtyard. He pushes Irving through the door, slams it behind him, and scoots back under the table just before the thunder of another volley.

"Jesus Christ!" he blurts out. "I haven't heard anything like *that* since the Marshall Islands!"

Mother seems calm, but the queer little smile on her face isn't a happy smile. It's a terrified, doing-my-best-but-I-don't-know-if-I-can-take-anymore smile. Her curly, dark hair is a tangled mess, her head pressed firmly against the underside of the table. Rivulets of sweat drip down her neck, darkening her red blouse. Her thin hands shake violently, and I realize she's on the verge of hysteria.

Suddenly, the color fades from her face and her expression goes blank. "Where's Lynn, for God's sake?" she asks, feverishly clawing at Doc's arm. The shakes have got a grip on her throat, too. "Does anyone know where Lynn went?"

Lynn, eleven years old, is my other younger brother. She's forgotten that he's hanging out with his friend David Phu, at David's house out near Cholon.

"He's at David's house," Lowell shouts.

The pop and whistle of yet another mortar sends Irving racing in circles, barking, whimpering, and jumping against the screen door. A deafening tank blast judders our front windows so hard that it seems like the glass should shatter into a thousand pieces, but it doesn't.

Doc peels Mother's clenched fist from his forearm and takes her hands in his. "It's all right, Miggie. He's all right."

"Well, why doesn't he call?" she asks. Tears roll down her cheeks.

"He's probably under a table, too," I say, and instantly regret it.

Doc puts his arm around her and shoots me an angry stare. "They probably shut the phones down, Miggie," he says, gently. "It's standard operating procedure in a coup."

Doc massages Mother's shoulder, reassuring her that Lynn will be safe at David's house. He gives her a cigarette, but she can't keep the match steady enough to light it, so he lights it for her. She sucks down a lungful of smoke and suddenly I feel ashamed for making wisecracks.

To me, nothing could possibly taste better than a cigarette, right now. Adrenaline loves nicotine. While the battle roars down the street, it occurs to me that Lynn has gotten the better deal in this nasty situation. He can hang out with his friend until the violence stops, but I'm stuck here with no pals and no way to sneak a smoke. Watching Mother crack up is making me antsy and nervous, and I want to run somewhere, do something, but there's nowhere to run and nothing I can do.

Doc is busy eyeing the front door as if he's expecting soldiers to rush in at any moment, so I slide closer to Mother and try to offer some sort of consolation, hoping I can calm her down a bit. But I'm not really sure how dangerous our situation is, or what to say. I suppose a misplaced mortar round could blow the house apart and kill us all, but it doesn't seem likely, although you wouldn't know it from the look on Mother's face. I put my arm around Mother's shoulders and peer out the open front door as an American Military Police patrol drives by slowly. Hopefully, the MPs will make sure the battling armies point their weapons in the right direction.

The Vietnamese radio stations have gone off the air, but according to Doc, the American radio station, AFRS (Armed Forces Radio Station), is still broadcasting. Until the assault on the palace is over, AFRS will provide the only information available beyond what we can hear or see happening in the streets outside of our house. "When things calm down," he says, "I'll turn on the radio and see if there's any news."

"Will you go get Lynn?" Mother asks.

Doc considers her request for a moment, then says, "Maybe when things quiet down a little."

'But what if they evacuate us?" Mother pleads. "What if they make us leave without him?"

Doc rubs her shoulder for a moment then looks into her eyes. "We're not going anywhere without Lynn, Miggie. I promise. Okay?"

She nods and swipes at her teary red face with her forearm.

"Do you guys know where he lives?" Doc yells.

"Yeah," Lowell says.

"No," I say.

"Over near the market, on the way to Cholon," Lowell adds.

Taxis won't be cruising the streets, but we're one of the few American families that own a car, a big black 1949 Ford. I think Doc is planning to go get Lynn, but the only person here who knows where David Phu lives is Lowell.

After an hour of huddling in fear under the table, Doc suggests we go upstairs and sit in the hallway between the bedrooms. "We'll be safer there—no windows or open doors."

Lowell runs to the stairs and goes up first. Mother sends me up next, and Doc follows her with the radio tucked under his arm. We sit down on the floor in the dark hallway and lean against the walls to wait.

It's quieter in the hallway. The battle is focused on the palace, so even though shells are still falling, they sound farther away. After a while, Doc decides to fetch a couple of cocktails from the downstairs bar. Mother needs a drink, badly. He crawls down on hands and knees.

A few minutes later, I hear shattering glass and Doc cursing: "God *damn* it to *hell*! Shit!"

I immediately think he's taken a bullet, probably from a well-hidden sniper with orders to shoot amateur bartenders on sight. When Mother hears the breaking glass, she's struck with terror, and Lowell looks like he's going to cry.

Mother gasps, lifting her hand to her open mouth. But before she can scream, Doc calls up, "I'm okay, I'm okay!"

I'm not sure who's most relieved, Lowell, Mother, or me. Hearing her shriek would have been scarier than having my hair set on fire, and Lowell's lower lip is still quivering.

Then Doc yells, "Leslie! Come get your mother's drink!" I slither downstairs and crawl back with a scotch and soda, handing it to my grateful mother. She takes it in her shaking hands, the ice cubes clinking against the glass like wind chimes. She lifts the drink to her mouth and drains most of the booze in one needy gulp.

About an hour before sunset, the shooting slows down, so Doc decides that there will be no better time to rescue Lynn. He mouths a few comforting lies to Mother, then Lowell follows him down the stairs and out the back door into the alley where we keep the car. I remain in the upstairs hallway with Mother, who looks like she's going to start crying again.

"Do you want another drink?" I ask.

She hesitates for a moment, then hands me the glass.

"Scotch and soda," she says softly.

I hurry downstairs and mix the drink as quickly as possible. I glance at the stairway to make sure Mother hasn't followed me, then rush into the alley behind the kitchen, fish a half-finished cigarette out of my pocket and light it. I take a few fast harsh puffs and crush the butt under my foot before hurrying back upstairs with Mother's drink (which tastes awful).

While she's nursing her drink, I tell her I'm going to close the door to the balcony in my bedroom. I know the door is already closed, but she can't see that from where she's sitting. I crawl in on hands and knees. Thanks to the battle, no one had noticed the bulge in my pants caused by the fat lump of bills in my pocket, money I'd made trading currency on the black market. I pull the bottom drawer out of my dresser and stuff the wad of cash way in back, where Lynn and Lowell won't think to look. I push the drawer back into place, then hurry back into the hallway where Mother is still quaffing her drink.

Around forty-five minutes later Doc comes through the back door with Lynn and Lowell. He pours himself a Scotch, straight up (plus a fresh drink for Mother), and they crowd into the upstairs hallway where Mother and I have been waiting.

"Is it bad out there?" I ask Lynn.

"Every street is blocked off," he says.

"If I didn't have my AFRS ID card they'd never have let us through," Doc says. "One of the benefits of being with the press."

Mother is calmer now that Lynn is back, or it could just be that her third Scotch has worked its magic.

At sunset, Doc suggests we try to get some sleep. "It could be a long night," he says.

We crawl into our rooms and flop on the bed, but a minute later Doc steps into the room. "*Under* the beds, guys!" Doc says. "If a mortar round hits the house you'll be wearing the ceiling!"

The floor under my bed is cool against my back, but the slats supporting the mattress are just a few inches from my nose. I see the legs of my desk on one side of the room, the dresser against the wall opposite. Lynn and Lowell are under their own beds, on either side of me. Our bedroom windows face out onto Phan Dinh Phung Street, where the lights of speeding police cars pierce the darkness of my room, red streaks racing wildly across the walls. In the distance, the sporadic crackle of small-arms fire and the mournful wail of an ambulance siren punctuate the uneasy silences. There's nothing to do but wait. Morning will come, eventually.

The gunfire continues all night, making deep sleep impossible. The bed is too low to allow for tossing and turning, so I remain on my back, like a corpse. When I finally manage to doze off, a fresh volley from the .50-caliber machine gun down the street snatches me awake and I whack my forehead against the slats, which amuses the hell out of Lynn and Lowell.

Since we'd arrived in Vietnam, I had concluded that a normal existence wasn't possible here—this coup d'etat was just the insanity du jour, part of the constant conflict between the Vietnamese Army (who had the support of the people), and the Ngo Dinh Diem administration which was on the verge of turning it into an all-out civil war. The profoundly disturbing events of the previous eleven months were just as extraordinary in their own way, a macabre carnival of anger, violence, and suffering. But every crisis seems to generate a new one in its wake; nothing is ever resolved. For months, I've watched in astonishment as South Vietnam's government careens from one disaster to another, like a drunk smashing into garbage cans as he staggers down a dark alley.

As I drifted into sleep, I remembered that I'd initially felt utterly miserable about leaving Florida to move to Vietnam, a country that was rapidly turning into an absolute madhouse. I realized how silly I'd been.

Saigon was the best place I'd ever lived.

Chapter Two

Orders: 1962

I n 1962, no map I had ever seen included a country called Vietnam. In late May of that year, my brothers and I had been looking forward to another long, hot summer in Florida when my father received orders from the Defense Department to report for duty in Puerto Rico. Doc had told us that in a few months, we would sever our ties to Pensacola and the dull, hot suburb of Warrington where we lived, and begin life over again at the Roosevelt Roads Naval Base in Celba, Puerto Rico. None of us wanted to move, but a military family isn't a democracy. Military transfers are commands, not suggestions or requests.

A couple of weeks later, on a sunny day in June, Lynn and I got off the school bus at our usual stop, the corner by the bridge over Bayou Grande, just down the street from our house. I was twelve, soon to be thirteen, and Lynn was eleven. We walked up the hill from the bridge, and I noticed my parents new Fiat in the driveway next to the black 1955 Cadillac belonging to my older brother, Lee. But it wasn't even three o'clock. Mother and Doc never came home early unless one of us was bleeding too much for a Band-Aid, so we hurried inside to see who was hurt.

Doc had come straight from his office at the Pensacola Naval Air Station and was still wearing his khakis. Stem to stern, he looked like the epitome of the Navy career man: above, a razor-clean, regulation crew cut; below, sharply creased pants ending at high-gloss brown shoes polished to a mirror finish. Five rows of colorful campaign ribbons decorated the space above the left breast pocket of his jacket—testaments to his service in the Pacific during WWII and Korea. His right sleeve was adorned with several long black hash marks, each stripe denoting a length of service, one for every four years. In the Navy's career system, the hash mark was the sign of the lifer.

Lee had picked up Mother early too, so we knew something important must be in the air. She was wearing high-heeled shoes, a slim red dress with large white polka-dots, and a necklace of fake pearls as if she were still at the bank, standing behind the teller window taking customer deposits and cashing checks. Her knees were touching Doc's as she sat catty-corner on the edge of the worn couch in our living room. About the only time my mother ever cried was when Doc was reassigned. When Lynn and I walked in, it looked as though she'd been crying for a while.

My three brothers and I gathered around to hear the bad news. Lee was perched on the arm of the couch, next to Mother. Lowell, my youngest brother, was sitting cross-legged on the floor, in front of the coffee table. The living room was dim; the drapes were closed, and no one had bothered to turn on a light. Lynn kneeled down on the rug next to Lowell. I dumped my saxophone case and books on the brown carpet and sat down. Then Doc said, "Vietnam." I had no idea where or what that was.

Mother apparently had never heard of it either. "Where?" she asked.

Doc gathered her hands in his before he answered. I wasn't sure whether he was trying to comfort her or if he was afraid that if her hands were free she'd take a swing at him. "French Indo-China," he replied.

She wrenched her hands away, and an irritated scowl settled on her face like a dark cloud. "I don't even know where the *hell* that is, Bryant. Isn't that in Asia?" My brothers and I were the only ones who called him Doc, a nickname he'd picked up as a corpsman during WWII.

Doc spoke in pillow-soft tones, every word carefully calculated to soothe my mother's fears, a technique he'd mastered out of necessity, long ago. "It'll be like when we went to Hawaii, only a little farther."

She raised her cigarette to her lips, fumbled her purse open and took out a handkerchief. She prepared to wipe her eyes, grimly stubbing out the cigarette in the ashtray and shooting Doc an angry glance.

"I'll be going over next month to get started with the radio station," Doc continued. "As soon as I find housing, I'll send for you and the boys."

The Navy had recently decided that Doc was needed more in Viet Nam than in Puerto Rico, so they changed his orders. In two weeks, he would be flying to Saigon without us.

Dark lines of makeup streaked down Mother's cheeks as tears ran from her red eyes. She dabbed at her face with the twisted hanky. "When will that be? How long?"

When Doc and Mother argued, they usually matched each other's tone and anger level tit-for-tat, but I think Doc knew better than to raise his voice to her today. "I don't know, Margaret. I won't know till I get there."

"What about Lee?"

"He's got a good job, and he'll be in college," Doc rationalized, trying his best to console her. "It'll be the same as if we'd gone to Puerto Rico."

Lowell looked like he might cry, too. A sickly child, he had developed an aversion to doctors and hospitals. "Are we gonna have to get more shots?" he asked softly.

We all hated the half-dozen vaccinations we'd already gotten for Puerto Rico, Lowell most of all. "Just you," I whispered, spreading my hands wide, "and the needle's *this* big." Lynn smirked, sharing my pleasure in watching Lowell's lower lip begin shaking like fresh Jello.

Doc glared at me and I clammed up. "Maybe a few, Lowell," he explained patiently. "Viet Nam has diseases they don't have in Puerto Rico."

Vietnam—I learned months later when two Navy nurses began jabbing multiple needles into both my arms—was the home of a vast smorgasbord of diseases, including cholera, plague, typhus, diphtheria, smallpox, tuberculosis, syphilis, malaria, dysentery, and leprosy. After the first few stabs, I stopped counting how many holes the nurses had poked in my arms. If Doc had entertained any fears about taking my asthmatic mother (who'd endured nine bouts of pneumonia) or Lowell into a disease-infested country like Vietnam, he didn't let on. I think he knew better than to get Mother any more riled up than she already was.

Mother was also upset because Lee would have to stay behind. Military Brats could remain dependents until they finished college, but unless Lee learned to speak Vietnamese, he couldn't attend college in Saigon. He would be the first of us boys to leave home. His transition from living at home to being on his own would be sudden and complete: Viet Nam was 9,479 miles away.

Lee worked evenings as a Top 40 disc jockey in Pensacola and took courses at a local community college during the day. He had a car, a job, and a steady girlfriend. Once he was settled into an apartment, he could start a new life. If he wanted, he could even put down roots, keep his friends and become part of the community—the normal life he had been denied during his years as part of our military family. For the rest of us, though, life was about to take a sharp turn into the feverish chaos of an unusual country on the other side of the world.

Chapter Three

Military Brat

I guess I wasn't cut out to be a military Brat, because the thought of leaving Florida filled me with despair. Like most military families, we'd been traipsing around the country for years, but until the Puerto Rico/ Viet Nam transfer came up, it didn't seem so bad. When we had moved from Hawaii to New Jersey, or from Philadelphia to Pensacola, I was too young to be unhappy about it. My brothers were my best friends and they were always there. But in the last couple of years I'd changed, and moving had become a thing to be feared and hated. We'd been in Florida for three years, and Pensacola was beginning to feel like home.

I hoped that when Doc's tour of duty ended, we might be able to return to Florida. I might even be welcomed back into the old neighborhood as something of a hero—an experienced globetrotter, spinning tales of adventure in the Far East. I was sure my old friends would be enthralled as I recounted my exploits, punctuating each tall tale with bits of Vietnamese slang and a droll wittiness gleaned from rubbing elbows with well-traveled strangers.

Sometimes I'd catch Mother ironing or doing dishes and badger her about moving back to Florida after Doc's tour of duty. Even if she was in a good mood, she always frowned if I whined about moving, a skill I'd only recently developed. Without looking up from her task, the stock answer would automatically come tumbling out of her mouth: "It's only going to be a couple of years, and then we'll come back, Leslie."

I had heard this line so many times I was sure that somewhere there must be a Department of Defense manual with a list of clichés to feed your children if they complained about relocating. "Yeah, sure," I would say, staring at the floor, resentful.

"Well, I can't control where the Navy sends your father any more than you can," she'd reply, irritated by my surly attitude. "He can ask to be transferred back here, but you know as well as I do they send him wherever they damn well please."

"But I never have any friends!" I argued. "As soon as I get to know anybody, we leave!"

At this point in the conversation, she always stopped what she was doing to say what she always said when we moved to another town. "You'll make new friends there." Then she'd stitch a custom-tailored silver lining around the cloud of bad news: "I'm sure the American school there has everything the schools here have. Besides, we're not going 'til your father sends for us. That could be months, so relax, already."

She must have had that manual memorized.

In Pensacola, I'd found a place for myself in the local social scene, and for the first time in my life, my best friends weren't my brothers and their friends. I had always been a transient, a nomad, the new kid in school, but now I wasn't an outsider anymore; I was an insider, privy to the secret pathways and privileges of my middle-class suburban neighborhood.

I knew the yards you could cut through and which ones had dogs that would take a hunk out of your ass if they saw you climbing their fence. I knew the homeowners who would pay me to cut their grass, what stores I could hang out in, and the hideouts in the woods where my friends and I could smoke without being seen. I even knew which cashiers would believe me when I told them the cigarettes were for my parents.

If I moved away, my best friends, Bill, Mike, and Harold, would gladly assume the pleasant task of keeping an eye on Betty Jo and Karen, two of the neighborhood girls currently in the process of sprouting breasts, experimenting with makeup, and squeezing into skin-tight Capri pants. I'd had my eye on both of them for some time, but now I'd be out of the picture, forgotten, forced into a life of exile in a foreign land I could barely find on a map. My newly blossoming social life would soon be dead. How many American kids could there be in a place as far away as Saigon?

I was trying to make sense of this mess when I saw the preview for a new movie, *The World of Suzie Wong*, "coming soon to a theater near you." After seeing the trailer for *Suzie Wong*, I began to fantasize about my imminent future in the Orient. Dramatic Technicolor visions of adventure, international intrigue, and romance sprang wildly to life in my adolescent imagination. In my mind, I could see myself bouncing along in a rickshaw, lazily lighting a cigarette as the driver drew me through the dank, crowded streets of Saigon. My fantasy destination was always a casual rendezvous with a sultry, long-haired Asian beauty in a tight, slinky dress, slit up to the middle of her sensuous curvy thighs. In her small (but tastefully decorated) second-floor apartment, we would while away the hours on a rattan sofa, smoking exotic cigarettes, reading exotic magazines to each other, making exotic love. Why a mature Asian beauty in a sexy dress would be romantically drawn to a thirteen-year-old American boy never entered my mind.

Eventually, I decided that Vietnam, being much farther away than Puerto Rico and therefore deeply mysterious, was not such a bad destination as Navy transfers go. If Saigon resembled what little I had seen of *The World of Suzie Wong*, then it might even be cool.

In June, Doc left for Viet Nam and I set about enjoying six months of carefree living while we waited for his call. It had been years since he'd been out of the house for more than a few days. Now I was old enough to take advantage of Mother's more relaxed, accepting approach to discipline. After school, I'd toss my books on the couch and take off to Navy Point Shopping Center. At the shiny linoleum counter of the drugstore's old-fashioned soda fountain, I'd hop on a stool and order a Coke with a dash of vanilla in it, a sophisticated choice, I thought. When my friends showed up, we'd pool our money, buy several packs of cigarettes and sneak into the woods behind the shopping center where we'd smoke ourselves sick.

I was pretty sure smoking was bad for me, but I'd been surrounded by smokers since the day I was born and developed a love for tobacco the first time I tried what the older kids called "weeds." And why *wouldn't* I want to smoke? In 1962, smoking was cool! Doctors smoked, athletes smoked, musicians, movie stars, my uncles, aunts, Mother, Doc, Lee. As far as I could tell, the entire world was lighting up, sucking down Big Flavor one satisfying puff at a time. Movie stars, doctors, and sports celebrities peered from the pages of every magazine and newspaper I saw, happily assuring me that the worst that could happen was the dreaded Throat Irritation. Of course, in those same newspapers and magazines, the cure for Throat Irritation was often advertised on the next page: Coca Cola!

It was easy to hide my smoking from my parents, because my constant tobacco reek dovetailed perfectly with theirs. But one day, shortly before Doc left for Vietnam, I made the mistake of trying to filch a pack of cigarettes from a freshly opened carton of Tareyton in his dresser. The crime took longer than planned, and Doc walked in and caught me red-handed. When he realized I was trying to steal his cigarettes, not his underwear, he began the first of what would be many short, nasty lectures. "Keep your hands off my *goddamn* cigarettes," he'd said, snatching the fresh pack out of my hand. "They'll stunt your growth, stupid."

When he left for Saigon, my fear of punishment went with him, but the peace and comfort of tobacco stayed close to me.

In spite of several sexual fantasies involving Suzie Wong, a handheld fan, and rattan furniture with soft cushions, I remained haunted by the prospect of a desolate future without friends or a real home. I couldn't shake the feeling I was missing something; that the parade of life was about to pass me by as I watched from the sidelines. We'd never returned to any of the towns we had lived in, and in my heart I knew this move would be no different. I soon began thinking of Pensacola as a place I *used* to live—and I wasn't even gone. Tobacco became the dear, understanding friend I could always depend on to lift me out of my adolescent misery, at least for a little while.

Doc finally sent for us in November, 1962, and a few days after Christmas we said goodbye to Lee at the Pensacola airport. When we might see him again was anyone's guess. Once Doc's tour in Viet Nam ended, we could once again be transferred anywhere in the world.

From Pensacola, we flew to San Francisco to wait for a military standby slot on a commercial flight to Saigon. Mother, Lynn, Lowell, and I took up residence in a cramped brick apartment at the Presidio, an old Army base near the Golden Gate Bridge. For two weeks, we lived out of our suitcases. Mother called the airport every day to ask about available standby seating for four on any flight to Saigon; every day she was denied.

The Presidio was a hub for military families waiting to fly to destinations along the Pacific Rim. Some of the kids I met there were on their way to Hawaii, some to Seoul, South Korea; some to Yokohama, Japan; but none except us were going to Vietnam. This confirmed my fears that *no* American kids lived in Saigon. Our stay at the Presidio seemed to be a microcosm of my life: Arrive, make friends ("acquaintances" would be more accurate), then leave, never to see any of them again.

Before we left Florida, Doc had wired enough money for what was supposed to be a one-week trip, but that week had passed, and we began running out of money. Mother put her pride aside and went to the International Red Cross for help, but they didn't have much sympathy for Navy wives and refused assistance. She finally managed to borrow a few dollars from Navy Relief (the Navy's welfare agency), but it still wasn't enough, so we squeaked by with only the most basic necessities. We could eat at the base cafeteria, so no one was starving, but we had little money for medicine (for Mother and Lowell), laundry, or toiletries.

Suddenly we were flying. After two weeks of waiting at the Presidio, Mother finally found a flight with available seats for all four of us. San Francisco faded into the distance behind us. Ahead, the blue Pacific Ocean extended to the long, gentle curve of the horizon. Our plane was a nearly obsolete four-engine prop-jet, packed to capacity with a hundred other people. We were suspended between sea and sky, gliding towards Hawaii and our ultimate destination, Vietnam.

Chapter Four

Vietnam

T he slow plane and extended layovers—a long wait in Hawaii, several hours in Guam, another hot afternoon at tiny Wake Island, and an overnighter at Clark Air Force Base in the Philippines—made an already long trip seem endless. It was early one morning in mid-January, 1963, when we departed Clark AFB for the final leg of our journey.

Once airborne, we lowered our tray tables and the stewardesses delivered breakfast: Tin TV dinner style plates of scrambled eggs, soggy toast, and limp bacon. When they brought us three meals instead of four, I thought they had goofed. Then I realized that Mother had paid for food for us boys, but not for herself. I tried to get her to eat mine, but she wouldn't hear of it. "You eat, dear," she said. "I'm not hungry, and we'll be there soon anyway." It was with no small amount of guilt that I ate my lukewarm breakfast, occasionally glancing over to see her staring forlornly out the window, blowing clouds of smoke into the air-conditioned cabin.

My mother, Margaret Mooreen Davis, was tall, rail-thin, and beautiful, with wavy dark brown hair and long, perfect eyebrows I always wished I had inherited. Her dark complexion and high, delicate cheekbones were the only visible evidence of a Cherokee ancestor: Her great-grandmother.

Miggie, as my father sometimes called Mother, was a small-town girl from a big family in Mission, Texas, less than one mile north of the Rio Grande river. Besides her brother and four sisters, she had more aunts, uncles, and cousins than she could remember, many of whom she had never met. Hers was an old Southern family with roots that predated the Revolutionary War; not rich, mind you, just old.

Before she met Doc, she had moved just once in her life, to Mission, from Hugo, Oklahoma, where she was born. She had come home from school one day during those dark years of the Depression to find that her home had burned to the ground, leaving only a chimney standing amongst a pile of smoldering ruins. Her parents salvaged what little they could, then loaded the entire family into her father's pickup truck and drove to the Rio Grande Valley. They lived on her uncle Quiller's farm while her father built a small house at the end of a short dirt road in Mission. It was the only real home Mother ever knew.

In south Texas, folks referred to women like my mother as 'High-Strung,' a catch-all term for anyone deemed sensitive or easily excitable. Because of her asthma and endless bouts of pneumonia, Mother always kept the medicine cabinet crammed full of a drugstore's worth of pills and remedies. These legally prescribed cures, however, were only for the run-of-the-mill diseases and ailments doctors treat every day. For the lifestyle of a High-Strung military wife (and High-Strung military men), the preferred anxiety-relieving medicine was generous quantities of booze. Mother's favorite was Hamm's Beer—but on the plane to Viet Nam she had so little money that she couldn't even afford one bottle of Hamm's.

Her stable, quiet family life in Texas couldn't have prepared her for the peripatetic life of a military wife, but she loved Doc and wanted to be with him even if that meant flying to the ends of the earth, which in this case, it did. I wasn't sure how long Mother went without eating on our journey, but on the final leg of the trip she chain-smoked her way through her last pack of cigarettes. As for myself, I had been without cigarettes for weeks and would gladly have traded any amount of food for the pleasure of one smoke, though I could never admit that to her.

We'd been flying over the South China Sea for several hours when Viet Nam finally appeared on the horizon. I pressed my cheek against the window, gazing past the ghostly spin of the propellers. Far below me, a thin ribbon of white sea-foam lapped against the coastline. Beyond that, a lush landscape checkered with rice paddies spread out like a dark green carpet. A network of canals and dirt roads separated the shallow paddies, an occasional water buffalo sloshing through the water as the owner prodded it from behind. A few minutes later, our plane tilted into a steep descent, and the crisscross runways of *Ton Son Nhut* airport came into view. In the distance I saw Saigon, the rusted rooftops of shantytowns on the edges of the city forming a shabby skirt around the modern buildings in the center.

The plane touched down and taxied to a low, white shoebox of a building surrounded by hangars, corrugated tin Quonset huts, and service buildings. At the opposite end of the terminal, the control booth jutted into the sky, shining in the sun like a diamond. I watched eagerly from my seat, craning my neck to look out the windows on either side of the aisle.

The engines chugged to a halt, and several Vietnamese men in overalls rolled a steel gangway into position.

When the door to the cabin swung open, I squeezed into line with the rest of the passengers, stepping out of the air-conditioned plane with my brothers and Mother behind me. The sun was directly overhead, bearing down with a harsh yellow intensity. I walked quickly down the stairs, blinking back the brilliant light. A light zephyr swept the dry airfield, filling my nose with the smell of asphalt, aviation fuel, and the dust of my new home. In the distance, shimmering waves of heat rose from the pavement, distorting the helicopters and palm trees until they looked like images in a funhouse mirror. The terminal was less than 100 yards away, but I was sweating by the time I reached the door.

Inside, soldiers wearing wide black armbands emblazoned with the bright gold initials of the Military Police stood silently near the open doors, tan khaki pants bloused into their combat boots, pistols snug in fat leather holsters. Vietnamese airport officials wearing filmy, white short-sleeved shirts hurried back and forth, checking documents and jabbering rapidly in Vietnamese, French, and pidgin English. The ceiling fans stirred a hot breeze through the building as GIs in green fatigues hustled in and out of the terminal, their sleeves rolled up to their sweat-stained armpits.

I couldn't see Doc anywhere. I wondered if he had forgotten we were coming.

"You boys stay here," Mother said. "I'm going to have your father paged."

A few seconds later we heard the page echo through the terminal. "Bryant Arbuckle, please come to the ticket counter. Bryant Arbuckle."

It was a small terminal, so he would certainly hear the announcement if he were there. Mother was still scanning the crowd when she rejoined us after the second page.

"Where's Doc?" I asked.

"I don't know, Leslie," she said, tersely. "I told him we'd be here at two o'clock."

Lynn pointed at the wall on the far side of the terminal. "The clock up there says it's twelve."

We had flown through nine time zones since leaving San Francisco, two since leaving the Philippines. Mother had called Doc from Clark AFB, but it was clear now that she hadn't calculated our arrival time correctly. She looked at her watch and frowned. "Well, *crap*. I told him the wrong time."

"Why don't you call him at home?" I asked.

"There's no phone at the house yet, honey, and he won't be at the station this late."

Mother lit her last cigarette, and blew grey plumes at the ceiling as she surveyed the terminal. She fidgeted with her purse for a moment, her eyes narrowing as little hills wrinkled up on her brow. "I'm going to get us a ride." She marched back to the ticket counter, and I saw the clerk point to the MPs by the terminal door. After a brief conversation, Mother and one of the MPs walked outside, out of sight.

Lynn, Lowell, and I stood with our hands in our pockets, gawking at this Asian/American beehive, fascinated by the fuss. A sensation of motion filled the air, a whirlwind of activity that was much more intense than I'd seen at the other military airports we'd passed through. Everything and everyone was moving except us. New arrivals shuffled by, looking confused, trying to get their bearings in the sweltering heat. Short, brown men pushed carts piled high with luggage as officials barked orders in Vietnamese, a dissonant new language to my ears. A few feet away, an American woman with three small children scanned the airport just as my mother had, standing on tiptoes to look for a husband or ride that wasn't there. We watched as she herded the kids toward the ticket counter, carrying the youngest in her arms.

After a few minutes, Mother walked back inside. "Let's find our luggage and follow the MP. He's getting a car for us."

We dug our suitcases out of a pile, cleared customs, and dragged everything outside. A black Mercedes pulled up. With the help of the Vietnamese driver, we loaded our bags in the trunk. When the MP showed the driver an address, the driver nodded enthusiastically. "OK," he said. "I go now, OK."

"Do you know where we're going?" I whispered nervously to my mother. Since the car pulled up I'd been sizing up our driver, ever aware of my status as man of the family, a position I'd earned by default. We were getting into a car with a Vietnamese man we'd never seen before, to be driven god-knows-where, in a strange city on the other side of the world. Plus, we were completely broke and knew not a single word of Vietnamese. This could be a mistake, I thought, fearing that we might be kidnapped and held for ransom, or sold into slavery in some jungle hellhole.

Mother didn't share my paranoid fantasies, though. "The driver knows." She dug in her purse, looking for loose change. "I hope your father's there. I don't have money for a tip."

Mother sat up front and the rest of us scrambled for the window seats in the back. Our car rolled out the front gate of the airport into the cultural environment of Vietnam—a civilization already thousands of years old when the United States was born.

When we reached the main road, our car merged into a swarm of bicycles, motorbikes, and little yellow-and-blue Renault taxis scurrying through the streets like ladybugs. A wide strip of dirt on either side of the road separated the blacktop from shops, stores, and restaurants. Whenever a driver turned off the pavement toward the shops, choking clouds of dirt billowed into the air. We quickly learned to roll up our windows when these miniature dust storms were blowing our way.

On either side of the street, narrow buildings two or three stories high were crammed together like books on a dirty shelf. Most were pale shades of blue, brown, yellow, or green stucco, separated by alleys barely wide enough for a person to squeeze through. Heavy rains had splattered mud up the walls during the monsoon season, and each building displayed a dirt-brown fringe running along its base.

Many of the stores had apartments on the upper floors, their balconies strung with clotheslines full of freshly-washed laundry drying in the sun. Behind the laundry, windows covered by tall wooden shutters were closed against the afternoon heat, waiting to be thrown open later in the day to summon a passing breeze. An erratic spider's web of telephone and electrical wires ran from one crooked wooden utility pole to the next, spanning the space above the crowded street.

In every direction, the unfamiliar competed with the unusual for my attention. A toothless old woman in baggy black pants and shirt, sandals, and a conical straw hat (a *cai non*) walked past the shops, balancing a long wood pole on one shoulder. She'd wrapped one arm over the pole to steady it, swinging the other at her side in perfect counterpoint to her stride. At each end of the pole, straw baskets heavy with ripe fruit and vegetables hung like weights on a scale. The baskets bounced gently as she passed the shops, her sharp voice cutting the air as she advertised her merchandise.

In front of one store, a tin roof supported by four poles cast meager shade on a group of thin, nut-brown men squatting flat-footed on their heels, smoking, talking, and throwing dice. A few feet away, a man in long, loose white pants and a white shirt leaned against an open restaurant door. He was thin and frail, lazily stroking his wispy white *Ho Chi Minh*-style beard as he watched children playing in the dirt. Except for sandals, the smallest of the children were naked from the waist down, a fashion choice that perplexed me. Like the adults, they had thick, straight, jet-black hair.

When we lived in Hawaii, the Filipino, Hawaiian and Japanese kids I played with had straight black hair, but they had been the minority. Now, I was the minority.

Above the shops, signs and billboards illustrated in brash shades of gold, red, yellow, green, and blue boldly proclaimed their specialties in Chinese or Vietnamese, with an occasional French or English word thrown in. Hundreds of years before, French colonists had converted written Vietnamese into the Latin alphabet, modified with a host of unusual accents and diacritics to achieve authentic pronunciations for words that traditionally had been written in Chinese.

We struggled to pronounce the words on the signs, and our driver turned to us with an amused expression. Our attempts at speaking Vietnamese must have sounded like hammers striking an anvil to him. I'd finally concluded that he was just a regular working man, not an unscrupulous blackguard bent on kidnapping us. I gave him a sheepish grin, embarrassed by my prejudice and tone-deaf attempts to speak his language.

The variety of motorized bikes swirling crazily around our car was this teenage boy's dream come true, and my eyes darted from one to the next in amazement. Lambretta, Itom, Suzuki, and Vespa motor scooters filled the air with soot and the buzzing of engines as they zigzagged their way between cars and bicycles with up to three passengers holding on tight.

Behind us, a garishly painted three-wheeled vehicle chugged along, a rhythmic popping spouting from its muffler. The contraption looked as if a motorcycle had slammed into the middle of a love seat from behind and taken it for a ride. Similar to a rickshaw, there were wheels on either side of the seat. The fenders above the front tires were a dull red, the rear fenders blue, the seat cushions upholstered in faded green plastic, the wheels and trim a dirt-encrusted chrome. A collapsible canvas canopy shaded two elderly Vietnamese women sitting on the dusty seat. On their laps they balanced a large, brown wicker basket containing several ducks that quacked in protest as the machine rattled noisily along.

Their driver wore a frayed, tan pith helmet, rubber sandals, grease-stained khaki pants rolled to mid-calf, and a wrinkled, graying, long-sleeved shirt that may originally have been white. A cigarette dangled from his lips, and between drags he worked the brake, clutch, or gas. Occasionally, he'd honk the little clown-horn on the handlebars at a cab or bike driver who swerved too close.

This was the *xich lo may* or *motor-cyclo*; cheaper to hire than a cab, but more expensive (and faster) than the single-passenger foot-powered *cyclo*. Among the motor-cyclo drivers, pith helmets and long sleeve shirts rolled up to the elbow were common attire. Like a uniform, the outfit set them apart from the cyclo drivers who usually wore a pith helmet or cai non with shorts and a T-shirt—a cool alternative when engaged in the hard labor of pedaling a cyclo in the tropical heat.

Suddenly, a young girl whizzed past our car on a black Solex moped, weaving and jousting for space as she stared straight ahead into the traffic, one hand atop her cai non, the other gripping the handlebars. She was elegantly dressed and couldn't have been more than a few years older than me. She was perfectly proportioned in face and physique, as beautiful as any woman I'd ever seen. I was mesmerized by the way she swerved through the dust and dirt of the busy street, her full-length white dress split from each ankle to each hip. Beneath the dress, she wore loose-fitting white pants of what looked like silk or satin.

I eventually learned that this outfit was an *ao dai,* a traditional Vietnamese outfit worn by educated and middle-class women. She was the only woman in traffic wearing an ao dai, but many of the motorists and pedestrians wore the cai non. Having felt the blazing intensity of the sun, it was easy to understand why.

After a couple of miles, the traffic backed up, forcing us to stop. A moment later, an odor as repugnant as the smell of rotting garbage wafted through the window and into my virgin nose. I scrunched up my face at the stench. "What's that smell?" I said.

"He who smelt it dealt it," Lynn said, trying to mask his disgust. Lowell held his nose and laughed.

"I did not!" I defended. Fart accusations were serious business among us kids. "It's coming from outside, stupid."

Our driver turned once again to look at us from behind his Army-issue sunglasses. His otherwise hairless chin sported a small mole from which three long black hairs had sprouted. Several teeth were outlined with gold trim. "*Nuoc mam.*"

"Nook bom?" Mother repeated.

The driver grinned and gave us the thumbs-up sign. "Nuoc mam numba one fish." He pointed to the right, and we saw racks of fish drying in the sun next to a roadside café. "Nuoc mam OK."

"I think my nose is scarred for life," I muttered under my breath.

"Now it's like the rest of your face," Lynn said.

"If you don't *shut up*, you're gonna get some scars," I said.

Lowell was eyeballing us closely, preparing to get out of the way if fists started flying. He'd been trapped in our backseat fights often enough to have developed a finely tuned evasive strategy involving equal amounts of ducking, weaving, and crying.

Mother spun around in her seat and shouted, "*Cut it out!*" She rarely yelled at us, but after the long trip, her nerves were shot, and she was about as High-Strung as I'd ever seen her. The car started moving again and we continued quietly gaping at the new world flickering around us like a slide show. Soon, the traffic thinned to a trickle and the car picked up speed. We saw fewer shops and more swatches of undeveloped land.

We were passing through the *Gia Dinh* district, a suburb between the airport and downtown Saigon. On either side of the road, I saw weed-covered fields surrounded by low brick walls. Several half-finished buildings sat in the center of the fields, an exoskeleton of bamboo scaffolding hugging their exterior walls. Shirtless workers wearing cai non hauled bricks and mortar as they crawled over the scaffolds like sailors climbing rope to man the sails.

Moments later, we turned off the blacktop onto a dirt road. Along the side of the road, hardened tire ruts cut deep into the dirt, leftovers from the rainy season. Another turn put us in front of six chalk-yellow townhouses facing an empty field. The houses were cookie-cutter identical. The car crunched to a stop, and we exited into a big cloud of dust.

For months I'd imagined we would be living in the city, surrounded by the thrill of a vibrant urban center. I noted with disappointment that downtown Saigon was miles away. Except for a few dusty trees, everything around me seemed to be concrete, dirt, or scrub brush. The new neighborhood looked like hell.

Two kids I took to be Americans ran through the field in front of the houses, throwing a football. While Mother went to the door of 26A-11 Chi-Lang Street and rang the bell, Lynn, Lowell, and I propped ourselves against the car, staring at the kids.

The taller kid's hair was combed into an oily-looking pompadour, his shirttail hanging over his pants like a flag. I instantly thought of the greasers who used to hang around the hoagie shop near the apartment in South Philly where we lived when I was nine. The greasers were all bigger than me, and they smoked, cursed, and beat on the pinball machines with impunity, irrefutable evidence they were bad kids. I was afraid if I got too close they'd want to beat on me, too. Now I felt the same uneasiness, as if South Philly had followed me to Vietnam.

Fortunately, this greaser-kid was my size. He looked in our direction, raising the ball as if to throw it my way. "Go out," he said.

I took off, sprinting across the rubble-strewn lot to catch a pass from my new neighbor. After we exchanged a few tosses, he introduced himself as Herbert "Spike" O'Reilly. He lived next door with his parents, brother, and two sisters.

Lynn, Spike, and I began throwing the ball to each other while Lowell and Spike's younger brother Freddy ran through the field begging for us to heave it their way. Spike finally gave in. "Okay, but you'd better catch it." He reared back and threw a perfect high spiral pass. Freddy ran as fast as he could, but the ball sailed over his head, landing in a patch of weeds. "Not so hard!" Freddy yelled.

"Run faster!" Spike demanded.

"I can't!"

Spike flashed me a smile, then shouted at Freddy. "Well, *shut up* then!"

Torturing little brothers has always been a privilege reserved for older brothers. Like me, Spike was a master. Lynn was too big to tease without getting into a fight, but as far as Lynn and I were concerned, Lowell was fair game.

Freddy retrieved the ball and lobbed it into the dirt several yards in front of me. Spike rolled his eyes in disgust. "He throws like his sisters."

Out of the corner of my eye I saw our front door swing open, revealing a matronly Vietnamese woman wearing a green ao dai decorated with gold embroidery. Her gentle, round face was ringed by black hair pulled into a tight bun. I recognized her as Thi Hai, the maid in a photo Doc had sent us months before. When she saw Mother, her eyes opened wide with surprise.

"Is Bryant here?" Mother asked, turning to look at the numbers next to the door.

"Oooohh, Madame!" the woman said. "OK, OK! You come in *now*."

Mother waved at us to follow her into the house, so we left the driver to struggle with our bags and ran through the gate, eager to see our new home. I waved goodbye to Spike and followed Lynn and Lowell inside.

Chapter Five

Chi Lang Street

Thi Hai showed us in, then put her palms together next to her ear, tilting her head. "Monsieur *here*."

"Sleeping?" Mother asked. "Let's go wake him."

Before we could get to the stairs, Doc clomped down with a bleary-eyed look of surprise on his face. He was wearing only Bermuda shorts and flip-flops, an outfit that ensured I would never bring girlfriends home for fear they would keel over at the specter of my shirtless, hairy-chested, middle-aged father.

"Christ, Miggie, you're early," Doc said. "I had my driver all set to take me to the airport."

"We took so many flights," Mother said. "I think I'm still on Honolulu time or maybe Guam. She gave Doc a long, tight hug and smiled for the first time in months. "I missed you so much. Can you get me something to eat? I'm starving."

If ever someone needed fattening up, it was my mother. She usually rang the bell at about 100 pounds, but I was sure she'd lost a few on the trip.

Doc patted Lowell on the head, looking us over. "Have you guys gotten bigger or have I gotten smaller?" There would be no hugs from Doc, manly or otherwise. "You met Thi Hai already, I guess. Come on in the kitchen."

"Can we go back outside?" Lowell asked.

"Yeah, but stick around," Doc said.

While Doc showed Mother the new house and fixed her something to eat, Thi Hai tipped the driver, who had brought our luggage into the house. Lynn, Lowell, and I ran outside to see what Viet Nam had to offer. Nothing inside the house could possibly be as exciting as what lay just outside our front door.

Spike and Freddy were still tossing the ball in the field, and they waved us into the action. Lowell and Freddy resumed their pleading, running eagerly through the field even though we ignored them. After several throws, Spike tossed the ball over the gate into his yard. "C'mon, I'll show you the village."

The five of us walked down the dirt road and took a left. Around the corner, I saw more pastel stucco row-houses on one side of the street. But on the other side, only a few yards from the village, were several large, single-family French colonial homes.

We stopped in front of one of the homes, hanging on the wrought iron gate, ogling the house like a pack of street urchins. Behind the gate was a two-story stucco villa with garage and driveway, a terra cotta tile roof, and separate servant's quarters. High brick walls protected it as if it were a castle. Along the top of the walls, shards of broken glass jutted from of the mortar like the teeth of a dragon. Above the broken glass, razor-sharp strands of barbed wire, taut between metal posts, ran the length of each barrier. A burglar who tried to climb over this wall would be cut to the bone, a nasty but effective deterrent to petty thievery.

Les, Lowell, and Lynn
Front courtyard, 26-A 11 Chi Lang Street, Saigon, 1963

We walked past the last house on the street, pausing at the head of a wide dirt trail that led into the village. Just beyond where we stood, a makeshift sidewalk of boards wound its way between dozens of shacks that were jammed tightly together, leaning one on the other. The walls and roofs of the shacks appeared to be jerry-rigged from whatever could be found and nailed down: hunks of plywood, sheets of tin, flattened beer cans, palm fronds, tar paper, rotting bamboo mats. The huts resembled the improvised forts Lynn and I built for fun when we lived in Florida.

No power lines or telephone wires went into the village, nor did it appear that the residents had running water. Hygiene, Spike explained, was primitive; a toilet was a pail or basin, emptied into the street or into one of the small murky canals nearby. The shacks seemed barely high enough for an adult to stand erect inside. An errant fire in this maze of alleys and refuse would have burned most of the village to the ground within minutes.

Gaunt women, some carrying babies on their backs, hauled water from the filthy canal in rusty buckets. They went about their chores, laboring under the weight of the water and babies without a glance at us. A few children noticed us and smiled as they passed by. Having seen where they lived, I couldn't imagine what they had to smile about. This village was nothing more than a slum, the lowest rung of the economic ladder in Saigon. The next step down was living on the street.

I'd never seen slums as extreme as these, but I must admit that they didn't bother me much. I was only thirteen, and a full understanding of the hardships I was witnessing had yet to find resonance within me. As awful as the spectacle of poverty and wealth side by side was, I easily accepted its reality as the way things ordinarily were in Vietnam. The length and breadth of this slum, like all of the many slums I would eventually see, was hard to reckon, but the depth of its wretchedness was obvious at a glance.

"Are we going in?" I asked Spike.

"No. My dad says it's too dangerous." He jerked his thumb at Freddy. "'Specially if I take shit-head here."

Freddy managed an embarrassed grin.

"I go in to buy firecrackers sometimes," Spike continued, "but my folks always yell at me if they find out."

We stood there for a bit, then walked back the way we came. Lynn, Lowell, and I said goodbye to Spike and Freddy and went inside our new house. We'd been gone a while, and I hoped that Doc hadn't been looking for us. The moment I had laid eyes on him, I remembered how hot-tempered he could be. Sooner or later, one of us would piss him off, but I didn't want it to be me.

After six months on a waiting list for American soldiers with dependents, Doc's number had come up and he was able to rent a suitable home and bring us to Viet Nam from Florida. Our townhouse was in the middle of a row of six, all formerly tenanted by French families, but now all occupied by American military families. An open living room and dining room took up the ground level; two bedrooms and a bathroom were upstairs. The flooring throughout was cream-colored ceramic tile, cool in the shade and easy to keep clean. A small paved courtyard separated the dining room from the kitchen and maid's quarters at the rear of the house. In front, a high wall topped with barbed wire enclosed a postage-stamp-sized cement yard decorated with several potted palms. A wooden double gate opened onto the dirt road where we had first arrived. Like the more luxurious homes we'd seen, several strands of barbed wire protected the top of our gate. There seemed to be more barbed wire in Saigon than in the entire southwestern United States.

I had yet to see the entire house, so I ran upstairs for a look around our new home, expecting to see three bedrooms. In the first bedroom, I saw my parent's bed and dressers. Overhead, a wooden ceiling fan turned slowly. Three windows faced the dirt street out front. A door next to the windows opened onto a tiny balcony. But in the only other bedroom, three identical beds were set up, spaced a few feet apart. Our dressers were set against the wall next to my desk. We'd been delayed in San Francisco for so long that our furniture had arrived before we did.

That our new home had only two bedrooms was bad news. I was now going to be crammed into a room with Lynn and Lowell. In Florida, I had shared a room with Lee, but because he attended school during the day and worked at night, he wasn't around much. It was almost like having my own room.

Lee was the golden boy of the family. In high school, he'd lettered in football *and* band (trombone), earning straight As with little apparent (to me) effort. He had a way with the girls too. I didn't even kiss a girl until I was seventeen, but Lee was hiding condoms from my mother when he was still in high school. He had a car and a steady girlfriend, too, so I was sure he was getting laid. As a teen, he'd risen to the exalted status of Life Scout, and was privileged to wear a Boy Scout sash that displayed what I believed to be every merit badge known. How he accomplished this while remaining an avid smoker was, like everything else he did, beyond my comprehension.

Aside from the fact that we were brothers, smoking and playing in the school band were about the only things Lee and I had in common. In academics, girls, and sports, I had resigned myself to the fact that Lee could do anything I could do, but better. Now I was being forced to share a room with Lynn *and* Lowell, as if I were living in some kind of sniveling little Romper-Room kiddie-barracks. This state of affairs was worse than uncool—it was a demotion.

After exploring the upstairs, I found Mother, Lynn, Lowell, and Doc in the kitchen. Doc was giving them the scoop on the local drinking water. "Don't drink from the tap or you'll get Ho Chi Minh's revenge," Doc said.

"What's that?" I asked.

"Dysentery, diarrhea. The runs. You'll get stomach cramps and spend all your time on the toilet. We have to boil and bleach the water before we can drink it." He held up a large vodka bottle. "If you need water to drink or brush your teeth, get it from one of these bottles in the refrigerator."

For fear of dysentery, we quickly learned to drink only from the gin and vodka bottles in the fridge. If one of us poured a glass and couldn't finish it, we put it back in the refrigerator to minimize waste. As you might imagine, this led to some confusion, like the time a few months later when, hot and sweaty from running around the neighborhood with Spike, I went to our refrigerator for a drink.

When I opened the refrigerator door, I saw what I needed on the top shelf: a frosty glass of water, pure and clean, beckoning me like a siren, its cool wet pleasure the perfect antidote to my hot, dusty thirst. I lifted it to my lips in eager anticipation, tilted my head back, and filled my mouth with ice-cold refreshment.

A shock wave of heat seized my mouth and throat. Rivers of tears burst from my eyes. My esophagus burned like a blast-furnace. Holy crap, I thought, I've swallowed mother's fucking *asthma* medicine! I gripped my throat as alarm bells went off in my head. She'd warned us to be careful not to take her medicine accidentally. It could kill us, she'd said. Now, I'd gulped a shit-load of it. I thought I was going to die. I set the glass on the countertop and wheezed like a broken saxophone.

The fumes were nauseating, and I felt a sharp knot taking hold in my stomach. I'd never been poisoned before and wasn't sure what to do. After a minute, I realized that except for the brush-fire that had raged its way down my throat, I felt okay. I wasn't weak or dizzy, and fainting didn't seem to be in my immediate future. The house was empty, so I decided to wait it out. If my condition deteriorated, I could always stagger next door and unleash a desperate scream for help.

A few minutes later, Mother and Doc walked in. I leaped from my chair, full of questions, hoping for salvation. "What was in that glass in the fridge? Was it medicine? I drank some and my stomach hurts."

Mother stared into my eyes with dark concern, obviously wondering how much time I had left. "You weren't supposed to drink *that*."

"It was *terrible*," I said, worried that I might die, or worse, end up going to the hospital to have my stomach pumped. "What was it?"

She smiled a little, as if amused by my unscheduled flirtation with death. "That was gin, hon. We needed the bottle to hold water."

"Gin?" My shoulders sagged with relief. "God, that stuff tastes bad."

"Well, you're not supposed to drink it straight," Mother said

"*You're* not supposed to drink it at all," Doc added.

I explained what had happened. "That's the worst thing I've ever tasted. I thought I was going to die."

"If you drink enough gin," Doc said, "you'll get so sick you'll wish you *were* dead."

I swore then that I would never drink gin.

Once Doc had finished scaring the hell out of us with his dysentery speech, he showed us the maid's quarters behind the kitchen. It was a tiny apartment which had an equally small bathroom with just a toilet and sink.

Another wood fan spun lazily overhead as a single fat gecko basked in the hot air above the fan. In one corner, a dresser and a single bed were pushed against the wall next to the room's only window. A private servant's entrance led to a wide dirt alley. Thi Hai slept here most weekdays, Doc explained, and went home to her family on weekends.

The acute poverty of the nearby slums had dealt me the first blinding shock of cultural dissonance. The toilet in the maid's quarters was the second.

Our family shared one upstairs bathroom between the two bedrooms. It had a western-style white porcelain sink, bathtub, and toilet and a tile floor. But the maid's quarters had a Vietnamese-style toilet. This consisted of an eight-inch hole in the floor centered between two crosshatched cement foot-markers. Behind the toilet, a thin pipe snaked into the hole from a rectangular water bin placed high on the wall. Pulling on the long chain hanging from the bin started the flushing action.

The toilet looked impossible to use, but I quickly discovered that the secret was the ability to squat low, a position the Vietnamese cultivate from early childhood. Chairs were a luxury in Vietnam, especially among the poor. At the markets, on the sidewalks, and in the slums, most Vietnamese (and Chinese) routinely squatted or stood, unless they were in bed or lucky enough to have a stool or chair to sit on.

In our household of five, the upstairs bathroom always seemed to be in use whenever I needed it the most. On these occasions, I ran downstairs and hurriedly asked Thi if I could use her toilet. My bowels had no preference for toilet style, so I quickly and reluctantly mastered the Vietnamese squat.

Chapter Six

The My Canh Restaurant

S liced green scallions floated on clear broth like life preservers thrown to the rice paper dumplings and thin strips of red pork floating on the bottom of my bowl. The delicate aroma of ginger and soy sauce rose from the broth in a steamy wisp. I held an odd spoon, a flat-bottomed ceramic affair that matched the blue-and-white Chinese countryside scene on the bowl. Across the table, Doc cupped his rice bowl under his chin, tilting it up to push rice into his mouth with chopsticks.

Mother looked at him with disdain. "If Grandma Margaret saw you do that, she'd have a fit, Bryant."

Doc put down his bowl and picked a grain of rice off the front of his white short-sleeved shirt. He seemed to be teasing my mother by showing off his familiarity with the local customs. "That's the way the Vietnamese do it," he said, proudly.

Although it was 7:00 pm in Saigon, I was still on San Francisco time and felt like I hadn't slept or eaten in days. A few hours after we arrived, Doc had insisted we go to dinner downtown, at the Floating Restaurant, the My Canh. Situated atop a barge on the Saigon River, the restaurant had two stories. The kitchen was on the first level, but the second story, where we sat, was an open-air dining room. The canvas roof was supported by steel rods, but instead of windows, large glass panels had been installed around the perimeter to prevent Viet Cong guerillas from tossing in grenades.

A thin trail of rice led from my bowl to my lap dotting the white tablecloth in testimony to my failed attempts with chopsticks. Bits of egg, pork, onion, and peas were mixed with the golden-brown fried rice, but it was a struggle to get a sizable bite up to my lips. Picking up a dumpling or piece of chicken was easy enough, but rice was impossible. I decided to imitate Doc, lifting my bowl to push the rice into my mouth with the chopsticks. Lynn and Lowell quickly joined in.

Mother frowned at our rebellion, unhappy that we had so easily cast off the manners she'd drilled into us at the insistence of Doc's mother. But after a 9,000-mile journey and two weeks of lousy food, manners would have to wait.

The My Canh swayed gently as a motorboat with a red running light passed by the dock. Less than 200 yards away, the lights of downtown

Saigon glowed brightly, but on the opposite shore, the coalmine blackness
of the jungle pressed against the riverbank, where few lights were visible.
On that side, a few miles inland, the sparkly red trails of what looked like
Roman candles flashed against the night sky. Had I been in America, I
would have assumed it was fireworks.

"Mortars," Doc said. "The Vietnamese army's having a scuffle with
the Viet Cong."

On the Saigon side of the shore, couples held hands as they strolled
the bank of the Saigon River, enjoying the evening's cool stillness. Women
wearing cai non washed clothes and filled buckets with water while
raggedy children played on shore, laughing and running, chasing each
other as children do everywhere. As twilight gave way to night, I noticed
rows of saloons, shops, and restaurants on a nearby street. Above the bars
and shops, office buildings rose as high as five stories, their crisp lines
evoking the elegance of the age of French colonialism. The avenues and
boulevards were crammed with cars and motorbikes, horns honking, the
glare of brightly lit signs and streetlights reflected in their fenders. Under
the garish neon lights in front of the saloons, bargirls in white *ao dais*
teased the soldiers strolling the street, working hard to lure them into the
bar. As shopkeepers and office workers turned out lights and locked their
doors, the Saigon bar scene blossomed to life.

All evening, a thin, well-dressed Vietnamese man had been hovering
near our table, apparently telling a waiter to refresh my parent's cocktails
again and again. He wore a pinstriped black suit, white shirt, and brilliant
green tie emblazoned with an ornate embroidered red, yellow, and gold
dragon. His shiny black hair was slick against his head. He navigated
his way to our table and clasped his hands in front of his chest, smiling.
"Everything okay tonight, Mr. Arbuckle?"

Doc set down his chopsticks to dab at his mouth with a napkin.
"Excellent as usual. Margaret, this is Mr. Phu, the owner of the My Canh
and Cheap Charlie's."

Mother nodded and extended her hand gingerly. After seeing my
father use chopsticks like a shovel, she may have realized that in this part

of the world, etiquette might be quite different than what she'd learned in South Texas.

She seemed relieved when Mr. Phu shook her hand, bowed, and excused himself. He began moving among the tables, greeting customers with a smile and a nod. Waiters scurried from the lower deck with trays of drinks and food. Other diners talked softly, and the sound of clinking silverware rose above the My Canh restaurant as it swayed under the January moon.

I saw several Vietnamese (or possibly Chinese) families at nearby tables, but most of the customers were either American or, I guessed, French. At the table beside us, two sailors in brilliant white uniforms held chairs for their dates—beautiful, long-haired Vietnamese girls. Once the girls were seated, the sailors folded their canvas Dixie-cup hats into their belts and sat down. From the other side of the room, an American couple's children, a boy and a girl, each about Lowell's age, stared at us with curious eyes.

As I picked up my spoon to resume eating my wonton soup, Lynn elbowed me. "Les, look," he whispered, pointing to the Vietnamese family. "They're using forks."

The crowd on the My Canh began to thin out as we finished dinner. Mother swirled her drink impatiently, watching as Doc talked business with Mr. Phu, a regular advertiser on Saigon's Armed Forces radio station where Doc worked. I learned that because my father was the announcer for the My Canh's commercials, we would always receive preferential treatment at both of Mr. Phu's restaurants.

I placed my crumpled napkin next to my bowl and stood up. Lynn, Lowell, and I asked to be excused, then hurried down stairs and walked the gangplank to shore. When we'd arrived at the restaurant, I had noticed a tobacco stand in a kiosk near the end of the gangplank. It was still open, so I strolled over and peered with longing at the colorful packs of smokes. The surprising number of French, English, and Vietnamese brands I saw lining the shelves showed me that Saigon offered a rich new world of smoking to explore. But even if I'd had money, I couldn't risk buying cigarettes when Lynn was around. He'd rat me out in a minute.

I leaned against the stall and watched as several young, well-dressed Vietnamese men strolled hand in hand. It had never occurred to me that there might be places in the world where people were openly homosexual, something I'd never seen. When Doc and Mother finally came ashore, I asked, "Are they . . . you know . . . homos?" Lynn and Lowell giggled, but how else could I put it? Queer was such a derisive and offensive word, and in 1963, "gay" still meant "happy" to my friends and me.

Doc smiled at my question. "No, it's just a sign of friendship here."

We hailed one of the blue-and-yellow cabs that seemed to be everywhere. Doc and Lowell sat in front and Mother, Lynn, and I squeezed in back for the ride home. I even got a window seat without having the usual fight with Lynn. Doc gave directions to the driver, occasionally turning around to provide little bits of information about landmarks such as Notre Dame Cathedral and the presidential palace.

The full moon followed us through strange streets and dimly lit boulevards as the cab wound its way through Saigon. I wanted to see as much as possible, but my eyelids grew heavy. After a few minutes I dozed off. I felt Lynn shove me, pushed back, and awoke confused, my cheek stuck to the window. The cab was in front of our new house. I sleepwalked my way upstairs and flopped into bed with my clothes on, still jet-lagged from our trip.

_____

Chapter Seven

Spike

The next evening was "welcome to Vietnam" night at the O'Reilly's house. While the adults settled into an evening of booze and conversation, Lynn and Lowell went upstairs to play with Freddy and his sisters, Brenda and Roberta. Spike and I were alone in the dining room when he whispered, "Do you smoke?"

I couldn't believe my good luck. For weeks I'd been starving for nicotine, and I couldn't wait to rekindle the flame of addiction. "Yeah."

He swiveled his head in all directions, checking to make sure no one had an eye on us. "Follow me."

We walked into the kitchen, paused, then slipped through the maid's quarters and stepped into the warm night. I ducked the hordes of bugs swarming around the lamp above the rear door as Spike closed it softly behind him. We hurried into a narrow passageway between the town houses on the other side of the alley.

The way was dark, but the brilliant moonlight allowed my eyes to adjust quickly. Twenty yards in, we stopped where several passageways intersected near the light outside someone's rear door. Spike pulled a fresh pack of Marlboros from his pants pocket and offered it to me. I slid a cigarette out and passed it under my nose, savoring the sweet smell of tobacco. "Where'd you get these?"

He held out a match. "I buy 'em on the black market or sometimes from a GI. Sometimes if my folks aren't home I can swipe a pack."

"What's the black market?"

"Bootleg. GIs buy 'em by the carton at the Post Exchange and sell 'em to the street vendors, who jack up the price and sell 'em a pack at a time. They're fifteen cents at the Exchange, but fifty Ps on the street. A lot of the stuff you can get at the Exchange ends up on the black market."

"Fifty Ps?"

"Piasters. Dong. Vietnamese money."

I had a lot to learn, and Spike was a valuable source of guidance, filling in the huge gaps in my knowledge with information crucial to living the good life in Saigon. Compared to me, he was worldly. "What's with this 'numba one' stuff?" I asked him. "Our driver said it a couple times."

"It means it's the best. Numba ten means it's the worst. Everything's either numba one or numba ten around here." He took a big drag and blew dusky smoke into the air. "Marlboro numba one."

Suddenly, Spike whispered, "Ditch it." I threw my cigarette in the wet gutter behind us. Spike cupped his behind his back. At the entrance to the passageway, I saw Freddy peering into the darkness.

"What'd you want?" Spike yelled at Freddy.

"You're smoking! I'm gonna tell Dad!"

"I'll beat the *shit* out of you!" Spike screamed. Freddy turned and bolted for the safety of home. Spike had a way of getting right to the point.

"Will he squeal?" I asked. Doc would be pissed off if he found out I was smoking.

"Little asshole," Spike said, irritated. "He might. We better go in." He took a last drag from the cigarette and flicked the butt into the gutter. "My sisters definitely would."

Later that week, Spike and I agreed on secret code words to signal one another when we wanted to catch a smoke. *Hai Ba Trung* was one of the main boulevards in Saigon, and its name became one of our verbal cues for a trip around the block for a cigarette. *Phan Dinh Phung* was the street the American Commissary was on, but when we used the word, it meant, "let's ditch the little brats and go to the pool hall."

We eventually created enough passwords to keep our brothers and sisters guessing, but our code didn't always work, because they liked to follow us around and try to catch us smoking. With this information, they could lord it over us for special favors. The best way to escape their spying eyes was to leave the neighborhood completely, something they were forbidden to do.

Spike's dad was a Navy Chief who ran the print shop at *Ton Son Nhut* airport. They'd moved here from Oakland, California, the year before. Spike seemed eager to teach me what he knew, and I figured he was glad to have a fellow weed-fiend living next door. Though we were about the same age, he was in seventh grade and I was in eighth.

We sneaked inside through the back door, opened a couple of sodas, and went into the living room to sit among the adults. Freddy had taken up a safe position next to his mom's chair, opposite Spike. If he intended to tell anyone about our trip to the alley for a smoke, he'd have to do it while Spike looked on.

Spike's mother had brilliantly vivid red hair, and her skin was dotted with big, brown freckles. She wore ruby-red lipstick that was as brilliant as her hair, and her mouth was usually set in a good-natured smile. She had a deep, throaty laugh that was contagious; hearing it always made me want to laugh, too. But she wasn't laughing when we sat down on the floor—she apparently had noticed the hawkish way Spike was looking at Freddy. She looked at them both and frowned, as if to say, "Don't you two dare fight in front of our new neighbors." Spike briefly locked eyes with Freddy in an intimidating stare, then turned away. Freddy wouldn't squeal.

During a break in the conversation, Spike said, "You should have been here last year. A couple of Vietnamese soldiers stole two planes and shot up the palace where *Ngo Dinh Diem* lives."

Ngo Dinh Diem had been Vietnam's Prime Minister since 1954 and President since 1956. He'd brought one of his brothers, *Ngo Dinh Nhu*, to power as head of the country's secret police.

"There've been demonstrations against the government for persecuting the Buddhists," he continued. "And these two guys decided to try to kill Diem and Madame Nhu."

"Who's Madame Nhu?" I asked.

"She's Ngo Dinh Nhu's wife," Spike said. "Everybody hates her and Diem." Because Diem was a lifelong bachelor, Madame Nhu had assumed the role of first lady of Viet Nam, becoming the feminine face of the Diem regime. Her quick temper and abrasive, outspoken personality infuriated Americans and Vietnamese alike. The local and international press and wire services had begun calling her the "dragon lady" of South Vietnam.

This was the first time I'd paid any attention to political developments except for the recent Cuban Missile Crisis, when I figured we were all going to be incinerated in a nuclear blast. When they heard Spike, the adults turned the conversation to local politics.

Doc was sitting in the chair beside me, stirring his drink. "Things are heating up fast around here," he said, looking from Mother to Spike's dad,

Kevin. "The South Vietnamese Army got the hell beat out of them over in the Delta last week. Diem tried to make it sound like a victory, but the guys at work think he's full of crap."

"If Diem and Nhu don't get their act together, there's going to be hell to pay, that's for sure," Kevin said. "We've got too many Americans here for them to be screwing around."

"More planes are landing at Ton Son Nhut everyday," Doc added, "and every one is full of advisors."

Mother looked concerned. She knew the United States was involved in what the government liked to call a "police action," but what she had just heard went beyond any information she could have gotten stateside. "How many advisors are here now?" she asked.

"Officially, about 2,000," Doc said. Kevin nodded in agreement.

Doc paused, looking from Kevin to my mother, as if what he was about to tell her might be upsetting. "Unofficially, about 16,000."

"They're supposed to just help the Vietnamese soldiers with battle strategy," Kevin said, "and not get involved in the actual fighting, but that's hard to do when the VC are trying to shoot your ass off."

The next day, Spike invited me to a pool hall a few blocks away where we could hang out and smoke without interference. "There's usually a guy selling weeds out in front, so bring some Ps," he advised.

I begged some piasters from Doc under the pretext of getting a Coke from one of the local street vendors. Money in pocket, Spike and I casually strolled to the middle of the field in front of our homes, idly kicking rocks around, doing our best to appear innocent. If our siblings saw what we were up to, they might try to follow us, but I didn't see Lynn or Lowell or any of Spike's family. We walked to the far edge of the field, by the main street. After one last, furtive survey of the area, we moved quickly out of sight, down the street towards the pool hall.

As we walked, Spike told me that the pool tables in Viet Nam had no pockets. "They play billiards here," he said. "I'll show you how."

As we walked down the street, we passed a restaurant with a rickety shed next to it. Behind the open door of the shed were rows of slanted wooden racks covered with drying fish. On the floor of the shed, a metal pan gathered the juices as the hot sun desiccated the meat. I recognized the odor immediately.

"Nuoc mam smells like shit," I said.

Spike sucked a big whiff through his nose, savoring the awfulness of the stench. "Naw . . . shit smells better than nuoc mam."

"How can anybody eat rotting fish?"

"Nuoc mam ain't the fish, it's the sauce they make with the juice. Fish sauce."

I walked a little more quickly to get away from the smell. "Smells like numba two to me."

"You got it."

A block later, I saw the cigarette vendor standing outside the pool hall, a dilapidated tin building beside a row of small stores and shops. I gave Spike my money and he bought me a fresh pack of Pall Malls.

We went inside and after my eyes adjusted to the darkness, I saw two pool tables standing on a dirty wood floor. The only light in the room was a bare bulb hanging by a cord above the tables. As Spike had said, the pool tables had no pockets. On each table, three ivory balls sat on the green felt like snowballs on grass.

The proprietor, a man as bent, gnarled, and brown as an old tree, sat on a stool at the back of the room. Like most of the Vietnamese people I'd encountered, he was thin and short, with thick black hair. Spike approached him and held up four fingers. *"Bon muio dong* (forty piasters)?" he asked. The old man nodded and Spike handed him the money while I tried to remember the words he'd used.

Most of the Vietnamese phrases I knew I had learned from Spike over the previous two days, including the most popular profanities. He taught me that *du mamia* meant "fuck your mother," *mai bu cac* meant "eat my dick," *mai bu lo* meant "eat my pussy." He patiently showed me how to pronounce each profanity with the correct accent and nasal inflection. When insulting someone in another language, it's important to be understood.

While Spike explained how to play billiards, I unwrapped my Pall Malls and took a look around. The pool hall was little more than a well-built shack, the walls constructed of a random selection of boards, corrugated tin, and plywood and riddled with holes and gaps. Through one crack I saw two children squatting in the bright sun of a small courtyard, staring at the ground in front of them. They wore only shirts and sandals. Occasionally, they raised their heads to laugh. I bent down and peered through the opening to see what they were looking at.

Each child held a long thread, looped around the body of a live cricket like a cowhand's lasso. Whenever a cricket leaped into the air, one of the young tormenters jerked it back to earth. Spellbound, I watched as the children led the insects around like tiny dogs, prodding them with sticks to make them jump.

"You gonna play or what?" Spike said, snapping me out of my trance.

For days, I had seen children like these running around naked from the waist down. I figured that they were the less fortunate kids in the neighborhood. "Why don't the kids wear pants?" I asked. I stood up and lit my cigarette.

"The Vietnamese think that if you put pants on a kid under the age of four or five, they'll get tuberculosis."

I put my smoke down on the edge of the pool table, taking careful aim with my cue stick. It was easy to hit the first ball, but my angle was wrong and the cue ball missed the second by several inches.

"Not as easy as it looks, huh?" He lined up a shot, squinting down his stick for the correct angle. "Will your brothers rat on you for smoking?"

"Lynn will, but Lowell's too scared." I marveled at his ability to shoot pool with a cigarette dangling from his lips. The smoke didn't seem to burn his eyes and nose the way it did mine.

"Freddy's scared, but my sisters ain't. They know if I hit 'em, my Dad'll slap the shit out of me."

While we played, he gave me a crash course in how to hide my smoking from my parents. He seemed to know all the tricks. "You have to kill your breath before you see your folks, but don't use milk, 'cause that makes it worse. And be careful where you hide 'em. If you stick 'em in your socks, then you can't sit down, because they'll show. If I think my sisters have ratted on me, I hide my smokes outside the house, but usually I put 'em down my pants next to my balls. I know they won't search there."

One day after we played billiards, Spike stayed at the pool hall to play the owner's kid. When we played the kid, the games were free. I walked home alone. As I turned onto the first dirt road leading to our house, I noticed something moving in the dirt. I crouched down for a closer look and was shocked to see a hairless, filthy puppy, its stomach scraping the ground as it struggled to crawl along the side of the road, a thick crust of pus and scabs sealing its eyes. The gray mottled skin on its back was covered with sores, like little volcanoes oozing blood. The dog couldn't have been more than two or three weeks old. It looked to be near death, so I did what any normal American boy might do. I picked it up and took it home.

Mother was in the kitchen helping Thi Hai with the chores. When she saw the repulsive blob in my arms, her face wrinkled in disgust. "What's *that*?"

"A puppy. I found it on the side of the road."

Lowell had followed me into the kitchen, standing on his tiptoes to get a look. "A *puppy?*" He said. "Let me see!"

Thi Hai put down the wash and came over. Mother looked closer and her eyes widened. "Oh, my God! Thi Hai, go get Bryant!"

When Doc came downstairs, he looked at the dark clump of scabs and sores I had set to crawling on the kitchen floor and said, "Damn! That thing's almost *dead*. Don't just stand there, Leslie—get some water!"

I fetched the smallest bowl of water I could find, but the puppy was too weak to lift its head. It was a pitiful sight, struggling just to move. I thought it might have escaped from the village, but it had more likely fallen from someone's carryall or bicycle basket. The spot where I found the dog was blocks away from the village or a house. It couldn't have crawled that far on its own.

"Hold on, I'll get an eyedropper," Mother said.

Doc picked up the puppy and wrapped it in a soft towel, holding it next to his chest. When Mother returned with the eyedropper, she filled it with water from the bottles in the fridge. Doc fed it the water a little at a time, nursing it like a newborn.

The back door to the maids' quarters slammed shut and Lynn entered the kitchen, He joined us around the new dog. "What's its name?"

"I found it, so I get to name it," I said. We had owned many dogs before, but the privilege of naming one had never fallen to me.

"Why should you get to name it?" Lynn said.

I expected him to challenge my authority. He always did. I gave him a dirty look. "'Cause I *found* it, that's why." I thought for a moment. "Irving."

"Irving?" Lynn sneered. "What kind of name is that for a dog?"

"You know, like the plant in *Mad* magazine." Scribbled at random in the margins of *Mad* magazine was a drawing of a scraggly, potted avocado plant. "Irving" was scrawled on the side of the pot. I was never quite sure what the joke was, but I thought it amusing to see a plant called Irving.

Lowell laughed, but not Lynn. "You're kidding," he said.

"Oh, stop it you two," Mother said. She poured a small glass of milk and sucked some up with the eyedropper. "Let's see if he'll take some food."

Irving lapped up the milk eagerly, draining several eye-droppers before putting his head against the towel to rest. We gently wiped the crusty goo out of his eyes with a wet washcloth, and put ointment on his sores to help them heal. I stuffed a towel in a small box to make a bed, and Irving quickly fell asleep.

Irving grew into a healthy miniature Belgian shepherd, his tail curling into a loop that touched his back. We taught him all the obligatory dog tricks: sit, down, stay, roll over, shake. He was a lightning fast ball-chaser, as good-natured as any dog we'd owned.

Our family had begun breeding champion-level boxers when we lived in Hawaii, but when Doc was transferred back to the mainland, we were forced to leave behind Tinker, our blue-ribbon winner. When we departed Florida for Vietnam, we left behind another boxer, also named Tinker. The scene was always the same: four boys gathered around their dog (who had no idea what was going on), each boy sniffing back tears as he gave her one last hug. Like death-row lawyers, we always turned our sad faces to Mother and Doc, praying for a last-minute reprieve, but it never came.

TV shows like *Lassie* and *Rin Tin Tin* had instilled in us the notion that all dogs were heroes-in-waiting, ready to bite a bad guy or rescue a drowning child from a burning building. Each dog we owned was like a perfect brother whom we could love without reservation. We never fought or argued with our dogs, only with each other. We still complained when we had to clean up the occasional pile of dooky on the floor, but the family dog was like a best friend: loyal and always ready to play—the traits that we valued most.

Not long after Irving's rescue, we were horrified to learn that in Vietnam, dog meat, or *thit cho*, was a delicacy among men wishing to boost their flagging libidos. But for slum dwellers struggling to survive, what Americans considered a pet might be the only meal available. Though they might let a dog grow a little to fatten it up, they wouldn't have hesitated to eat Irving. As Doc warned, "You boys better watch out for him, or he'll end up as someone's lunch." To us, the notion of eating a dog was unthinkably repugnant. We would as soon eat one of our relatives.

Chapter Eight

Saigon

Meeting Spike intensified my hair envy, an affliction I suffered from more than any teenager I knew. Everyone, even Vietnamese teenagers, seemed to have better-looking hair than mine. I longed for "cool" straight hair, but my brown locks were too curly, turning upward when they should turn downward and downward when they should flip upward. Every day I thrashed at my hair with comb and brush, but it refused to be tamed, to submit to the style trends that taunted me from every magazine, newspaper, and movie.

In 1963, three hairstyles dominated the pates of American adolescents: the pompadour, the Ivy League, and the crew cut (the flattop was just a variation of the crew cut). The pompadour, always a popular choice, crowned such famous heads as James Dean, Marlon Brando, and Elvis Presley, handsome icons of American entertainment. Slick and shiny, it was held in place by generous amounts of hair oil that we called grease. Prep school boys, Troy Donahue, Pat Boone, and clean-cut men everywhere seemed to favor the Ivy League: medium-short dry hair, parted neatly on one side, combed across the forehead in a gentle wave. The crew cut was the regulation style for American military men around the world, including my father. Lean and mean, it left little hair for combing or fussing with, activities vital to my slowly blossoming sense of style.

But none of these styles suited my head. When I tried to comb my hair into a pompadour, it mocked my failure, exhibiting generous amounts of dour, but not a whiff of pomp. My current attempt at an Ivy League style yielded a literal interpretation of the phrase: it looked like ivy had seized my head. Ivy that was in League with the Devil. The crew cut was strictly for military men, hard-asses, baseball players, and little kids, not me. Besides, a crew cut would do away with my thick carpet of unruly hair and everyone would realize what I had known for years: my exposed scalp was lumpier than a bag of golf balls.

Spike had groomed his long, dark hair into a magnificent Elvis Presley style pompadour, and carried a black comb in his rear pocket so he could whip it into shape if it strayed from perfection. He wore his shirts greaser-style, unbuttoned to the middle of his chest, short sleeves rolled up a notch or two, shirt tail out. If he was feeling cocky, he would raise the back of his shirt collar. He was an inch taller than I, thin and lanky, and sometimes stumbled over his feet as he walked, as if they'd suddenly grown too big. His complexion was pimple-free and dotted with freckles—thoroughly Irish.

Soon after we met, Spike took me into his bathroom to show me the complex techniques involved in creating a pompadour of significance. The secret to his hairstyle was Top Brass hair cream. "Use plenty of grease," he instructed, squeezing a white stripe onto his palm. "At least an inch to an inch-and-a-half."

He rubbed his hands together and began stroking the Top Brass into his hair. "Make sure you cover it all," he said, his expression as serious as a cop at a crime scene.

After drenching his hair in a fresh coat of grease, he wiped his hands on a towel and pulled out his long, black comb. With his free hand following the comb across his head, he raked his hair straight back, slicking it down. Once he had it smoothed into place, he used the first three fingers of his right hand like the tines of a fork, pushing them into the hair above his forehead. He squeezed his fingers together, gently pulling the hair forward and down a little. Elvis would have been proud to know he'd inspired such a beautiful, elegant pompadour.

"It's important," Spike explained, "to push the fingers in until you can grab plenty of hair."

I asked Spike to work with me for a few minutes to see if we could perform a miracle on my hair, figuring that a good pompadour would be better than a poor Ivy League. If anyone could properly sculpt my hair, it had to be Spike.

But after saturating it with Top Brass and screwing with it for a while, even Spike conceded defeat. "You're right, man," he said, tossing me a towel. "It looked better the other way."

I gave up all hope of ever having cool hair.

I was no stranger to big cities. I'd lived in Philadelphia for a year and had visited Manhattan several times to see my paternal grandmother. I'd also been to San Francisco and Honolulu, and had seen my share of tall buildings (the Empire State!) and crowded streets.

In 1963, Saigon was a city in transition; it had grown from around one million people (in 1950) to over two million people. It wasn't particularly big by my worldly standards. But so far, I had only seen this strange new city from a cab, at night, on the way to the My Cahn for dinner and back. We'd been in Viet Nam for three unexciting days, so I recruited Spike to back me up when I asked Mother if we could go into the city.

"We're just going to look around," I said. "Maybe go to the market."

Spike was quick to add, "I do it all the time. It's really safe."

Mother was skeptical of my new friend's claims, so she called Spike's mom who verified what I initially thought was a lie meant to impress me.

"Well, I guess it'll be okay," Mother said. "But I don't want you riding in any of those damn motor-cyclos."

"We'll take a cab," Spike said. "It's cheap."

I begged a few piasters from her, and we hurried out to the street and started walking, leaving the neighborhood quickly, before my brothers saw what we were doing and tried to tag along. When we were out of sight, we flagged down the first empty motor-cyclo we saw and climbed in. Cabs were cheap, but motor-cyclos were cheaper, Spike explained. We could use the extra money to buy weeds.

The motor-cyclo chugged along, fanning up a weak breeze in the hot, dusty streets, its metal springs creaking and squeaking as we bounced along the rough roads into town. I put my feet up on the bumper bar in front and we broke out a couple of Spike's cigarettes. We were free. Next stop Saigon.

We followed the road out of the Gia Dinh neighborhood and took a right on *Duong Hai Ba Trung*, a straight shot into the heart of Saigon. Hai Ba Trung began to look cleaner and wider, and we passed into an area with stately Colonial-era townhouses and tall elm trees lining what had gradually become freshly paved roads and sidewalks.

Spike gave a shout and the driver turned right, approaching the Notre Dame cathedral from behind. Twin Gothic spires jutted hundreds of feet into the sky above a neatly landscaped square, and for a moment I imagined I was in Paris. On either side of the square, rows of four and five-story office buildings lined the streets, their elegant arched windows and high porticos sheltering the busy cafés and stores on the ground level.

We passed the cathedral and cruised slowly down the Flower Street, *Duong Nguyen Hue,* basking in the intoxicating smell of roses, carnations, apricots, and orchids. The rich scent of flowers blended easily with the exhaust of the motor-cyclo, street dust, and cigarette smoke, the sweetness of perfume followed by a lungful of soot. Nguyen Hue came to an end at the Saigon River, its dirty brown water reeking of oil and dead fish. Near the shore, a group of small, thatched-roof bamboo boats and sampans bumped against each other in the current.

We reversed our path and cruised past the elegant Majestic Hotel. The Majestic had once been the residence of Graham Greene while he worked on his prophetic novel, *The Quiet American,* in the 1950's. The characters in his novel stayed at the nearby Continental Hotel, a well-known hangout for foreign journalists and intelligence operatives. Spike directed our motor-cyclo driver to stop at the Continental. We got out and began walking towards the market.

Traffic in this part of Saigon was thick and noisy, horns blaring, bicycle bells ringing, engines sputtering. Of the two million people in the city, I was sure at least half of them rode bikes, motorcycles, or mopeds. They ruled the streets by sheer numbers, weaving between the crushing throng of taxis, cyclos, and motor-cyclos their drivers honking, cursing, and gesturing at anything and anyone they deemed deserving. I saw little evidence that Saigon had traffic laws.

The most common form of unmanned traffic control in Saigon was the rotary, a word which when translated into Vietnamese, means "circle of death and dismemberment." Downtown rotaries were overrun with a bewildering stampede of cabs, bicycles, motor-cyclos, and motorbikes, all flowing in the same direction. Why there weren't thousands of accidents bloodying the pavement every day was a mystery to me.

"Check out the white mice," Spike said, pointing to a cupola in the middle of a four-way intersection. "White mice" was the American name for Vietnamese policemen.

On the cupola, Two Vietnamese policemen in white uniforms stood back to back, waving at traffic and energetically blowing their whistles in mostly futile attempts to bring order to the swarm of vehicles.

One of the white mice blew his whistle and held up one palm to a Citroen, a shiny, black armadillo-on-wheels that was attempting to bully its way through the crowd. The driver of the Citroen was a balding, doughy-looking expatriate Frenchman wearing a wrinkled white suit. He stopped the car and threw his hands up in frustration. The policeman turned and waved to a large green Army truck and the vehicle rolled through the intersection with dozens of bikes and mopeds eagerly stealing across in its wake.

The Central Market was a few blocks away and would have been an easy walk except that we had to cross a busy street, a Herculean test of willpower, nerve, and raw courage. As I stood on the curb intently watching the free-for-all going on in front of me, Spike explained that once you had committed yourself to crossing a street, you couldn't flinch, slow down, or stop.

"If you do," he said, "they'll run your ass over."

When I stepped into the street to enter the fray, my first impulse was to dodge the hordes of vehicles that seemed dead set on squashing me like a bug. But in spite of every instinct I had screaming at me to run for my life, I did what Spike told me, walking steadily across the street as drivers swerved around me with just inches to spare. After what seemed like an eternity, I arrived at the opposite curb, sweating heavily, but alive.

As we drew near the Central Market, the crowds became dense. Everyone was working or shopping. The streets and sidewalks were like a living thing, undulating, moving this way and that, an entire city in itself, buzzing with life and motion in the thick afternoon heat.

We slowly made our way down the street, dodging people carrying baskets of fruit and produce on their heads, one hand touching the load for balance. It was easy to see the difference between the upper-class Vietnamese—shopkeepers, office workers and students—and the lower classes of laborers and vendors. Upper-class men generally wore long pants, short sleeve shirts, and leather shoes or sandals, maybe even a suit and tie. Women often wore the ao dai, or a western-style skirt and blouse.

But the lower classes commonly wore a traditional outfit, the Áo *bà ba*: a pair of baggy silk pants and a buttoned-down-the-front silk shirt, usually black. These "black pajamas" would eventually become known as the uniform of the Viet Cong.

We rounded a corner and I saw the Central Market. Along its outer walls, a necklace of street-vendor kiosks pressed tightly against one another. Baskets full of unusual vegetables, strange-looking fruit, mounds of rice, hardware—every vendor had his or her specialty displayed on the pavement or on makeshift tables. Covering each stall was a canvas awning nailed between upright boards or an umbrella fixed to a pole or stand.

Bicycles with aluminum boxes the size of small refrigerators situated between two front wheels plied the pavement around the market. The owners pedaled slowly, shouting out offerings of food, their closed umbrellas sticking up from the cart like flagpoles. Spike said it was okay to buy soda from these carts, but he warned me to avoid the mysterious noodle soup (Pho') I saw the locals enjoying. Although the soup looked tasty, dysentery was guaranteed if your body wasn't accustomed to Vietnam's pushcart food. It takes years to become acclimated to unfamiliar strains of bacteria in food and water, and I'd only been in Saigon for a few days.

Americans called these pushcarts "Howard Johnsons"—a Vietnamese version of the iconic American restaurant. Like a rolling fast-food restaurant, they traveled through wealthy neighborhoods and poor ones, providing quick, cheap meals to servants and laborers. The day before, I had seen Thi Hai buying lunch from one of the carts that worked the streets around my home.

Cigarette hawkers elbowed their way through the mass of people with wooden trays hanging from their necks, stacked with packs of American and French smokes. The hawkers shouted, "Winston! Marlboro! Ruby! Camel!" with a sharp Vietnamese twang, two or three packs held aloft in one hand. Some of the packs had been peeled open to allow the vendors to sell individual cigarettes to those without enough money for a pack. Ruby, a Grade C French cigarette, cost only a couple of piasters, so I bought one.

I liked my cigarettes strong, but this one was like smoking a rug. I took a few drags, coughed hard, and threw it away.

We stopped briefly to watch a cyclo driver sitting on a small stool, gripping its edges as a sidewalk dentist stood over him, tugging on one of the driver's teeth with a pair of pliers. The driver grunted in pain, the dentist grunted with exertion and the rotted tooth suddenly popped out. The dentist smiled as he held up the bloody tooth stump for the cyclo driver to see.

On the corner ahead, a man wearing shorts and a cai non squatted in front of a disconnected bicycle wheel. A thatch of grey whiskers jutted from the chin of the grizzled old man. His hands were black with bicycle grease and soot from the small fire in the clay pot next to him. Using a couple of screwdrivers, he worked the tube out of the wheel and began dragging it through a large pan of dirty water, watching for air bubbles to find the leak. When a few bubbles appeared, he said something to the owner of the bike who was watching as intently as we were. He showed the owner where the leak was and said, "*muoi dong*," (ten piasters). The owner nodded and fished the money for the repair out of his pants.

Spike finally led me to a clock tower that marked the entrance, and we strolled into the cool shade of the market's interior. It looked much like the area just outside—narrow aisles crammed with shops offering food, clothing, jewelry, magazines, vegetables, plastic toys, transistor radios, condoms, cookware, bootlegged American whiskey and shaving cream, bottles of Vitalis, Top Brass, and Revlon products.

In the center of one tiny stall, a man in a sleeveless undershirt sat on a stool reading a newspaper, his short-sleeved shirt hanging from a hook nearby. The walls of the stall were papered with diagrams of the body and its "meridians," with Chinese and Vietnamese text. Small shelves held fluids, bandages, and other tools of the trade. Four long, thin needles protruded from the back of the man's neck, just above his shoulder blades.

A scholarly-looking man I took to be Chinese stood behind the seated patient, holding a small vial with several needles soaking inside. He selected one and prepared to place it in the man's skin. I felt uneasy about watching what I thought was a painful procedure, so I turned away before the needle struck. Unlike me, the customer seemed calm and relaxed. Acupuncture may have been common in Asia, but it was entirely new to me.

After a quick pass through the interior of the market, we emerged into the heat and headed back toward the Majestic. Glancing across the street, I was horrified to see what appeared to be small children, skinned and decapitated, hanging upside-down in the window of a butcher shop. Their hands and feet had been cut off. Droplets of blood lingered at the tips of greasy red arms. Stringy blue veins covered the wet, oily flesh.

"What's *that*?" I asked Spike. The sight nearly made me sick.

"That's what they do with the orphans."

He was bullshitting me. At least, I hoped he was. "Come on."

"It's monkey," he said. "They eat monkey, too."

It was hard enough to wrap my mind around the fact that dogs were considered food, but eating monkey seemed almost cannibalistic. For days I found it difficult to shake the grisly image of the skinned monkeys from my memory.

At the next street over, we came upon a few toothless old women squatting on the sidewalk in front of large woks on a charcoal fire. They idly pushed meat and vegetables through the hot oil of the wok with wooden spoons, jabbering away at each other and the throngs of shoppers passing by. I wondered if they were serving monkey or dog.

As we moved through the market, my eyes were drawn to wooden trays and bins of food unlike anything I'd ever seen. Pig's ears, tails, feet, and snouts were piled high beside a line of large, green frogs. A tangled bin full of webbed duck's feet took up the end of one table, followed by row upon row of squid, catfish, octopus, and long red slabs of pork ribs. Many of the vendors specialized in black-market American goods, such as cartons of cigarettes, Dove soap, ladies' nylons and cosmetics, Crest toothpaste, Scotch whisky, and perfume. One young man sat happily in front of a cornucopia of peppers spread neatly across a bamboo mat, large green and red peppers piled next to smaller yellow peppers, alongside pointy, rust-colored ones. I saw at least a dozen varieties, as different, I assumed, in heat as in size. Next to him, a fruit vendor stood behind a display of vegetables and fruits, including the Durian fruit, a thorn-covered football-shaped melon that smelled like feet and rotten eggs.

Farther along, we came upon a sidewalk pharmacy that featured a display with several tall glass jars of oil, each with a snake coiled at the bottom. Beside the jars were boxes of potions and powders made of insects, rhinoceros horn, mushrooms, and herbs. A hand-lettered sign written in four languages (Vietnamese, Chinese, French and English) touted these ancient remedies as guaranteed cures for arthritis, glaucoma, warts, impotency, shingles, hives, and dozens of other illnesses. I couldn't imagine what diseases the snake-in-oil might cure. Had Mother prepared a teaspoon of that particular oil for me on days when I moaned about being "too sick to go to school," I would have declared myself healthy faster than you could say "detestable."

A few vendors shouted, "You OK buy nuoc mam, GI?" laughing at me as I held my nose. Unlike the *nuoc mam* I'd smelled in my neighborhood, the commercial version was tightly bottled. But with so many strong odors assaulting my senses, one more wouldn't have made a difference.

We drifted through a maze of stalls and umbrellas, examining everything that piqued our interest. None of the merchants let us pass without giving us their sales pitch, spoken in the unique pidgin of Saigon—a potpourri of Vietnamese, French, and English, woven into a complex and sometimes amusing verbal tapestry. Their rapid-fire mishmash of phrases were accompanied by hand gestures, nodding, and good-natured grins, like mimes imitating a used car salesman.

One young vendor noticed me staring at her as I strolled by. She picked a silver watch from her tray, strapping it to her wrist. Brushing it against her cheek, she gave me a smile of sensual delight, as if to convey the pleasure such a watch might bring to its lucky owner. "Hey, GI!" she called out. "*Bookoo* numba one watch! OK you? *Chinh-muoi dong!* (eighty piasters)" She held out her wrist for my approval.

She was the most beautiful, sensuous girl I had ever seen, and I wanted to buy the watch immediately, fall to one knee, and declare my undying love, but I shook my head. I didn't have *chinh-muoi* dong. Heck, I didn't even have *hai-muoi dong* (twenty piasters). As she put the watch back into the tray her face went blank.

The word bookoo is a slang version of the French word *beaucoup,* meaning very much, a lot, or an abundance of. In all the former French colonies and most of Asia, you can hear bookoo used as part of the local pidgin in every imaginable situation, as in "bookoo numba ten" or "you bookoo OK." The word is bookoo useful.

Spike wanted to buy weeds, so we looked around for the nearest cigarette hawker. "Watch how I get 'em to cut the price," he advised.

On a nearby corner, a man wearing black pajamas was standing next to a tray of smokes on a collapsible wooden stand. He leaned against the wall of a building on the shady side of the corner, picking his red teeth with his fingernail. As we approached, Spike touched two fingers to his lips to mime smoking. "Marlboro? *Bao nhieu?*" (How much?)

The man smiled. "Marlboro, OK." He held up a pack between his nicotine-stained fingers. "*Bay-muoi dong* (seventy piasters)."

Spike frowned. "No *bay-muoi* dong. You *dinky-dau* (crazy)." He held up two fingers. "Hai-muoi dong (twenty piasters) OK."

"No, No!" the vendor shouted enthusiastically. "*You* dinky-dau, GI! *Sow-muoi dong* (sixty piasters) OK."

Spike spoke slowly, as if he was insulted that the man would try to charge so much. "*Sow-muoi* dong? Noooo . . . you numba ten. No sow-muoi dong." He assumed a sad expression and turned to walk away.

The man held up five fingers. "OK, OK, GI!" He waved the pack of Marlboros with his other hand while nodding emphatically. "*Nam-muoi dong* (fifty piasters) OK!"

"*Bon-muoi dong* (forty piasters)," Spike offered.

The man's grin vanished. He put the Marlboros away and turned his head, staring down the street with silent resignation.

Spike gave me a shrug before facing the man. "Okay, okay. *Nam-muoi dong.*" The man beamed as Spike dug the money out of his wallet and handed it over. "I can never get 'em cheaper than fifty Ps," Spike said. "They always try to get more." He put the cigarettes in his pocket. "Merci bookoo."

The vendor grinned and nodded in appreciation.

"I wish we could get 'em at the PX," I said. "Fifteen cents is dirt cheap,"

"Yeah, I got a GI to buy 'em for me once, but usually they tell me to fuck off."

On the streets of Saigon, it seemed that everything was for sale, and all prices were negotiable. At times, the bargaining could get heated, especially among the locals, but if you didn't haggle over price, you were considered a sucker and a tourist. No self-respecting Vietnamese street shopper would ever pay the first price quoted. The vendors around the market always caved in on the initial offer, but the indoor shopkeepers had overhead to consider and always held tight to the prices marked on their sales tags. Selling cigarettes to kids wasn't a problem either: If you had the money, you got the weeds.

I'd tried not to stare while Spike was haggling, but I'd noticed that the cigarette vendor's teeth were coated with syrupy, reddish-orange goo. "What's that stuff on his teeth?" I whispered as we began moving away.

"Betel nut. Some kind of drug, kind of like chewing tobacco."

Betel nut turns the mouth a bright red-orange, eventually turning the teeth black as it accumulates in the tooth gaps and darkens with age. It has a mild euphoric effect, like strong coffee. "It looks disgusting."

"It's mostly old women you see with the orange mouth. Not too many of the men chew it."

"And the fingernail there on his pinky," I said, pointing at the curled nail on the old man's hand. "That thing's two inches long!"

"They grow 'em like that to show that they aren't manual laborers. You know, ditch diggers and stuff."

I would eventually see fingernails on taxi and cyclo drivers that were so long that they spiraled into the finger. It was a sign of class that allowed the drivers to distinguish themselves from common laborers and farmers. Maintaining a long fingernail is nearly impossible for a person involved in strenuous manual labor.

As we resumed touring the market, I noticed that some of the merchants were covering their merchandise with plastic tarps. "It's siesta time," Spike explained. "Every day, the whole damn city shuts down for a nap around one o'clock."

Most of the shopkeepers had locked their doors and turned off their lights. Cyclo drivers pulled to the curb, climbing into the passenger seat for a snooze. Commerce in Saigon ground to a halt. A few feet away, a woman placed a small, rectangular wooden block at the end of a straw mat stretched out on the pavement in her stall. She curled up on the mat and gently laid her head on the wood block. It looked incredibly uncomfortable.

I was still looking at the woman on the mat when I bumped into a child holding a rope. The kid may have been six or seven. "Sorry," I said, and he looked at me and smiled. His mouth was a checkerboard of rotting teeth, his blind right eye a milky white. His hair was so raggedy it looked like it had been cut with a pocketknife. His filthy T-shirt and shorts wouldn't have been considered useful rags at my house.

As he held out his free hand to beg, my eyes followed the rope. It was attached to a makeshift wooden cart with metal wheels, about two feet square and four inches off the ground. A shirtless old man sat on the worn planks, his collarbones threatening to poke through his taut brown skin. At first glance, it appeared that the old man's legs were folded beneath him, but when I looked more closely I saw scarred leg stumps protruding from his shorts where knees should have been. His fists were at his sides, pushing against the ground, rolling the cart slowly through the crowd with help from the kid. His knuckles were swathed in calluses as thick as the pads on a dog's foot.

I had never seen people who looked as desperate and hopeless as these two, yet they smiled, as though their situation was a joke that I didn't get. I wanted to smile back, but I couldn't find anything to smile about. I glanced from the man to the boy and reached in my pocket for change.

"Don't give 'em anything," Spike warned, "or you'll never hear the end of it."

"Why not?" I said, handing the kid a dime. The kid smiled gratefully at me and showed the money to the legless man before they rolled away.

"Fuck," Spike said. "Take a look."

Beggars surrounded us. Several children on makeshift crutches elbowed their way forward, jamming together with their hands extended, pleading, "OK, me" or "You numba one." A hollow-cheeked woman with a naked baby over her shoulder squeezed through the crowd. Like several other beggars, her face and arms were dotted with huge smallpox scars. She removed her *cai non*, thrusting it in my direction, upside down. "OK, you same-same me," she said, nodding earnestly.

"Hold onto your wallet," Spike said. "We're gettin' outta here,"

He'd warned me about pickpockets, especially children with their small, fast hands. I put my hand in my back pocket and followed him as he forced his way through the crowd and began a slow jog. Behind us, the crowd dispersed as the beggars sought more viable opportunities. We jogged for a block before slowing down.

"If you give one of 'em a dime, you gotta give 'em all a dime," he said. "You ain't got enough dimes for all the beggars around here."

A dime didn't seem like much to me, but I'd learned that in Saigon, a beggar could survive easily on less than ten cents (fifteen piasters) a day. The average annual wage earned by a Vietnamese worker was just $250 U.S.D.

I quickly became aware that the streets around the market were overrun with orphaned children, disabled war veterans, and helpless, emaciated women carrying babies, squatting in the shade with a look of sheer desperation on their faces. The beggar-children had an unfocused gaze in their eyes I had only seen on deathly ill people. They wandered the streets like zombies, their faces blank, shell-shocked, and empty of hope, right up until the moment they approached a stranger. Then they grinned automatically, extending a hand to beg, their forced smile like a mask they wore so as not to inflict too much of their suffering on the living.

The festering stink of extreme poverty seemed to inhabit every corner of Saigon, and I soon concluded that poverty in Asia was not the same beast as in America. In Saigon, poverty didn't mean going to a lousy school, living in a run-down housing project, and eating junk food for dinner. It meant *no* school, *no* apartment, *no* food—and no hope. Compared with these beggars, the slum-dwellers in my part of town were well off.

Months later, I noticed a family of four that had set up housekeeping on the corner near the American bowling alley. The mother wore the loose black uniform of the workers, but the father was attired in a white short-sleeved shirt, blue cotton pants with cuffs, and leather shoes—too well dressed to be a beggar. They'd spread out blankets and mats on the sidewalk in the shade of an office building. In one corner of their space, dishes and cooking utensils were stacked by size. Neatly folded clothes had been placed next to shoes and assorted household goods. A small hibachi-style charcoal stove sat near jugs of water and drinking cups. Two small children, naked from the waist down, rolled a ball on the sidewalk as their mother watched. It was as if they were living in a house that, by some odd twist of space and time, had been stripped of walls, roof, and furniture.

"They're refugees from up north," Spike explained, "trying to escape the war or the commies. They don't have any relatives to stay with, so they live on the street until pop can find a job. You can tell by their clothes they're not farmers or beggars. Definitely upper middle-class."

The family lived on the corner for a few weeks, and then one day they were gone. They may have moved to a better street corner, or maybe they found a long-lost cousin or relative. It's even possible that Dad found a job and could afford to rent an apartment. It's equally possible, though, that they moved into one of the squatter slums on the outskirts of town. Many such families lived on the streets of Saigon. Some were poor, some middle class, but all were seeking a better life than the one they had fled in the countryside or North Vietnam.

As we walked back to the Majestic Hotel, we passed nearly a dozen nail parlors/hair salons. Their windows were plastered with colorful posters featuring men and women who looked vaguely Asian, but who were most likely *matisses*—half-French, half-Vietnamese women (and men), born to Vietnamese mothers and French fathers. None of the models were small in stature, like most Vietnamese, nor did any poster show a face with the broad nose and wide, high cheekbones so common among the people of Southeast Asia.

The models sported hair that was straight and silky-black, but their skin only suggested brown. The women's styles seemed to have been copied from the latest Ann Margaret/Elvis Presley movie: beehives piled high, held firmly in place by several applications of hair spray. Some posters showed women posing with smooth, toil-free hands that featured long, beautiful nails, like the hands you might see in a Palmolive commercial between *Father Knows Best* and *The Ed Sullivan Show*. Long eyelashes, pouting red lips, and dainty noses as straight as a ruler completed this idealized version of the modern, urban Vietnamese woman.

Other posters depicted handsome Vietnamese men peering confidently over their high, starched collars, their hair swept into glossy duck-tailed pompadours that rivaled Spike's in size and slickness. They stood next to shiny new motorcycles, idly chatting with tall, pretty girls. With their hands in the pockets of their tapered pants, a sharp crease running all the way to slick leather loafers, these young Vietnamese models looked more American than I did.

Some of the female models were dressed in the modern version of the ao dai, its style updated to mimic the fashion of Vietnam's acting First Lady, Madame Nhu. She'd angered the traditionalists by westernizing this classic outfit, changing the customary high, narrow collar to a low boat-neck and shortening the sleeves to three-quarter length. Saigon was a fashion chameleon, casting off the old French styles in favor of new American trends in clothing, beauty, and music.

But the most compelling example of America's influence on Vietnamese style was the appropriation of the cowboy image by Saigon's teenage motorbike gangs. The romantic appeal of American cowboy culture left a lasting impression on every nation that imported Hollywood movies, but nowhere more effectively than in Saigon.

John Wayne, Gary Cooper, Hopalong Cassidy, and the Lone Ranger were heroes to millions of boys like me, and apparently to every teenage gangster in Saigon. Movie cowboys, be they outlaw, rancher, gambler, or sheriff, were often portrayed as rugged mavericks, men to be feared and respected. But the Vietnamese cowboy aesthetic leaned exclusively to the outlaw side. Their reputations as thieves, hustlers, gamblers, black market traders, pimps, and switchblade-carrying thugs were well deserved.

As we walked through the streets, Spike pointed out a group of draft-age Vietnamese teenagers blazing through the traffic on motorbikes, knees spread as wide as a bowlegged cowpoke on a horse. They were hunched over the handlebars or leaning back, steering with one hand, dark sunglasses shielding their eyes, shirts unbuttoned to the waist. Several of them wore Australian bush hats—cowboy hats with one side pinned flat against the head. Their cigarettes protruded from lips twisted into insolent, angry sneers, and I have to admit, these cowboys looked a lot tougher than the kids I'd been afraid of in Philadelphia. Watching them weave recklessly through the traffic brought to mind Marlon Brando in *The Wild One*, with a nod to James Dean and a side order of nuoc mam.

It took almost an hour to get to the Majestic because I paused to gawk at every arcade and window front, ogling antique stores full of Chinese and Vietnamese ceramics from ages past, carved ivory elephant tusks, ancient jewelry, statues of Buddha, and lacquered furniture. We passed shoe stores, banks, nail parlors, and several cubbyhole-sized stores crammed with transistor radios, electric shavers, and record players, their smiling shopkeepers trying in vain to wave us into the store.

At the hotel, we hired another motor-cyclo for the ride home. Spike directed the driver to take us down Tu Do Street, then to the zoo, past the Presidential Palace, the American bowling alley, and the theater. I didn't want to take a chance on being seen in a motor-cyclo by my family, so we stopped a few blocks from our neighborhood and walked the rest of the way home.

As soon as Mother laid eyes on me, she asked, "How was downtown?"

I could have told her about the hordes of beggars, bizarre foods, strange sights, unfamiliar sounds, and the overwhelming hodgepodge of smells and odors. I could have gone on about how the Vietnamese people I met were friendly and seemed a bit shy, not at all like I had once imagined them. Maybe I should have explained how the crusty decay of Saigon was far more interesting and colorful than I had ever envisioned. But, like most teenagers, I was loath to share my feelings with my parents. "All right."

Chapter Nine

The American Community School

The American Community School 1964

S chool was prison. From the first day of first grade, I daydreamed my way through each class, wanting nothing more than to be set free to explore all the fascinating things the world had to offer. Most days, while the teacher droned on and on, blandly reciting whatever nugget of wisdom was in their lesson plan for that day, I stared out the window or nodded deeply as my eyes fluttered shut, bored beyond tears. I loved to read, but I had no taste for the lifeless chapters in the textbooks that made up the bulk of our history and English lessons.

School was bad, but homework was worse: It meant I had to take a little bit of prison home with me every night, a cruel reminder of what awaited me the next day, and the next, and the next, and so on, into infinity. Whenever a homework assignment included sentence diagramming or math problems, I prayed for an illness or an accident to strike me down, giving me a plausible excuse to avoid completing the assignment. Nothing too serious, just the plague, or maybe a broken arm.

By the time I arrived in Saigon, my feelings about education had matured into a bitter acceptance of the inevitable.

Early one morning a few days after we arrived, Spike and I caught the American Community School (ACS) school bus. School was only a few miles away, near the airport. We rode in silence with our siblings and the rest of the American kids. "It's too early for this shit," Spike muttered. I agreed silently.

Half awake, I watched as we passed a group of Vietnamese Catholic school kids walking along the side of the road in two columns, led by an older girl. They were upper-middle-class kids who looked to be about six years old. The girls were wearing dark plaid jumpers over white blouses; the boy's outfits consisted of dark blue pants and a white shirt, similar to what I'd once worn in Catholic school. Several of the children held raw eggs to their mouths, slurping the innards through a small pinhole in one end. Going to school's a drag, I thought, but at least I don't have to suck raw eggs on the way.

When we approached the American Community School, a guard pulled open the wide metal gate (topped with the requisite rows of barbed wire) and the bus rolled into a concrete slab plaza. The guards quickly closed the gate behind us. I followed Spike off the bus and down the long, covered corridor leading to the eighth-grade classrooms. It was my first day at the new school, and I would rather have been anywhere else.

The American school was small compared with what I was used to, with grades one through twelve crowded into seven white stucco buildings that were lined up like dominos and connected on one side by a tiled breezeway. The first building housed administrative offices and the principal's office. Upper-school classes were held farthest from the front of the school, in a three-story building with exterior halls and stairs. This arrangement gave Spike and me plenty of time to wallow in regret whenever we were forced to walk the long, lonely path to the principal's office.

All of the classrooms had their windows propped open to allow air to circulate. Because of the climate, our school day consisted of morning classes and little or nothing in the afternoon, when the heat was so intense it could melt asphalt as easily as it melted the spirit of academic inquiry.

The abbreviated school day left us plenty of free time to explore Saigon, something my mother had ceased worrying about after my first couple of trips downtown.

Most of the students at ACS and the American Community High School (ACHS) were American, but students from the Philippines, India, China, Indonesia, Vietnam, and Thailand also attended. ACS students were the sons and daughters of American military personnel, diplomats, civil service workers, and well-connected foreigners. A few, like Mr. Phu's son, David, were lucky Vietnamese kids whose parents possessed enough money and influence to buy their way in.

At the American Community School, I was an outsider among outsiders, a stranger among strangers. I immediately felt more comfortable than in any of the six schools I'd been to previously.

ACS Sentry On Duty

But unlike my previous schools, ACS also looked like a prison. In addition to high walls topped by razor wire, Marines stood guard on the roof of the breezeway and around the school's perimeter, pacing constantly, rifles slung over their shoulders or propped on their hips, a holstered handgun tight against their belts. While I sat in class, my eyes were often drawn away from the blackboard (or a daydream) by the silhouette of an armed sentry moving back and forth, always visible, ever vigilant. It was easy to imagine myself in prison, doing hard time under the watchful eyes of "the screws."

No prison would be complete without a warden, and we had ours: Mrs. Rehnquist, a puffy-looking bulldog-of-a-woman. Her son and daughter were students at ACS, and though she may have been a wonderful mother, I felt nothing but pity for them. I couldn't imagine a more gruesome fate than to come home after a hard day at school and see the school principal standing in the kitchen wearing an apron and stirring some viscous concoction in a big iron kettle. Their mom was the harshest principal I'd ever met, a woman who could kill a bug by looking at it.

On more than one occasion, the well-armed Marines who accompanied us on the school bus reported Spike and me to Mrs. Rehnquist for smoking. My adolescent mind was stung by the irony: The soldiers, who were supposedly there to protect us, ratted us out to the warden! Mrs. Rehnquist promptly suspended us every time.

The constant presence of armed guards at all of the American facilities was an ongoing reminder that the edge of civilization was close by, and that beyond that edge lurked chaos and turmoil. Doc had informed my brothers and me that during the waning years of the French occupation in the 1950s, downtown Saigon would sometimes experience as many as eight grenade attacks in a single night. "It could happen again," he warned.

The constant warnings from Doc and our teachers made us careful not to eat at outdoor cafés or restaurants where grenades could be easily tossed into the midst of unsuspecting patrons. Some parents were so concerned that they wouldn't even let their kids out of the house unless an adult was with them. Luckily, military dependents didn't seem to be on the Viet Cong radar, but I knew that could change. Eventually, the political climate heated up to the boiling point, and I was able to peek over the edge of civilization into the maelstrom.

We were immersed up to our eyebrows in a culture that was weird and wonderful but frequently disconcerting. On one occasion, I was alone and bouncing along a city street in a motor-cyclo on my way to the bowling alley when I suddenly realized that I'd told the driver to take a wrong turn three blocks back. Or maybe it was four… I was now adrift in a wild, unknown neighborhood of Saigon, a lone American lost in a sea of Vietnamese and Chinese faces. Stores, townhouses, shacks, and narrow dirt streets teeming with bikes, cars, and motor-cyclos offered no clues about where I was. Street signs were nonexistent. The neighborhood even smelled different. Nothing I saw or heard (except the constant sputtering of engines) seemed familiar. I was overcome with cultural vertigo.

After a few trips around a busy rotary that I'd never seen before, every avenue looked as if it led in the wrong direction. Alone and lost, I grew uneasy as I contemplated the treachery of the Viet Cong, one of whom, in theory at least, could be driving the motor-cyclo in which I sat.

Desperate, I grabbed the frame of the canopy and stood on the seat of the moving motor-cyclo, looking for a landmark. In the distance behind me, I spotted the radio spire on the Rex Hotel, shining in the sun like a beacon of hope. I shouted to the driver to turn left *(Tai mot! Tai mot!)* and sat down, relieved. I could simply have asked him to take me to the bowling alley, but who knows where I would have ended up?

The American bowling alley was an oasis of burgers, French fries, Cokes, and rock 'n' roll, and walking through the front doors into its air-conditioned grandeur was like taking a trip to the America we had left behind. Ten glossy wood lanes, a rental counter with cubbyholes full of two-tone shoes arranged by size, bowling balls of various weights and colors lined up in racks, and a cafeteria staffed by hair-netted women dressed in white, slinging food short-order style—everything about the bowling alley smelled, sounded, tasted, and looked American, except the pin boys.

Because automated lanes had not yet come to our remote Asian outpost, local teenagers were hired to reset the pins manually. They were relegated to a high bench behind and to the side of the pins, climbing down to collect and return the balls and rack the pins after each frame. Bowlers could see only their legs dangling a couple feet off the floor as the pin boys sat waiting for the next clash of balls and pins.

Monday night was League Night, and sometimes Spike and I went to watch his parents bowl. Spike's dad, Kevin, was a serious bowler who toted a vinyl bowling bag crammed with impressive-looking gear, including a custom-made wrist brace, a swirly green-and-black bowling ball with holes drilled specifically for his hand, talcum powder, a hand towel, and shoes that fit perfectly.

Like several other burly he-men, Kevin could toss the ball with brutal power. We were awestruck at the symmetry and grace of his technique as he sent the ball rocketing down the lane, curving into the V of red-and-white pins with a resounding blast. He consistently scored in the mid 200s, an impressive feat. But for us, the most entertaining aspect of Monday night bowling was when a throw by Kevin (or one of the other he-men) transformed the pins into weapons. With each loud *ka-whappp!* the pins whipped through the air, slamming into the sides of the lane, often whacking the pin boys' legs.

Teenage boys are connoisseurs of pain (especially when it's someone else's), and Spike and I appreciated a good bruise, cut, or scrape with the same disgust and perverse fascination we reserved for a loud belch or fart. At the bowling alley, we watched with amusement as the pin boys' skinny legs jerked a frantic puppet-dance of avoidance, but the heavy pins often smacked into their bare shins and ankles. Whenever the pin boys cursed and swore in pain, Spike and I laughed as though we were watching an episode of *The Three Stooges*. Unlike the *Stooges*, however, the pin boys' pain was real, a fact that only enhanced our enjoyment of this popular sport.

With a constant flow of pimply new Brats arriving and old ones shipping out, the teen social scene was always fresh and interesting. Although we lived in one of the largest cities in Southeast Asia, television, like automated bowling lanes, had yet to make its debut. Its absence left a gaping hole in our entertainment options. We couldn't just plop down in front of the boob tube after school, so the desire to get out of the house and mingle was more urgent than it would have been stateside.

We banded together as immigrants in America often do, with little regard for class or rank, held together by the glue of estrangement from our native soil. Transportation by taxi or motor-cyclo was dirt cheap, so meeting friends was easy. Another bonus was the short school day. We were finished before one o'clock, so we had plenty of time to escape the critical eyes of our parents and hang out in the city. Saigon was our amusement park. Admission was free.

The best places for getting together with friends were the bowling alley, the Capitol *Kinh-Doh* Theatre, and the *Cercle Sportif Francais*, all within a block of each other. The Cercle Sportif had tennis courts, showers, a steam room, and a long, clean swimming pool surrounded by cabana chairs and umbrellas. It also maintained a snooty colonial-era vibe the administrators perpetuated by excluding as many Americans and Vietnamese as possible. In addition to completing a written application, officers, diplomats, and their dependents were required to submit to a personal interview, after which, if the interview went well, they were permitted to become members. Even though enlisted personnel and their families were forbidden membership, Doc could easily have gotten our family in because of his position at AFRS. Unfortunately, coaxing Doc into joining *any* club would have been as difficult as getting him to go to the bowling alley: "Not a chance in hell," as he put it. Except for the Navy, Doc was never a member of any club, association, sporting group, society, or organization, It was only as guests of Bob Harding that Spike and I were ever able to see the inside of the Cercle Sportif.

Bob was a Foreign Service Brat. Nothing about his short, skinny self suggested an interest in sports or familiarity with athletics. His brown crew cut covered a head that looked like an upside-down pyramid, his wide, high forehead perfectly counterbalancing his narrow chin. The first time I saw Bob, I thought he looked like Brainiac, the evil genius from the Superman comics.

Although Bob was born in the United States, most of his thirteen years had been spent overseas. When he was three, his family moved to Karachi, Pakistan, so his memories of the United States were few and hazy. He'd been in Saigon for five years, long enough to become fluent in French, and with a little help from his family's servants, Vietnamese. In Pakistan, he'd even learned to swear in Urdu, the national language.

I met him on my first day at ACS while standing next to Spike in the third-floor exterior hall during mid-morning break. Spike was leaning on the railing holding a paper cup of water over the side, aimed at the head of an unsuspecting student in the courtyard below. A voice behind me said, "Better drink up; Rehnquist is coming."

I turned in time to see Bob grab Spike by the shirtsleeve and pull. "If Rehnquist sees that cup fall, she'll have your head."

Spike thought better of his prank and drank the water. "See, man," he said, crushing the paper cup. "He's always fucking with me."

Principal Rehnquist stepped out of the stairway, walking toward us with her usual sour expression. Spike had already been to her office twice in the last year. She paused to look us over. "You boys are behaving, I hope."

"Yes, ma'am," Bob said, ginning up a phony smile. "We were just discussing last night's homework."

She gave us a doubting sideways glance and walked away.

"You lucked out that time," I said.

"She's always got a case of the ass," Spike whispered, glaring at her back.

After school, Spike and I dumped our books at home and took a motor-cyclo to Bob's house. Unlike the small townhouse apartments we lived in, Bob's home had three bedrooms, a formal dining room, and a separate servants' quarters. The yard was half as big as a football field and surrounded by a high brick wall with an imposing iron gate that opened onto a gravel driveway.

Eventually, General William Westmoreland would move in next door. Other wealthy or important people occupied similar homes in the neighborhood. Bob's older brother and sister had been shipped to boarding school in the States, so now just three people lived in the Harding house on *Duong Hien Vuong*, six blocks from the presidential palace. Compared to my home, it was a mansion.

We passed through the gate, stepped onto the veranda, and knocked on the front door. No one answered, but we heard Bob shouting in anger, so we went in.

We opened his bedroom door. He was standing in the middle of his room screaming, "You little fucking *asshole!*" He ripped the covers off his bed, throwing the sheets at a cage on the floor. "Look at this shit," he said. The floor was littered with books that had previously been on shelves. Bob's wounded Akai reel-to-reel tape recorder lay on its side with yards of brown tape-intestines curled in front of it. A plastic ship model lay in ruins, snapped in half like the *Titanic*. The ceiling fan was cocked at an odd angle, hanging by a lone wire. The white curtains had been torn down, the rods bent beyond redemption. Next to the window, a broken mirror glinted from the top of Bob's desk.

"Damn, man," Spike said. "What happened?"

"I left this asshole in here, and he broke out of the cage. Fuck!"

The asshole was his pet spider monkey, Alfred E. Neuman. Like me, Bob spent way too much time reading *Mad* magazine.

Bob picked up the tape recorder. "I was being nice, letting him stay in my room instead of out in the yard. It took me twenty minutes just to catch the little fucker."

We helped Bob straighten out the books and curtains. Bob snatched up the monkey pee-soaked sheet and we carried the cage outside. I took a good look at the devil who had caused all the trouble. It was hard to believe a spider monkey could do so much damage.

Many of the kids at school dressed in an Ivy League style, especially the Brats from the Washington D.C.— Virginia area. Some, like Spike, dressed like greasers, and a few students from the Deep South stood out just by opening their mouths. But Bob had none of the identifying clothes, speech, or hairstyles of any group. His style was no style.

His father worked for the United States Information Service (USIS), but I never knew his occupation. The acronym had a sinister ring to it, as if it were a CIA-sponsored cloak-and-dagger outfit. For years, I imagined Bob's dad involved in all kinds of dangerous, nefarious activities, slinking around in the back rooms of Saigon, meeting with dark strangers, wheeling and dealing in the kind of machinations I'd seen in Charlie Chan movies.

It wasn't long before Bob's house became a launching platform for our late-night forays into Saigon. His father was frequently away on business, and his mother was usually asleep by eleven pm, so three (or more) of us could sleep over with room to spare. We began staying at Bob's every night we could.

With Bob as our mentor, we learned the fine art of trading money on the black market, a common but illegal activity. The most common trade was the exchange of U.S. dollars for Vietnamese piasters at a higher-than-market rate. Fortunately for us, the police looked the other way most of the time.

Saigon's thirst for a strong, stable currency was unquenchable. As the fortunes of the Diem administration waxed and waned, Vietnamese politicians, businessmen and government employees bought and hoarded U.S. currency as their insurance policy against a time when it might be necessary to flee the country. The dollar was life itself.

American dollars could be sold anywhere in Saigon, but the jewelers on Tu Do Street were the safest and most popular buyers. In a jewelry store, you didn't have to worry about getting swindled with counterfeit bills, or robbed as you might on the street. *Tu Do* Street, known by the French as Rue de Catinat, was well known for glitzy bars and glitzier prostitutes, all patronized by a growing number of newly arrived U.S. soldiers. Tu Do Street was also the home of "Brodards," a popular restaurant frequented by French, Vietnamese, and American customers intent on sampling the best French ice cream and croissants in Saigon.

You could judge the relative stability of the government in Saigon by tracking the exchange rates on Tu Do Street. The more the jewelers paid for dollars, the more volatile and unstable the government. At the PX, we could buy and sell dollars ("green") at the official rate of 73 Ps to the dollar, but the rate on Rue de Tu Do was much better.

"So here's how it works," Bob instructed us one day. "You get some green from your mom. Let's say you get three bucks. You take it to Tu Do Street and sell it to one of the jewelers for 100 piasters to the dollar. Then you go to your dad and try to get him to exchange your 300 piasters back to green at the *official* rate. That'll get you about four dollars. If you go back to Tu Do Street and exchange it again, you'll have 400 Ps. That's about five-and-a-half bucks in green. As long as you have someone to change Ps to green, you can keep increasing your profit. Jewelers prefer the big bills and always pay more for tens and twenties. If you do a couple of exchanges, it's like getting free weeds."

Bob didn't just look like Brainiac—he *was* Brainiac.

It didn't take long for us to figure out that booze was easily available in Saigon. We were only thirteen, but the average Vietnamese adult was about our height, so it was possible to go to a bar or restaurant and order a beer without showing an ID because we "looked" like adults. We often heard "Hey, GI" from the locals, who assumed we were soldiers, but we didn't make the mistake of going to bars where real soldiers were drinking. I knew the GIs would throw us out, or worse, get the MPs to grab us and drag us home to our angry parents.

We had our own watering hole though, the little restaurant next door to the *Kinh Do* Theater, just around the corner from the bowling alley: the Cafe' "33." It was too run-down and dirty for most American adults, so it was perfect for us. It was close to our other favorite hangouts, plus we could avoid being seen by sitting at a table that wasn't visible from the street. Bob and Spike took me there for my first beer, "*Ba-Muoi-Ba*," (pronounced bah-me-bah), Vietnamese for "thirty-three." It was served warm in a glass, with a big chunk of ice.

"You have to drink it before the ice melts, or the water'll give you diarrhea like you won't believe," Spike explained. He pointed to Bob. "He doesn't have to worry about that."

"Are you immune or something?" I asked.

"No, but I've lived here long enough to get used to it. I can still get the runs if I drink too much, but mostly I'm okay."

I poured my beer in the glass, patiently waited for the foam to subside and took a sip. The initial flavor was nice, but the sour after-taste was horrible. With Spike's admonitions in mind, I drank quickly, draining my glass in less than five minutes. When I finished, I felt woozy and a bit lightheaded. It doesn't take much when you're thirteen.

The three of us quickly became inseparable. Distinctions of class— Bob's parents made much more money than either Spike's or mine—were ignored. It wasn't that we didn't notice; we did, but we didn't care. The most glaring difference in our attitudes was that Bob was less likely to get in trouble at school (except for smoking on the bus), while Spike and I courted trouble.

Early in the spring, Spike and I had been caught sneaking an after-school smoke on the bus ride home. We always picked out the bus our siblings were taking and then boarded one of the others so we could open the rear windows and light up. Unfortunately, the MP in the front of the bus had a keen nose for tobacco. He quickly sniffed us out and reported us to Mrs. Rehnquist. The infraction meant an automatic week-long suspension from riding the bus. While the suspension was in effect, I had to take a motor-cyclo to and from school.

Spike's folks had been unusually candid when talking to my parents about the antics Spike had been involved in at school and elsewhere. "We don't know what to do with him," his Mom said. "Nothing seems to work." I had never been suspended before, so Doc began to dislike Spike, believing that he was the cause of my troubles at school. In one way, at least, Doc was right. I had never had a friend so quick as Spike to test the boundaries established by parents, schools, and authorities bent on taming the wildness of youth. But though I may have been led into trouble, I was an eager follower, as was Bob.

After the first suspension, I learned that I had to be cagey when asking my parents if I could stay overnight at Bob's. On one occasion, I slipped up, mentioning that Spike was staying over, too. "You know I don't like you hanging around with him," Doc reminded me.

I backtracked hastily, trying to cover my error. "Did I say Spike? I didn't mean him. I meant Bob, I'm staying at Bob's."

"I know what you meant," Doc said. "I'm not stupid."

The quick reverse wasn't working, so I went on the attack, provoking a direct confrontation. "Well, who am I supposed to hang out with?" I protested. "Lynn and Lowell?" No reasonable parent, I thought, would suggest such an ugly, distasteful thing.

But Doc pressed his advantage, rocking me onto my heels: "Why don't you get some friends who aren't screw-ups, like that Bates kid...."

Fortunately, my mother took up my defense with a stinging rebuttal of Doc's ad hominem attack on my pals: "That was back in Florida, Bryant. Spike's a nice boy."

Now that I had my mother on my side, I felt the battle shift in my favor. "Yeah," I said. "He's just unlucky."

"You keep hanging around with him," Doc said, "and you're going to be unlucky too." He sat down on the couch, reaching for his cigarettes and a magazine, a position of withdrawal. Victory was within reach.

"So can I go?" I asked.

He didn't even look up. "Ask your mother."

Once he threw the ball to Mother, the game was over. Mother always trusted me more than Doc did, but to avoid conflict, I learned to keep Spike's name out of the conversation.

Chapter Ten

Fight!

The author kneeling in the alley behind 26-A 11 Chi Lang Street

W hen military families move overseas, they usually live in a base housing development, especially where there's a large base, like Yokahama, Japan, or Rhoda, Spain. Those huge bases provide a protective bubble that insulates military families from the indigenous people and their culture.

But Saigon didn't have a large central military base, nor did it have such a protective bubble. We lived several miles from Tan Son Nhut Airport, a few miles from downtown Saigon, and were immersed in Vietnamese, Chinese, and to a much lesser extent, French cultures. American institutions, such as the theater, school, bowling alley, and U.S.O, could give us a taste of America, but with one glance at the world outside, we knew we weren't in Kansas anymore.

Hundreds of Vietnamese kids lived in our neighborhood, but the closest we came to interacting with them, at least intentionally, was when we swam at the nearby public pool, a leftover from the era of French colonialism. On any hot day—which was every day—dozens of locals (and a few brave American kids) crammed into the water seeking relief from the heat. Although the water was heavily chlorinated, it had a cloudy, brownish tint to it, more brown than green. It was so dirty you couldn't see the bottom, even while standing in the shallow end. My "vaccination" by baptism in that murky, urine-infused, hepatitis pond may be what has kept me healthy all these years.

Though we swam and dived side by side with the local kids, we didn't socialize with them. Rather, we observed them, taking note of our differences while ignoring our similarities. We were rich; they were poor. We were white; they were brown. We didn't understand their language; they didn't understand ours. They knew little about our culture and we knew as little about theirs.

Our one common denominator was that we were all kids, living in Vietnam, watching each other from a distance, separated by thousands of years of civilization along divergent paths. But in spite of the differences in language and culture, there was one way we got to know the local kids a little better. Boys have used this approach for ages. It was test of manhood as old as any civilization: hand-to-hand combat.

In the field in front of my house, Spike had introduced me to boxing, the sweet science. What we did wasn't real boxing, of course. We had no gloves, no ring, no protective gear or coach, so we had to be careful not to knock each other's heads off. We just sparred for fun. Spike was a more experienced boxer than I, but he hadn't been able to practice with (or on) his brother because of the differences in their age and size. Freddy was so much smaller than Spike that punching him, even if justified, would have been viewed by his parents as bullying. My brother Lynn was a year and a half younger than me and almost my size, so our fights kept me in shape.

One day, Spike and I were sparring in the open field when we noticed two local kids heading down the dirt road toward us. The taller of the two had round, thumbnail-sized smallpox scars covering his skin, just like the beggars I had seen at the Central Market. His friend was about my size and rather muscular-looking with a mouth that slanted down on one side, giving him a cruel look.

Spike looked at me and shrugged, and I began wondering what was going on.

Their expressions were grim until they were about a dozen feet away, when they suddenly broke into sheepish grins. The short, muscular one kept advancing until he was face to face with me. His smile vanished when he rammed his fist into the air an inch from my nose. "Me whip you!" he shouted.

Before Spike or I could say anything, Shorty repeated it, more loudly: "Me whip you!"

"I think he wants to fight, man," Spike said. "He's calling you out."

"What for? I've never laid eyes on this guy!" I was shocked, and more than a little nervous. Why would someone I'd never seen or met want to fight *me*?

"I don't know," Spike said. "Maybe he's a VC." He pointed to the taller of the two. "You Viet Cong?" he asked him.

The tall, scarred one—taller than both of us—grinned nervously. "No! No VC!" he said, emphatically. My new enemy was shorter than Scarface, but he looked strong and healthy.

Spike pointed at Shorty. "You cowboy?"

Scarface stuck up for his pal. "No! No cowboy! *You* cowboy!"

Shorty stepped closer to me. Again, he shouted, "Me whip you!" and slapped me in the face with the back of his hand.

I felt the sting of his knuckles on my cheek and flushed with anger. I didn't want to fight, but I wasn't about to let someone my size slap me around.

"That's it, asshole!" I yelled.

"Want me to hold your weeds?" Spike asked.

I checked to make sure my brothers weren't around, reached into my socks for my cigarettes, and handed them to Spike. I untucked my shirt and squared my shoulders, trying to look tough.

My opponent stepped out of his rubber flip-flops, and we backed away from Spike and Scarface. I assumed my usual right-handed boxing stance. Shorty crouched into a right-handed stance also, but he held his right fist cocked way back by his ear. He kept his left arm straight out in front of him, like a ramrod with a fist on the end. It looked as though he was going to try to knock me out with one punch, so I watched his hands and eyes intently.

I figured these two guys had been watching us spar from a distance. They certainly seemed confident that they could take us. How else would they find the nerve to pick a fight? As I stared at my opponent, I thought I might be in for a pounding.

We circled one another for about thirty seconds, each squinting at the other, sizing up the enemy, hoping to shake his nerves. Suddenly, Shorty dropped into a squat then leaped into the air. His foot shot out, striking me hard in the left shoulder.

I landed in the dirt on my ass. The kick wasn't painful, but it stunned me like a bolt of lightning on a clear day. This fight was getting off to a bad start.

I scrambled to my feet and began circling to my left, eyeballing him warily. I saw him preparing for another kick, so I circled out of the way, just like Spike had taught me. Shorty kicked again and missed, but he'd left his hands down. I swung fast, smashing him in the jaw with a solid right.

"Come on, motherfucker!" I yelled, encouraged by my throbbing knuckles.

He held his hand to his jaw. "No-no," he said, waving me off. He began smiling again.

It seemed odd to me that he was grinning. No American I knew would be grinning after a punch in the jaw, but I had no understanding of "face."

In Asia, face is the way you present yourself to the world and how you are perceived. To lose face is to be diminished in the eyes of others, to lose some of your sense of self. Shorty had presented himself as a badass who was going to teach me a lesson, but my right cross put an end to such thoughts. Now, he'd lost face. His smile conveyed the nervousness and embarrassment of his failure. "No whip you, OK," he said, backing up.

It only took one punch to knock the fight out of him, which was fine with me. I was glad to be done with it. As the two headed back toward the village, Spike and I used our fists and fingers to wave goodbye. When they were out of sight, Spike handed me my cigarettes. His wide grin suggested that he had enjoyed my fight more than I did. I was relieved to have won so easily, but my victory didn't feel complete; after all, I was the only one who'd gotten knocked down.

"That kick was cool," he said. "He hit you right in the shoulder."

"Yeah. Didn't see that coming." I brushed Shorty's footprint off my shirt. "At least I got in one good punch."

"We should practice kicking like that. What if they come back? We could be ready for 'em." He clearly relished the idea of kicking ass.

I hoped Spike was wrong. I didn't like fighting, especially when it involved strangers. "I don't know; I hit him pretty hard. I don't think they'll be back."

We immediately began to incorporate kicking into our repertoire whenever we sparred, imitating the style Shorty had demonstrated so well. Spike had the edge when we boxed because he had a longer reach, but when it came to kicking, I had the advantage. I'd learned the hard way that a good kick is a potent weapon.

Several weeks after the fight, Spike and I were heading toward the swimming pool, searching for a private place to have a cigarette. To get to the pool, we had to walk around the corner and cross a small field covered with dirt mounds where a building had been torn down. The field looked like a battleground, heaped with rocks and brick shards between well-worn dirt footpaths crisscrossing randomly. As we neared the stone arch leading to the street the pool was on, we spotted Shorty and Scarface entering from the other side.

When they saw us, they paused, and Scarface spit angrily on the ground. Then Shorty pointed at me and stomped across the lot, his scar-faced buddy following closely. "Me whip you!" he shouted. Shorty had lost face; now he wanted it back.

I rolled my eyes at Spike. "Shiiiiit, I don't want to do this again," I said. "Why don't you fight him?"

"Go on, man! He wants to fight *you*! I'll keep my eye on the big one."

Seeing no honorable way out, I raised my fists and we started to circle, just as we had the first time. Our posturing reminded me of grade-school square dancing, every foot shuffle matching my partner's. But this time, I was ready for his kick, and when it came, I latched onto his ankle and pushed him to the ground.

He jumped to his feet and charged me like a bull, grabbing me around the waist. We spun in circles and fell onto the rubble with a thud. Our knees and elbows banged together in a frenzy as we rolled over and over in the dirt, the impact of our fists accompanied by our grunts and cursing. Shorty was nothing but muscle, bone, and sinew. Fighting him was like wrestling a big wire coat hanger.

With considerable effort, I managed to clench his waist from behind and wedge my left arm around his throat, turning him onto his stomach. My other hand gripped his right wrist as I struggled to pull his arm behind him. Shorty's fingernails ripped into my skin as he clawed at my arm, tight around his throat. The fight had swung to my favor.

Then, out of the corner of my eye, I saw Scarface shuffle towards me and lift his leg. I took a deep breath and rolled Shorty in front of me. Scarface kicked hard, missing me, but hitting Shorty squarely in the chest. Spike leaped over us and went after Scarface with fury, rocketing a brutal punch into the side of Scarface's head. What had begun as a one-on-one fight escalated into a street brawl.

While Shorty and I writhed on the dusty lot, Spike began beating the hell out of his opponent. Scarface was taller and meaner-looking than Shorty, but he was weak and slow. Watching Spike hone his boxing skills by repeatedly punching the crap out of Scarface filled me with envy. Boxing, I thought, was so much more elegant and manly than rolling around in the dirt like a couple of pissed-off second-graders.

Shorty finally pushed me away, and I struggled onto my knees. We separated and stood up, straining for breath. As we squared off again, I noticed that Spike had Scarface in an unusual chokehold, the kind of position you might see in a professional wrestling match. The back of Scarface's head was wedged into Spike's crotch, and Spike's forearms were wrapped around Scarface's throat. Scarface had both hands locked onto Spike's belt, but was unable to push his way free. Spike suddenly began jerking upward in bursts, exerting maximum pressure on Scarface's Adam's apple, bouncing him higher with each pull. They rotated until they were next to a townhouse wall. Suddenly, a sickeningly hoarse croak erupted from Scarface's throat, like the mating call of a giant bullfrog.

Shorty ran to his pal's aid, but I chased him down, grabbed him by the arm, and yelled to Spike, "Watch out!" Shorty swung a vicious roundhouse at me, but I ducked under, grabbed him around the chest, and pushed hard. We fell across a dirt mound, sliding to the ground on a slope of crumbled brick.

Filthy rivulets of muddy sweat traced trails on our skin, staining our clothes. My pants were ripped out at the knees, but Shorty, who was wearing only soccer shorts, had shredded the flesh on his knees into bloody ribbons on the rocks and rubble.

Spike was still choking Scarface when Shorty wriggled out of my grasp and ran straight for Spike. By the time I got to my feet, he'd taken a running jump into the air, both feet aimed at Spike's head.

I shouted, "Spike!" But I was too late.

Shorty's feet grazed Spike's head and the three of them slammed into the wall. I hurried over, swinging wildly at Shorty, catching him on the side of the neck with my fist. He grabbed my arm and we fell to the ground.

Scarface scrambled to his feet. He coughed hard staggering over to where Shorty and I wrestled in the dirt. I could see him moving into position to kick me again if he got the chance, but Spike stood guard with his fist raised, ready to clobber him if he made a move. After a few more minutes of vigorous wrestling, I shouted in Shorty's ear, "No more whip me, okay?"

"OK, OK!"

With his face held against the ground it was hard to hear him concede, but I slowly let him go. We rose to our feet. Scarface and Shorty stood shoulder-to-shoulder, backing away from us. They were panting as hard as we were, trying to wipe off the dust and blood. When they'd retreated far enough to feel safe, they started shouting insults.

"Du mamia! You numba ten!"

Spike picked up a rock. "Your mama-san wears combat boots!"

"You numba ten!" I yelled. "Fuck you, *nuoc mam* breath!" We heaved rocks, then ran a few paces, pretending to chase them. They bolted through the arch toward the village. I dropped my rocks to survey the damage.

"You okay?' Spike asked.

"Look at this shit." I slapped my hands on my dusty pants. "My mother's going to kill me."

Spike wasn't dirty at all. "Did you see me choking that guy? I thought he was gonna die, but then I thought, naw . . . I'll let him live." He pulled his comb out and passed it through his hair. "I'm glad I got the big one. He couldn't fight worth shit." He put his comb back in his pocket and began flexing his hand. "My knuckles hurt from hitting him so much."

The back of my neck felt as gritty as sandpaper. "Yeah, well, next time I'll fight him and you fight Shorty. I hate wrestling."

As we moved away from the scene, I noticed that a big crowd of kids and a few Vietnamese women had gathered to watch the fights. Lynn slipped out of the crowd, catching up to us, excited by the rumble. "Is that the same guy as last time?" he asked.

"Yeah, the fucking asshole." I held my elbow out. "I'm bleeding, see?" Blood ran down my arm, making a rusty-colored trail as it mixed with the dirt and sweat.

"I thought the big guy was going to kick you until Spike hit him."

"Maybe I should've choked him some more," Spike joked.

All this was obviously great fun for Spike, but not so much for me. I never understood the attraction of fighting except as an expression of anger. I never wanted to fight unless I was hopping mad. But Spike wasn't particularly pissed-off after our battle. He seemed to enjoy it.

When we got home, Lynn told Doc about the fight.

"Did you win?" Doc asked.

"I think so."

"Did he try to kick you? The French are famous for that. They call it 'savate.' The art of kick-fighting."

"We didn't do much kicking. Just a lot of wrestling in the dirt."

"Well, don't take any crap and keep your guard up. If you want to hurt him, give him a slap in the ear with your cupped hand." Doc stuck his palm out as if holding a small bird. He put his hand on my ear to show me where to hit. "He won't hear anything for a week."

He seemed proud of me for standing up to them. I couldn't recall Doc ever being proud of me, so I was confused by his reaction to my fight. He rarely approved of anything I did.

When my mother saw my pants, she said, "I buy 'em and you rip 'em up. Someday, you're going to have to buy your own. Then we'll see how you like it." Disgruntled, she cut my ripped pants into shorts. I hated cutoffs, though. I thought they were for rednecks or little kids, and wouldn't wear them.

Fortunately, we never saw Shorty or Scarface again. I couldn't bring myself to hate them, though. I'm sure plenty of the Vietnamese kids must've felt that we invaders needed to be taught respect for their country. It could be that they just wanted to measure how tough we were, to test our mettle. I'm also sure their fathers and grandfathers had initiated the same sort of fights with the French Brats who preceded us. To the Vietnamese kids, we must have looked like spoiled, rich interlopers, Little Lord Faunterloys, ripe to be challenged and dominated. That Americans were there to help them fight the North Vietnamese was of no consequence to the kids from the village.

The hostility we faced always seemed to come from the Vietnamese kids who lived in the slums. When we passed them on the streets, they'd usually ignore us or smile silently, without drama or hostility. But the invisible wall created by the relative wealth and privilege of American dependents was a more profound obstacle to friendship than language. If not for fighting in the streets, I would have had no interaction with the local kids at all.

It seemed to me that at some point these kids would have to decide whether they would become part of the South Vietnamese military forces and fight with the Americans, join the Viet Cong and fight against the Americans, or do what so many did—nothing. Avoiding the draft was easy for the destitute boys from the villages, since they had no real address. The decision to fight or not was entirely up to them, but the distress of extreme poverty had long ago siphoned their will to fight, which made it easier for the North Vietnamese to take over the country. The slum-dwellers and beggars had nothing to fight for but poverty and despair. Who would defend that?

A few weeks later, I was in our living room hanging around the radio waiting to hear the Top 40 playlist. "The Sound of the Sixties" came on at four pm, and I had already staked my claim to the radio so that I could check out the new hits without distraction—that is, until Lynn ran into the house shouting, "Les, come on! Some kids are picking on Lowell!"

Lynn and I were the only ones allowed to pick on Lowell, a right we defended religiously. We ran outside. Around the corner, I saw Lowell facing off against two Vietnamese kids from the village. They were bigger than Lowell but about the same size as Lynn and me. The kids were stomping Lowell's toy soldiers into the dirt while little Irving growled, straining at his short leash. Irving wasn't yet big enough to scare anyone. Apparently, Lowell wasn't either.

Lynn and I didn't say a word to Lowell's tormentors. We rushed to the scene full of swinging fists and flying feet. A full-scale rumble ensued, with Lowell yelling encouragement from the side.

The kids were at least a year younger than Shorty and Scarface, and weren't as experienced or dangerous. We quickly got control of our opponents, forcing the battle across the street, into an empty lot bordered by bamboo and brush. I was punching away when I suddenly heard Lynn scream. I turned and saw him backed up against the bamboo. He had his opponent stuck in a headlock, but the kid had a grip on Lynn's balls and was squeezing away like he was crushing a tin can.

I took three giant steps and kicked the kid in the hips as hard as I could. Both he and Lynn slammed into the bamboo, thrashing and cursing. With the death grip released, Lynn began beating the kid senseless, extracting revenge for his sore testicles.

When I turned around, the kid with whom I'd been fighting was right behind me, raising his fist to strike. I plunged back into the fight, but after a few minutes, both of the kids broke free, turned tail, and bolted down the street. Once they'd achieved a safe distance, they started shouting the usual insults, and we responded with our limited vocabulary of Vietnamese curses: "Du mamia!" "My bu cac!"

The kids suddenly stopped retreating, reached into their pockets, and pulled out homemade slingshots. Unfortunately for us, the road was covered with pebbles of all sizes and shapes, like an ammunition dump designed specifically for their crude weapons. The kids quickly unleashed a barrage of stones, and we scrambled to duck and dodge their shots the hard little rocks streaking by our heads.

Lynn yelled, "I'll be right back," and sprinted for home. Lowell leashed Irving to a nearby fence, and we started heaving rocks as fast and as hard as we could, but our efforts were no match for their slingshots. Their shots made us dance, but our throws fell short by several yards.

A minute later, Lynn returned with heavy artillery: a Daisy BB gun. The cavalry was here! We were saved! He loaded up, giving the gun an extra crank for more power.

"Watch this," he said, drawing a bead on one of the kids.

Vietnamese slingshots couldn't compare to the accuracy and power of a spring-loaded Daisy BB gun. After a few BBs stung their bare legs, the kids ran into the village. I didn't feel the least bit guilty about Lynn turning a BB gun on them. Even spoiled rich kids have a right to defend their brothers. They didn't come back for more, and we didn't dare follow them into the slums.

Chapter Eleven

Cathouse

We'd only been in Saigon a few months when Bob, Spike, and I began sneaking out of Bob's house after bedtime. We wanted to see the sleazy side of Saigon, the side that we believed could only be found late at night. Spike and I had stayed overnight at Bob's a few times, and one night we decided to wait until his mom was asleep—his dad was usually out of town on weekends—and slip out of Bob's bedroom window. Fortunately, his mom was a heavy sleeper.

"We have to be real quiet," Bob warned, "'cause if the servants hear us, they'll tell my mother. Don't talk until we're outside."

Once we'd dropped to the ground, we moved silently to the grassy side of the driveway to avoid the crunching gravel and opened the creaky gate just enough to squeeze through. We walked until we could flag down a cab to head for town, usually to the Tu Do Street area.

We were afraid to hang out in the bars—they attracted too many MPs who might start asking questions. Instead, we cruised Tu Do slowly, basking in the craziness of the scene, watching the bar girls and soldiers haggling with each other under the neon lights.

At our age, we could only watch the Tu Do Street carnival from the sidelines, wishing we were old enough to take part in the good times we saw everyone else having.

One night in early spring, we left a classmate's party when it ended at around 11:00 pm. We were about to get in a cab to return to Bob's house when Spike pulled me aside. "Hey man, we're going to a cathouse later. You want to come?"

I was already committed to spending the night at Bob's, so if they were going, I didn't really have a choice, although I suppose I could have stayed at Bob's while they went. "What's that?"

"You know, a chicken house. Whores. Prostitutes," Spike explained. "It's cheap."

This new proposition was unnerving. Sex was something I'd only imagined or read about when I could sneak a peek at one of my brother's Playboys. The subject never came up at home. At our house, even curse words referring to sex acts or body parts were, by unspoken agreement, never used. Mother and Doc might say "damn," "hell," "shit," or "God damn it," but words like "fuck," "cock," and "ass" were off-limits. In my home, only adults could curse, and their profanities were selected from a short list of "acceptable" words, none of which my brothers and I would ever dare to utter in the presence of our parents.

Most of what I had learned about sex came from the lies, half-truths, and innuendos that boys pass around, never quite knowing what was true and what was bullshit. Doc had never sat me down for the man-to-man talk every father is supposed to give his son, but I didn't mind. It would've been too awkward, and I doubt I would've listened anyway.

In Playboy or Gent or one of the other men's magazines that I found in my brother's dresser in Florida, I'd read about that bygone era when a father might take his son to a brothel and instruct the madam to teach him what he needed to know. In that respect, unfortunately, my dad wasn't the old-fashioned type.

Now Spike was inviting me to cast off my virginity, and I was well aware of the considerable risk involved. We'd have to take a cab to a slum on the outskirts of town and risk robbery, kidnapping, or worse. That was dangerous enough, but I'd also heard frightening stories about rampant sexually transmitted diseases, curable only by hideously painful medical procedures.

One alleged procedure, nicknamed "the steel umbrella," gave me shivers just thinking about it. If a soldier contracted gonorrhea and his genitals became sufficiently infected, so the tale went, a doctor would have to insert a thin metal tube into the man's urethra. When the doctor pressed a button on the exposed end of the tube, four tiny, thin razor blades, extending a fraction of an inch above the steel shaft, popped out at the other end. The doctor would rotate the tube as he pulled the steel umbrella out of the penis, effectively cutting away the lining of the urethra, and with it the infection.

I believed those tales of venereal woe with all my heart. Plus, I knew that getting caught in a cathouse by the MPs would disgrace my family in the worst way. Catholic boys who patronized whorehouses, I believed, could expect to burn in the fires of hell forever.

"Yeah, I guess so," I replied calmly. "What does it cost?"

"Fifty Ps," Spike said. "I've been a few times. You're not a virgin, are you?"

"No," I lied, "but I've never been to a cathouse." Bob's mother was expecting us to show up after the party, so I would have plenty of time to think about my decision.

"Now's our chance," Bob said. "Once my mom's asleep, we'll sneak out."

Bob was a virgin too, but that wasn't a fact that thirteen-year-old boys liked to admit to each other. Only many years later did I learn the truth: we were all virgins that night.

Spike had heard some of the older guys at school talking about cathouses and was careful to pick up on the correct way to find a good one. If there was sex to be had, he was game. Later that night, we slipped out of Bob's bedroom window and hailed a cab.

When we got into the cab, Spike patted the driver on the shoulder, offering him a couple of American cigarettes. "Taxi, you go numba one girl, OK?" The driver turned around and gave us a big grin as he accepted Spike's Marlboros. By the dim ceiling-light of the cab, I could see gold rims on several of his teeth.

"Numba one girl, OK!" the driver said, nodding enthusiastically. "Me OK take you numba one girl."

Turning to face us, he raised his right hand, folding the third and fourth fingers and thumb into his palm, holding them down as if he was going to give us the Boy Scout sign. He used the tip of his second finger to grasp the first finger's nail, bending both fingers into an oval that approximated the shape of a vagina, as much as that can be done with two fingers. I'd never seen the female counterpart of the finger before. With his left hand, he made the male version and thrust it through the right hand oval.

"Bookoo pussy OK!" he said, slamming the car into gear, racing into the steamy Saigon night.

"This guy's a real horndog," Spike said as we howled.

"Taxi numba one!" Bob said. "Bookoo pussy OK!"

We practiced making the new sign until our fingers hurt.

The driver stopped the car on the edge of a slum near the Saigon Country Club, not too far from Tan Son Nhut airport. He parked under a streetlight, but we hesitated a moment. Past the light, I saw the crooked outline of the shacks lining the road. Beyond that, there was nothing but inky darkness.

I got out, trying to look calm. Spike threw his cigarette in the dirt and smiled bravely at me. The cabbie disappeared into an alley, and we followed closely, single-file through the maze of shacks. Getting lost in this blackness might be fatal.

He led us to a door and knocked. A skinny, wrinkled old woman opened the door. She was grey-haired, nearly toothless, and wore the standard black pajamas. Her head was covered by a faded, thickly-wrapped red and white cloth, like a miniature turban.

"He's got to be kidding," I muttered. "There's no way..."

"Shhh," Bob said. "She's the *mama-san*."

Then I saw six young girls standing inside the shack.

The driver explained who we were and she welcomed us in. He'd obviously done this before. He'd probably asked the mama-san to teach us what we needed to know.

While the mama-san and the cabbie talked, we stepped through the doorway into the cathouse. I figured the mama-san was a retired prostitute herself and had assumed the role of pimp and protector for the girls.

The mama-san closed the door, and I tore my eyes away from the girls and glanced around the shack. Four wood-frame beds were set against walls of rusty corrugated tin. Flimsy, see-through curtains hung in front of each bed, providing the illusion of privacy, but not the fact of it. Old rugs that were as much dirt as cloth covered the floor, and clean straw mats lay on top of the rugs in front of the beds. The shack had a few washbasins and tin pitchers, but I saw no source of running water or indoor plumbing. The beds were the only furniture. Oil lamps had been hung from the ceiling rafters, providing a weak yellow light that cast our shadows against the walls, adding a touch of the surreal to an already unusual night.

In one corner of the shack, an altar had been set up in the center of a wooden tray on the floor. A brass incense bowl, wallet-sized pictures of deceased relatives, and a vase of flowers rested on the tray beside a foot-high inscribed wooden tablet sitting on its pedestal. Most Vietnamese homes I'd seen included a similar altar, a memorial to deceased ancestors. Confucianism, a philosophy of morals, ethics, and the worship of one's ancestors, was an important part of religious practice in Vietnam, even among Buddhists. This home, this sex barracks, belonged to the mama-san. The names on the tablet were her ancestors, many generations removed. Someday, her name would be etched next to theirs.

The girls smiled and pointed, talking excitedly as they sized up their new customers. Unlike the tall, thin, sophisticated bargirls downtown, these girls were short and average looking, older than us only by a few years. Sensing our shyness, each of them took one of our arms, pulling us away from the door into the center of the room. Like good hostesses, they rubbed our backs and stroked our arms, trying to make us relax. In just a few moments, the musky scent of those six women had made my senses bristle, heightening my desire as though I were intoxicated by an exotic liquor: the liquor of sex. In the dusky glow of the oil lamps, our silhouettes moved across the tin walls like shadow puppets.

It was obvious that we were younger than their usual GI clients, and this seemed to amuse them. When one girl referred to me as "Baby," the rest began laughing. Maybe they knew we wouldn't be there for long.

The mama-san smacked the bottom of one fist against her palm three times to get our attention, then held up five fingers. "*Nam-muoi dong!* (fifty piasters) *Nam-muoi!*"

We broke away from the girls, paying her fifty Ps each while glancing at each other for support, unsure of the proper whorehouse etiquette. There's no chapter for this in the Boy Scout manual, and Grandma Margaret never voiced an opinion on the subject.

One of the girls moved closer to me, smiling as I looked into her dark eyes. Suddenly, she slid her hand down my pants, and grabbed my already hard dick. I felt the shock of her warm grip and my eyebrows rose in surprise. She giggled and talked excitedly to her friend, who did the same to Spike.

"What are they saying?" I asked Bob.

"They said cherry-boy has a big dick."

As soon as they heard Bob say "cherry-boy" they all repeated it, laughing.

"They must be talking about Spike," I said, embarrassed they'd found me out.

"I ain't no chico," Spike protested. The girl with her hand down his pants pulled him onto the nearest bed. Before her shirt was completely off, Spike had cupped her breasts with both hands.

The mama-san assigned a couple of the girls to Bob and me. We sat down on the beds, drew the curtains, and began removing our clothes. Shy and nervous, I followed my girl's lead, but she was wearing only a shirt and baggy silk pants. She wore no underwear. She was bare in an instant. I stared at her smooth brown skin and small tight nipples. I had never imagined things would move this quickly. She laid my shirt aside.

I peered through the curtain at Spike in the bed next to me. I had no idea what I was doing, and I thought I might get a clue by watching him. He was sitting on the edge of the bed as his girl massaged his erect penis with both hands. His grin was gone. His hands were on her breasts, his eyes nearly closed, focused with pleasure.

As I sat on the bed, my eyes fell to the wisp of dark hair between my girl's legs. I'm in bed with a naked woman, I thought, and we're going to do it right here, right now. My heart pounded in my chest as nervousness mixed with desire.

My girl reached under the pillow and produced a gold-colored condom. She gave the foil a quick twist and uncoiled the lubricated latex over my erection with a practiced skill. Taking me by the hands, she rolled onto her back, spreading her legs. She put her feet on the front of my hips, her heels tight against her butt. With one hand, she guided me into her slippery sex.

I felt her hot breath on my shoulder as my hips rode her feet in a gentle rocking motion. Soon, her wet heat sliced through me. I pressed forward and closed my eyes. The sounds in the room faded to a pinpoint and then vanished as I climaxed quickly and intensely, with the uncontrolled eagerness of a thirteen-year-old.

She pulled away and I sat back on the bed, waiting for the blood to rush back into my head. I had no notions about how long sex should last, but it seemed to end almost before it had begun. I winced as she squeezed my condom off with her thumb and forefinger. She tossed it into a trashcan next to the bed, stood and walked away, dispassionate and uninterested. I began pulling on my clothes, amazed that she could be so casual about something that was so powerful to me.

While we got dressed, the three girls, still naked, retreated to the back of the shack and squatted over the washbasins. They splashed water on their crotches, rubbed it in, and dried off with the threadbare towels hanging on the wall, laughing and talking the whole time. I felt like I had stumbled into some kind of strange girl's locker room and was surreptitiously viewing a secret ritual. It was the most erotic gathering of women I'd ever witnessed.

Spike, Bob, and I said a hasty goodbye, and as we entered the blackness of the alley, Bob joked, "Don't forget to write." The mam-san closed the door, leaving us in the darkness.

We stumbled over wood planks, navigating our way back to the street by moonlight. Our cab driver was where we'd left him, waiting faithfully. He leaned against the cab smoking one of Spike's Marlboros, contemplating us with a knowing smile, like a proud father.

As we emerged into the hazy light of the street, we were approached by a raggedy, one-legged beggar. The man must have been waiting in the shadows, because he appeared out of nowhere, like a phantom from a B movie. He stumbled toward us, working his crutches with feeble arms. As the man strained to speak, the cab driver shouted at him in Vietnamese and waved for us to hurry into the cab. Bob's eyes widened.

"What'd he say, man?" I asked, crowding the door.

"Unclean," Bob said. "He's a leper."

"I never seen a leper before," Spike said.

"Me neither," I said, hurrying into the cab.

Once inside, I put the disturbing image out of my mind. I had other things to think about.

What we had just experienced was nothing like the fumbling around in the back seat of a car so common among American teens. No one got pregnant, and I doubt that the girls' feelings were hurt when we put on our clothes and left. No names were exchanged. No promises were made. Lovers we weren't, but even Casanova lost his virginity once.

We had suddenly stepped out of the world we'd known as children and into the world of adults. But our slow-motion foray into sex lacked the gentle preliminaries of dating, holding hands, making out, and the more natural evolution of a relationship based on shared values and feelings.

As we rolled away, Spike said, "Was that cool or what?"

I looked at him with disgust. "The leper?"

"Hell no, man. The girls."

"My rubber kept coming off," Bob said. "It was too big."

"Nah," Spike said, derisively. "Your dick is too small."

Bob frowned at Spike and passed a cigarette to the driver. "Taxi, you go Rue de Tu Do, okay?"

"I don't know why it is," Spike said, pulling a Marlboro out of his pocket, "but a cigarette never tastes better than after I get laid." He struck a match and lit his cigarette. "Did you guys see when my girl dropped her bra? I thought I was gonna pass out when I saw how big they were."

"They just seem big next to your tiny little head," Bob said.

"Naw, really. There was a lot more than a handful. They were bigger than any of the other girls'." Spike stared out the window for a moment, lost in thought. He turned to face us. "You think we could get a blow job next time?"

We immediately headed downtown to Tu Do Street, wandering 'til the bars closed, savoring our newly acquired worldliness. I began to view each of the tall, beautiful bar girls with a new perspective, imagining how thrilling sex might be with them. They were too expensive for us, though, and the chance of being spotted and questioned by one of the many MPs that frequented Rue de Tu Do made us careful to keep a low profile.

Finding a cathouse and getting laid became a weekly (almost) experience after that night. Sometimes we would go during the day— occasionally after school. For me, the experience generated an exciting combination of fear and guilt, blended with generous doses of pleasure. We weren't the only Brats spending our piasters on sex, either. For years,

American (and French) boys had been shedding their virginity in the cathouses of Saigon. It was a well-known secret: most of the older kids at ACS, even the girls, knew about it, but our parents and teachers apparently had no idea what we were up to.

Many of the women in these brothels hailed from rural areas of the country and had escaped to the city with no family support, and no friends or marketable skills. I couldn't imagine how harsh village life must have been to make life as a prostitute an acceptable alternative. But Viet Nam had no real social programs to feed the poor and indigent, and very little in the way of charity organizations to take up the slack. Death by starvation or a descent into malnutrition and disease were fearful alternatives for any woman engaged in prostitution.

We knew that what we were doing was wrong, but our sense of morality was as vague and undeveloped as our understanding of the deep wounds caused by endemic poverty. The girls at the cathouse were pathetic in their desperation, but we were just as pathetic in our desire for sex, even if we had to pay for it. Our raging hormones had yet to develop a conscience.

Chapter Twelve

Blast-Off

I was burning. I was suffocating. I was freezing. I lay sprawled across my
bed, staring vacuously at the pure blue sky on the other side of the open
window above my head. The ninety-five degree heat and body-drenching
humidity pushed in from all sides. I felt as if I were being gently smothered
with cotton gauze. With the side of my head pressed against the pillow, I
could hear the foom . . . foom . . . foom of my heart beating in my ears, like
the gentle tapping of a mallet on a timpani. I was stripped to my Fruit of
the Looms, but the sheets were sticky with my sweat.

I turned my gaze toward the ceiling, where a fat, green gecko stalked
an unsuspecting fly. The gecko darted forward, flicked its tongue, and the
fly vanished. An inescapable gush of saliva rushed into the back of my
throat. My vision blurred. I began to swoon, and a tsunami of nausea rose
up in my chest. In one quick motion, I turned and pointed my face at the
basin on the floor as my stomach knotted, but nothing came up. I dry-
heaved a few more times and weakly rolled back into the wet center of
the mattress. It had been days since I had been able to keep food or water
down, and my stomach was as empty as the day I was born.

For days some weird flu had racked my body, sending my temperature
soaring into the zone where delirium takes hold and insanity creeps in.
Every joint and muscle ached. My mother and Thi Hai took turns standing
sentry, applying ice packs to my head while I thrashed about and wallowed
in sweat. Eventually the fever broke, and I slept for what seemed like an
eternity. When I finally woke, Mother said, "You were blathering on like
a madman."

Despite all the vaccinations I'd received, I had contracted an ailment
that science has yet to conquer, a disease I had never been exposed to
and consequently, one to which I had no resistance. It might have been
the Hong Kong flu or Singapore flu, or it could have been a parasite or
intestinal bug. Southeast Asian countries have more than their share of
unusual infectious diseases waiting to kick your ass.

When I felt well enough, I called Spike to see what he'd been doing
in my absence. I hadn't been outdoors for a few days. After we talked, we
met out front and took a motor-cyclo to Bob's place, stopping for weeds
on the way.

At Bob's, we pushed open the wrought iron gate and walked up the gravel driveway under the cool shade of the trees. I saw Bob on his porch taking apart a bicycle pump. "I know how we can make a rocket," he said, holding up the empty pump-tube. "First, we'll take this to one of the motorcycle repair guys and get 'em to weld up the end hole."

That sounded like fun to me. "What do we use for fuel?" I asked.

"We could empty out the gunpowder from some firecrackers," Spike suggested.

"Gunpowder burns too fast," Bob said, "and it's too expensive." He held up the aluminum tube for us to examine. "I was thinking that we could go to the PX, buy a ton of matches, cut the heads off and stuff the rocket full of 'em. We could make a fuse with tape and match heads laid next to each other."

"How do we get it to stand up? "Spike asked.

"We'll get the bike repair guys to weld some legs on," Bob said. "Let's go see if they can do it, then we'll buy the matches."

The motorcycle repair shop was glad to help for a few piasters. When Bob explained his idea about the legs, they produced three pieces of scrap metal and welded them to one end of the tube so that it stood upright. We now had something that looked like a rocket, but we needed fuel. We took a taxi to the PX, where we bought four cartons of matches and some razor blades.

When we arrived at Bob's house, we poured the matches onto the dining room table and began cutting. After twenty minutes of slicing, I had only a small pile of match heads for my effort. "This isn't working worth a damn," I complained.

"My dad's office has a huge paper cutter," Bob said. "Let's go there." It was Saturday and the United States Information Service was closed, but Bob knew the guard and was able to talk us in. The paper cutter was big enough to cut reams of paper. It even had a device for holding the matches firmly in place. We lined up dozens of packs, lopping off the heads with ease, then returned to Bob's to stuff the rocket with our bag-full of freshly cut match heads.

Bob had already developed some advanced ideas about rocket construction. "Let's press 'em in tight. That way we can fit more."

"Where's the tape?" I said. "I'll make the fuse."

"Why don't we just use some firecracker fuses?" Spike asked.

"Cause most of 'em suck," I said. "Sometimes they burn too fast and other times they burn too slow or go out."

"Yeah," Bob agreed. "Too unreliable."

"You guys are always squashing my ideas," Spike said, disappointed.

I rolled out a three-foot length of tape on the floor, laying match heads end to end along the middle. Spike and I put another piece of tape on top to hold the match heads in place.

We stood up the rocket and examined our handiwork with pride and a bit of excitement. It was almost two feet high and an inch in diameter, a glorious and convincing rocket, as good as any I'd seen in Popular Mechanics.

But we needed a launching pad. "Where can we set it off?" I asked.

"How about Pershing Field?" Spike said.

"Now you're talking." Bob picked up the rocket. "Let's go."

We hailed a cab. Pershing Field wasn't far from where Spike and I lived. The ACS softball team played the military teams there, but today the field was deserted. A chain link fence surrounded it, and two sets of bleachers ran along the first and third base lines, enough to hold a crowd of fans for both teams. We hopped over the fence and set up our rocket on the pitcher's mound.

Bob had thought through the intricate problem of attaching the fuse, too. "First, we thread it through the hole in the bottom cap, then screw the cap back on," he explained. When it was all set, we laid the fuse out full-length along the ground, making sure it was flat.

Bob backed towards the bleachers. Spike, the bravest and most foolhardy among us, wanted to light the fuse.

Spike pulled a pack of matches from his pocket. Bob and I ran behind the nearest dugout as he touched the flame to the end of the fuse. The flame raced down the length of tape, the match heads crackling and popping.

The fuse burned slowly toward the rocket, hissing a cloud of smoke. Spike ducked into the dugout with Bob and me.

Then a loud BANG! split the air and the rocket disappeared. We ran to the launch pad, but saw no sign of it.

"Where'd it go?" Spike asked, looking to the sky.

"Must've blown up," I guessed.

"That was louder than hell," Bob said, with a nervous chuckle. "I hope nobody calls the MPs."

In a place as volatile as Saigon, any explosion might summon a herd of MPs and white mice, all prepared to count the dead and assist the injured. Had we been closer to town, we would've been overrun with police in minutes.

We'd just begun searching the outfield when we heard a clank on the ground a few feet from the pitcher's mound. It was our rocket, returned to earth from its brief trip into the heavens.

"It must have been *up* there," Bob said as he picked up the still-warm rocket. "I thought it blew up, but it must have soared."

"No shit," Spike said. "Where are the legs?" We searched the area around the pitcher's mound, but they weren't there.

"It took off so fast, it was like it vanished," I complained. I had hoped our creation would lift off slowly, like the rockets I had seen in Flash Gordon movies.

"Let's make another one!" Bob said.

We hailed a cab and headed to the PX for matches, then to USIS to cut them, and then back to the bike repair shop to have some new legs welded onto the metal tube. From there, we went to Bob's to assemble it. While Spike and I poured the match heads onto the dining room table, Bob went outside and came back with a short, thick stick.

"This time let's pack 'em in tighter," he urged us. Brainiac had become Werner Von Brainiac, amateur rocket scientist. I imagined us in a fantasy future, attired in goggles and white lab coats, taking notes on clipboards as we prepared to launch Bob's monkey into space on a bigger version of our match-head rocket.

We took a cab back to Pershing Field and set the rocket up on the pitcher's mound again. Bob lit the fuse. We were hiding behind the dugout when we heard a deafening KWHAMMM!!

"That was even louder than last time!" Bob yelled, as we ran out to the launch pad.

"Hey, look at this." Spike picked up a ripped, twisted piece of tubing lying in the dirt a few feet away. "It blew up."

"Good thing we weren't too close," I said. "I wouldn't want to be pulling a hunk of that out of my leg."

Bob began nervously scanning the area for police. American houses and Quonset huts were less than a half-mile away. Two explosions in one day might attract the authorities. "We better get out of here before they throw us in the brig."

About eight months later, in early 1964, the Viet Cong paid a nocturnal visit to Pershing Field and planted two bombs under the bleachers. The next day, during a softball game, they detonated the bombs, killing two GIs and wounding many more. The attack was one of several Viet Cong assaults that further escalated hostilities between the North Vietnamese and the Americans in Vietnam.

Chapter Thirteen

Marie's Party

When I arrived in Saigon, I quickly discovered that the hippest way for an American teenager to get around was by motorbike. The coolest and most envied of the ACS upperclassmen traveled in packs on their bikes, sometimes with a younger brother or friend behind them on the seat. If a guy was lucky—and it seemed that motorbike owners frequently were—a cute girl would be sitting behind him, her arms wrapped tight around his chest. It was easy for me to imagine myself driving a Honda 50 through Saigon with a girl on the back seat, circling the twin spires of Notre Dame Cathedral several times, then driving to Cho Lon or the eternally crowded Saigon markets, free and easy.

Spike, Bob, and I liked to sit on the front steps of the bowling alley, watching with envy as the older kids came and went on their beautiful machines. One hot spring day, we fell silent as Fred Hibbard buzzed off with Colleen Kelly on the back of his Honda 50.

As they pulled away, Spike said what we had all thought from time to time: "Man, if I had a bike, I'd be up to my neck in pussy."

"No way Doc's going to buy me a moped," I said. A motorbike was much too expensive for me to buy on my own, and my parents sure as hell weren't going to give me the money. "My mother doesn't even like me riding on them."

"My dad said if I quit smoking, he'll get me one," Spike said.

"What kind?" I asked.

"I don't know," Spike said. He took his cigarette pack out of his pocket and peered inside to see how many he had left. "I figure any kind is better than none."

While I was walking near the Vietnamese pool a few days earlier, I'd seen a white Harley Davidson for sale. I asked the owner the price (way too much), and he started it and encouraged me to mount the leather seat. I climbed into the well-worn saddle, gripped the handlebars and gave the gas a gentle twist, careful not to touch the gearshift next to my foot. The Harley felt massive, its weight and power like a prehistoric beast waiting to spring to life beneath me.

I immediately began to fantasize about taking the Harley with me when we moved back to Florida, cruising up and down Sunset Avenue from the shopping center to the bridge, a cigarette hanging from the corner of my mouth. From behind my sunglasses, I'd smile indulgently at the eager neighborhood girls as a warm breeze whipped through my hair, billowing my unbuttoned shirt.

Unfortunately, Doc didn't share my dream. "If dog crap was a penny a truckload," he'd said, "I couldn't afford a teaspoonful. If you want a motorcycle, buy it yourself."

But in Saigon, American teenagers were forbidden by the U.S. government to compete with the Vietnamese for local jobs. I could have eventually made enough money by trading my meager allowance of U.S. currency on the black market, but it would have taken years. With no employment prospects, I was out of money and shit-out-of luck.

"It'd be great to get a Honda or an Itom," Spike said, "but I'll take what I can get."

"My mom doesn't think I'm old enough to ride one," Bob said. "So I'm working on my dad. He can talk her into anything."

A few days later, Spike's dad bought him a new Ischia moped. It didn't have the sleek, modern style of an Itom or Honda, but it ran well and was extremely economical. Spike never quit smoking, either, despite having told his folks that he had, so his fear of getting caught became an obsession. We'd already been suspended for smoking on the bus on two different occasions earlier that spring, so maybe Spike's parents figured he'd stay out of trouble if he rode his moped to school.

"If I screw up again," he said, "they'll chain it to the fence."

Near the end of the spring semester, one of the kids at school told Spike, Bob, and me that there was going to be a party the coming Saturday night at the house of one of our classmates, an American girl named Marie who was new to ACS. She'd been in our school less than two weeks. The party was on Rue De Pasteur. He didn't know the address, but we made plans to go anyway.

When Spike wanted to stay overnight at Bob's, his parents made him leave his new motorbike at home. "I think my folks don't trust me," Spike had said. He seemed offended that his parents knew what he was capable of.

Saturday night, the three of us met at Bob's, caught a cab, and cruised down Rue De Pasteur until we saw a crowd of American kids hanging out in front of a detached French Colonial house, talking and joking under the streetlight and on the porch. In the United States, showing up at a party uninvited would have been considered party crashing, but among the American kids in Saigon, if you knew about a party, you could consider yourself invited.

The day had been broiling hot, but as night fell, a shower had rolled through, squelching the June heat. We exited the cab and followed Bob up the wet pavement onto the porch. We were about to step through the front door when one of the school's jocks, Ron Trump, slid in front of us, barring the way.

Ron looked like one of the he-men shown kicking sand in the face of the ninety-pound weakling in the Charles Atlas ads. Ron's shirt perfectly fit his narrow waist and broad shoulders, but his huge biceps stretched the sleeves as tight as his phony smile.

Most of the ACS jocks were overtly aggressive, and like jocks everywhere, they always put out their best efforts when trying to impress a girl, as if dating were a sports event.

"You guys aren't trying to get into *this* party, are you?" Ron said, holding his hand out, palm up. "Let's see your invitation."

Carrie Oldman, one of the way-too-happy cheerleaders, was standing nearby looking amused, apparently impressed by the manly hassle Ron was unleashing on us. I expected her to break out her pompoms any second.

Bob tried to push by, grunting, "If it was that kind of party, you wouldn't be here."

Ron easily bumped him aside and remained standing in the doorway with his arms across his massive chest. "Sorry, invitation only."

"Come on man," Bob pleaded, trying to squeeze past Ron's elbow. "Why start this shit?" I watched nervously, hoping Spike and I wouldn't have to try to deal with Ron.

Carrie finally giggled her approval and Ron moved aside to let us through.

Bob said, "Thanks, man," and stepped through the door. He turned back to Ron. "By the way," he said, smirking, "The patent-leather hair looks good on you." Ron shot him a fuck-you look, but before he could muster a comeback, we slipped inside.

It was only 8:00 p.m., but the house felt claustrophobic, packed with Brats dancing and rubbing shoulders, their energy level as high as if the party had been going on for hours. A few of the older boys already looked disheveled and sweaty, and I figured they'd probably stopped off for a beer or two on the way there. A lone floor lamp stood in a safe corner, giving off a waxy yellow light in the dim living room. The record player blared with the honeyed falsetto of Maurice Williams and the Zodiacs, singing their best-known hit, "Stay."

I recognized most of the kids, but it was Beverly Whealton, a hot redhead from my class, who finally got my attention. I squeezed my way through the darkened room, watching her out of the corner of my eye while she talked to the new girl, Marie.

Beverly was wearing a slinky, Asian-looking outfit: a figure-hugging, short white dress, slit up one side from the hem to the middle of her freckled thigh. It was exactly the kind of dress I had seen Suzie Wong wearing. Her flaming red hair was teased into a modest beehive hairdo with long bangs hanging almost to her eyes. Between the bangs and the beehive, she had added a small white bow. Occasionally, she'd sip her 7-Up through a straw, bouncing one knee to the music. She smiled and laughed, nodding as the new girl spoke into her ear. She was gorgeously sexy, but I was careful to avoid being caught staring at her, afraid that she might think I was a weirdo.

Most of the eighth-grade girls wore bloomers under their dresses while at school. Bloomers were a chastity belt of underwear that extended from the waist to the knee and had a frilly, flowery hem. They'd been created for the sole purpose of preserving the innocence of young girls by frustrating the roving eyes of teenage boys, most of whom would go to ridiculous lengths to get a glance at the forbidden regions of the female form. Tonight, though, Beverly was bloomer-free, and in the low light she looked like a clothed, airbrushed, and well-stacked centerfold.

I opened a can of soda and stood at the edge of the dancing crowd, feeling the old wood floor bounce as kids danced to the last strains of "Stay." Then I saw Beverly and the new girl walk outside, and realized I'd missed an opportunity.

Shit, I thought. I should've asked her to dance. She'd probably say no, but maybe she'd say yes, I imagined. She might even say "I'm delighted" or "Certainly," or "I thought you'd never ask," and we'd spend a couple of hours dancing only with each other. Then I'd look deep into her green eyes, take her hand and lead her to a couch in the darkest corner of the room. We'd sit down, our breath quivering in eager anticipation. She'd close her eyes, tilt her head and place her sweet lips next to mine...

Suddenly, the guy in front of me stumbled backwards across the crowded dance floor. I jumped out of his way, but he bumped into my soda arm, and my drink splashed onto his Ivy League Madras shirt, the kind guaranteed to bleed when washed. It was Chad Taylor, a bullish-looking older kid. He said, "Sorry, man," and disappeared into the crowd. He seemed oblivious to his wet shirt.

A few minutes later, as I was moving away from the dancers, I felt a tap on my shoulder. When I turned around, Chad slammed his fist into my cheek, nearly knocking me out. I fell to the floor. He vanished before I could even figure out what had happened.

"Are you all right?" a voice asked.

Stunned, I looked up into a gallery of faces. The new girl, Marie Martel, was bending over to help me up. I quickly rose to my feet.

"Yeah." I scanned the crowd. To my relief, I didn't see Beverly. "That was a surprise."

Marie was a grade ahead of me, a couple of inches taller, and had a curvy figure to match Beverly's, though not so top-heavy. Her wavy dark brown hair reached almost to her shoulders, and her hazel eyes glowed with good-natured incandescence, as if confidence and poise were her birthright.

The crowd lost interest and resumed dancing. I was trying to figure out what had happened, but was still in shock, too confused to get angry.

The whole mood of the party had changed. Before the punch, I'd felt like one of the crowd; now I wasn't so sure.

"Come sit down and I'll get you another drink," she said.

"That's okay," I replied. "I don't want another drink right now." I followed Marie and she led me into her room, next to the dining room. If there had ever been any swagger in my gait, it had been knocked out for sure. I sat down on the bed and ran my comb through my hair, but my wounded pride wouldn't let me look Marie in the eye.

"I'm glad my parents didn't see that," she said, plopping down on the twin bed opposite. "My dad would flip out if he saw a fight in our living room."

"I don't think you can call that a fight. What an asshole." The embarrassment of being punched out in the middle of a party was far worse than my throbbing cheek.

Spike and Bob poked their heads into in the room. "You all right, man?" Spike said. "I heard you got in a fight."

"No fight," I said, trying to make it sound as if nothing much had happened. "Just a sucker-punch."

"Who was it?" Bob asked.

"Chad Taylor," Marie offered.

"Why don't you call him out?" Spike asked, as though he was encouraging a Dodge City cowboy to shoot it out with a bad guy.

"You call him out," I said, "and if you beat him, I'll fight him."

"Shit, no!"

Neither of us would have had a chance in a fair fight with Chad. Chad was a year older and thirty pounds heavier—big advantages at age thirteen—but that didn't make me feel any better.

I wish I could say that I was a confident, secure kid who had no need for the approval of my peers, but the truth is that I cared deeply what they thought, although I had no idea what their opinion actually was. Up until now, I had been an anonymous new kid in a school full of new kids. But tonight's altercation made me fear that I had achieved an undeserved notoriety: I might forever be known as "the guy who got punched at the party."

"Why don't we stay here a few more minutes," Marie said, "and then go back out, okay?"

"I'm all right," I said. "Why don't we go now?" I didn't want her to know how crappy I felt, especially with Beverly hovering around. Challenging Chad was out of the question, too. It would only have gotten me a beating and made me look like more of a wimp than I was.

We filed out of the bedroom and took over a corner of the busy dance floor. Spike went to the living room and took charge of the record player. While he sorted records and cranked up the volume, Marie located Beverly and pushed her into Bob for a dance. I began dancing with Marie, but I continued to eyeball Beverly on the sly, noticing how soft and sexy her features were in the dim light. The bash chugged back into high gear. I hoped that Beverly hadn't seen me lying flat on the floor, but I knew she must have heard about it.

Beverly was hot, and, I hoped, not out of my league, but I had no moves and wouldn't have had the nerve to try them anyway. Actually, I wasn't even sure what a "move" was, though I'd heard guys talk about "putting the moves on her" all the time. I was pretty sure that getting knocked on my butt wasn't a move.

After we danced to the Beach Boys' "Surfin' U.S.A," "Catch a Wave," and "Little Deuce Coupe," Marie loaded the player with the Four Seasons hits "Sherry," "Walk Like a Man," and "Big Girls Don't Cry." It took a while, but eventually the sucker punch faded from my mind and I began to relax. It wasn't long before we turned our corner of the party into a group dance.

Bob got us started by demonstrating his take on the Monkey, a dance he had heard of, but had apparently never seen. His version seemed to be based on his observations of his spider monkey jumping around in his cage. Bob bounced around the room with his arms dragging, moving rapidly from side to side, occasionally scratching his armpit and rubbing his butt on the floor. When we stopped laughing, Spike went into a convincing Mashed Potato, his heels swishing back and forth, never touching the floor. I thought he danced well enough to be on American Bandstand.

Finally, my turn to choose a dance came around. The first dance that I thought of was the *Bristol Stomp*. According to the lyrics, "The kids in Bristol are sharp as a pistol" whenever *they* performed this magical, mysterious dance, so I figured it would do my image good to whip out a convincing Stomp. But like Bob, I had never seen anyone actually do the Bristol Stomp, so I settled into my jerky version of the Twist, a dance I'd mastered long ago.

During a break in the music, Marie invited me to come over the next day and hang out. I wasn't sure whether she was extending the invitation out of guilt or a genuine desire to be friends, but I told her I might come by. I doubted there was any romantic interest in her invitation. High school girls are rarely attracted to smaller, younger boys—even those who take a punch well.

After a while, Marie's dad, a Maurice Chevalier look-alike, walked downstairs and stood in the middle of the living room, idly surveying the scene. I took this to mean that the party was over, so Spike, Bob, and I said goodbye to Marie and went outside. Under the streetlight, groups of kids stood waiting for cabs, motor-cyclos, or parents. When I saw Chad Taylor walking my way, I panicked, assuming that he wanted to finish what he'd started earlier. I stuck my hands in my pockets, pretending not to notice that he was approaching.

"Sorry, man," he said, clapping me on the shoulder. "I didn't know what I was doing. You okay?"

"Yeah, I guess." I was surprised to hear an apology. When he spoke I smelled his breath, and knew that he'd had a beer or three before the party. He hadn't been sober when he hit me, but little facts like that never stopped a drunk from pursuing revenge.

"All right. See you around." He walked away and I loosened up, glad to see him leave.

"Let's get a cab," Bob said. "My mom will be waiting up for us."

"Hey, man," Spike teased. "You let him get away!"

I punched him in the shoulder. "Fuck off." I didn't like being teased about what had happened, especially by friends. I could get all the teasing I needed at home, from Lynn.

He held his shoulder and gave me a push with his free hand. "You horny *cob!*"

I'm still trying to figure out what the hell a 'horny cob' is.

Bob hailed a cab and climbed into the front seat. Spike and I jumped in back. On the way to Bob's house, I said, "I don't know if I told you, but next week we're moving right down the street from you."

"Where to?" Bob asked.

"Phan Dinh Phung Street." I had told Spike earlier in the week.

"Who's going to help Spike beat up the kids in his neighborhood?" Bob asked.

"His sisters," I said.

Spike smiled. After a short silence, he said, "That'll scare the shit out of anybody."

I knew I'd miss the old neighborhood and being next door to my best friend, but it wasn't as though we were moving out of town. Our new address meant that I wouldn't have to rely on a motor-cyclo or Spike's motorbike to get to Saigon. Our new home was so ideally located that I could walk downtown or to Bob's if I wanted.

The next afternoon, I took a motor-cyclo to Marie's house. The temperature was soaring, and even in the shade of the motor-cyclo's canopy, the humid heat enveloped me like an overcoat. It was hard to recognize the house without a horde of American kids standing outside, but I finally spotted her family's white stucco colonial near the intersection with Duong Hong Thap Tu.

A maid answered my knock and showed me to Marie's room, the only downstairs bedroom. The door to her room was open, and Marie was sprawled on one of the two small beds with schoolbooks and paper scattered around her. She wore white shorts and a pale yellow shirt with a round, flat collar, an Ivy-league style popular with the girls at school. A dresser and desk sat against the opposite wall near a double window that opened onto a driveway ending at a one-car garage.

Marie bounced onto her knees and took the pencil out of her mouth. "Come on in." She closed her book and sat cross-legged on the edge of the bed. Her dark hair was pulled into a ponytail, her face clean and makeup-free.

I noticed a small pimple on her cheek. My oily skin was constantly breaking out, enough to make me envy anyone without acne scars. I felt more comfortable knowing that I wasn't in the presence of yet another girl with a perfect peaches-and-cream complexion.

"How'd you get so many people to come to your party last night?" I looked around the room, glancing in the mirror atop her wooden dresser before taking a seat on the empty bed. "You've only been here what, two weeks?"

"I knew some of the kids from my school back in Arlington, Virginia. Harry Stuart was in my class last year before they moved here."

Harry and Mac were two of the most popular kids in school. Marie wasn't as much of a stranger to the kids at ACS as I'd thought.

"Harry put out the word about the party." She gave me a serious look, focusing on my face. "How's your cheek? Did it bruise?"

"No, it doesn't even hurt," I lied. The spot where the punch landed was still tender, but another fist in the face couldn't have made me admit that to Marie.

"Beverly invited me to the Cercle Sportif to go swimming, but I have too much homework to do. I'm still behind in my classes."

My ears perked up quickly when I heard Beverly's name, but I didn't let on that I was smitten. Marie was getting chummy with Beverly, and I knew girls liked to gossip about these sorts of things. I wasn't about to reveal my crush to anyone, much less to someone I'd just met. For a moment I was glad my parents weren't members of the Cercle Sportif. Watching Beverly stroll by the pool in a swimsuit would have been more than my young hormones could have handled.

For a while we talked about school, the other Brats we knew, where we were from. I'd never had such a long conversation with a girl before. Up until now, my feeling was that girls were an entirely different species, as different from boys as fish are from birds. This was probably because my family was composed of only one female—Mother—and five males, and only Doc got much time alone with her. In addition to their mothers, Bob had an older sister and Spike had two younger sisters. In my family, Mother was a small oasis of estrogen surrounded by a vast desert of testosterone.

In spite of our awkward introduction, I began to feel that Marie and I were friends, though I couldn't fathom the basis for our relationship. We had little in common except perhaps a mutual need for friendship.

Just before school let out for the summer, we moved to 172-B Phan Dinh Phoung Street so Doc could be closer to work. Our new home was two blocks from Ngo Dinh Diem's presidential palace. Phan Dinh Phoung Street was lined with tall trees that provided shade from the purgatorial heat and cover from the torrential rain that fell daily during monsoon season. Unlike our old neighborhood, this one had paved streets, sidewalks, curbs, and hardly any mud. There were no slums nearby.

Our two-story townhouse included a tiny front courtyard, just like the house on Chi Lang Street. The living room, dining room, kitchen and maid's quarters made up the first floor; the bedrooms and bathroom were on the second. Four other homes were lined up next to ours, all a washed-out yellow stucco, all occupied by Americans.

I was dismayed to discover that once again, our new home had only two bedrooms. With Lee in Florida, I had hoped that my promotion to Senior Son in Residence might land me my own room, but it didn't happen. I wasn't sure whether it was a matter of money or availability that prevented us from moving to a bigger house, but either way, I was still stuck in a bedroom with Lynn and Lowell.

Doc didn't even try to spur me on to work harder in school by promising me my own room; nor did he try to explain why it wasn't possible. When I asked whether better grades might lead to a room of my own, he replied, "The reward for getting good grades is getting good grades." His educational philosophy was more stick than carrot. I once overheard him saying to Mother, "Maybe without Spike next door, he'll start doing better in school."

My parents never seemed to mind if I spent the night at Bob's, but they had no idea that we were sneaking out late at night to roam the streets. They also didn't know that I was hanging out with Spike just as much as I had when we lived on Chi Lang street. Doc liked Bob because he was a clean-cut, polite kid, at least when he was around adults. Spike, by comparison, had a wise-ass, anything-for-a-good-time look on his face that most people, especially Doc, recognized immediately. Without Spike as a next-door neighbor, I began leaving the house alone and returning alone. During the daylight hours, my parents had no way of knowing where I was or what I was doing. This may have been a good thing, because my experiences greatly exceeded any anxieties or fears they may have had about my behavior or the dangers of the local environment.

Chapter Fourteen

Sax Education

D uring the first few weeks of school, I was excited to discover that ACS had a student concert band. Attending class was still an onerous burden, but the prospect of playing music made me think that school might be tolerable, maybe even enjoyable, if I could just come up with an instrument and join the band. In Florida, I'd used a rented sax, but as far as I knew, there were no musical instrument rental stores in Saigon, and Doc had no connections that could help. I was ready to give up on the idea when Bob informed me that his dad had once played the saxophone. His horn was in a closet at home.

"I'm sure he'll let you use it," Bob said. "He never touches it anymore."

After school, I went to Bob's to check out the sax. Bob went into his dad's bedroom closet and pulled out a black rectangular case plastered with colorful college stickers from the 1940s. He set the case on the bed and opened it, lifting out the saxophone and placing it in my hands. I was mesmerized by the horn, a silver-plated Buescher Aristocrat alto, with mother-of-pearl keys and a rose-gold finish in the bell. It was easily the most beautiful saxophone I'd ever seen.

I assembled the horn and blew gently into the mouthpiece, hoping to create dulcet tones worthy of such a glorious instrument. In spite of my best efforts, all I could produce was an ugly squawking. "I think the octave key's not closing," I said, giving it what I thought was a gentle bend. The key promptly snapped in half.

I held the broken part in my hand, wishing it was a knife so I could kill myself and get it over with. If Bob didn't kill me, I was sure his dad would. "Oh, shit," I said, horrified at what I'd done. "I screwed up."

"I think I know where we can get it fixed," Bob said calmly.

I didn't understand his cavalier attitude. If one of my friends had broken Doc's drums, Doc would have murdered both of us and buried our bodies in a shallow grave. I felt sick about the broken key and would gladly have paid every piaster I had to return the horn to its pristine condition.

"Really?" I asked, praying that Bob knew what he was talking about.

"The jewelers on Tu Do Street can repair jewelry," he explained. "They should be able to handle this."

We took the piece to a jeweler on Tu Do Street who did such a seamless job of repairing it that I couldn't tell that the instrument had ever been broken. When I tried the horn again, I was relieved to find that it played perfectly. To my delight, Bob's dad never found out about my mistake.

The ACS band was already in full swing when I joined in the middle of the spring semester, but with only twelve players, they always needed more musicians. In the States, most high school or junior high concert bands had between fifty and one hundred musicians. They were colossal ensembles, "as much for show as for blow," as Doc put it. The ACS band was composed of two drummers, two saxophonists, two flautists, two trumpeters, one trombonist, three clarinetists, and one electric guitarist.

On my first day of rehearsal, I took my place between the Stuart brothers, Harry and Mac. Harry was two years older than I and played alto sax. Mac, his younger brother, played clarinet and like me was in eighth grade.

In a large ensemble, mistakes can often be obscured or smothered by the mass of players, but in the tiny ACS band, our errors were left flapping in the sonic breeze like dirty laundry. "You have to listen to each other," our band director, Mrs. Schaffer, would say, "It's not enough just to play the notes, especially the wrong ones."

Tall, blonde, and bespectacled, Mrs. Schaffer never seemed to tire of music. In spite of the sweltering heat, we rehearsed with the windows closed to avoid disrupting the classes nearby. Although we were usually drenched in sweat by the time rehearsal was over, Mrs. Schaffer never wavered in her pursuit of musical excellence, as futile as it sometimes may have been. When all else failed, she banged out our parts on an old upright piano, leading us along by the musical nose. "Let's try it again," she'd say, waving her baton. "Slowly this time."

Later in the semester, Harry began quizzing me about songs. "Do you know this song?" he asked. He played a bit of "Cherry Pink and Apple Blossom White." It was a popular hit I'd heard many times, but I'd never tried to play it. "Kind of," I said, not wanting to seem totally uncool. I played the first few notes, then fumbled around searching for the rest. "Not exactly," I admitted.

"Well, if you can learn that and "Tequila," I might have a gig for you."

Harry was the saxophonist for the hippest teenage American combo in all of Vietnam: The Esquires. Actually, they were the *only* teenage American combo in Vietnam. The band consisted of Mrs. Schaffer's son, Harrison, on guitar, his brother, Paul, on trombone, a drummer I don't remember, and Harry on alto sax. The band had no bass player or singer, so their repertoire was limited, but Harrison cranked up his amplifier to fill out the sound and they did what they could with their odd combination of instruments.

The idea of playing a job with a real combo was the most thrilling musical opportunity of my young life. I had seen my father perform many times, usually at the base Chief's or Officer's Club with his combo, The Men of Note. Doc always seemed happiest when he was behind his drum set, swinging away.

When I was younger, I'd thought it odd that wherever we moved, Doc always gigged with a band called The Men of Note. I figured it was just a popular name. It finally dawned on me that Doc was the leader of all these bands, starting a new incarnation of the group with every fresh assignment. His ensembles usually consisted of three or four musicians playing a strongly jazz-oriented repertoire mixed with hits of the day. The flat, white, fiberboard music stands in front of each musician were painted with The Men of Note logo in big black letters next to two upright drumsticks and a few randomly placed jaunty-looking eighth notes. Doc's bass drum head sported the same sticks, but with his initials above: BA.

Now I had a chance to see what it was all about. Harry gave me the sheet music, and I quickly learned both tunes.

The Men Of Note, Saigon Edition—Doc on drums, piano and bass unknown

On the day of the gig, I took a cab to the home of an American woman who was hosting a cultural exchange luncheon for the Vietnamese/American Social Club. Our band set up on the veranda, positioning ourselves under several large umbrellas. The Vietnamese women and their American hosts chatted, sipped tea, and ate finger sandwiches in the shade. After a brief introduction, we played our two tunes and retreated to polite applause: our only pay.

When I got home, Doc asked about the gig. "Did you make any money?"

I'd never even thought about getting paid. Actually, I probably would have paid them to let me play the job. But Doc's question got me thinking of music, something I liked to do, as a way to make money. Maybe it was a way to win Doc's approval, too. He never seemed to approve of anything I did, but this, I thought, could be different. I imagined myself someday taking the stage as saxophonist with The Men of Note, playing confidently as my father looked on proudly from behind his drums.

But that day would never come to pass. I received no encouragement from Doc, not even an inquiry about my musical interests or tales of his musical exploits growing up in New York, the jazz capital of the world.

During my last year in high school, I began working as a professional musician, but by then, Doc had quit playing. He never said why he had quit, but it may have had something to do with the lack of available gigs for non-union musicians.

When I was seventeen, I made the mistake of telling him that I intended to make a career of music. We were eating dinner. He pointed at me with his fork and angrily declared, "You can't."

In the three years since I'd played saxophone with the Esquires, I'd taught myself how to play guitar, and had also begun playing upright bass in the high school concert band. After a year of practice on bass, I'd auditioned for the Virginia All-City, All-Regional, and All-State bands. I became first chair and section leader in all three. I believed that I had what it took—at least on bass, if not saxophone—to be a professional. But Doc seemed determined to squash my only career aspirations.

"Why not?" I asked, shocked to the verge of tears.

"You're not good enough," he said.

Catching a smoke in the boy's room at school was one of my favorite ways to spend time during our mid-morning break. During one such interlude, I was puffing away with some of the other Brats in the school's third-floor bathroom when I noticed a new kid had joined us. He was peering under the stall door, trying to see what the Vietnamese janitor was doing to produce the gurgling noise we heard.

The noise stopped. The janitor opened the door and stumbled out. He ignored our stares as a cloud of sweet-smelling smoke trailed him, his eyes glassy and unfocused. Fumbling his way out of the bathroom, he wobbled back to work. Behind the toilet of the stall, I spied a small brass pipe-bowl atop a metal tube. A short hose protruded from the bulbous base.

Frankie, the new kid, threw his cigarette into the toilet and pushed the flusher with his foot. "Dang," he said. "He only took a couple of drags. Son of a bitch can barely walk."

In 1963, the ritual of smoking opium—the lingering evidence of generations of Chinese influence—remained common among lower-class Vietnamese. ACS had four or five janitors, and it seemed like they all smoked opium. Their pipes were stashed in bathrooms throughout the school. The administrators didn't condone the practice, but as long as the janitors showed up and did their jobs, it was tolerated.

As inclined as I was to experiment with anything new and dangerous, I didn't want to mess with dope. I was even careful to check the cellophane wrappers on the cigarettes I bought on the black market to make sure they hadn't been tampered with. I wasn't even certain what dope was, but after witnessing the blank stares of the janitors, I thought it might be a good idea to leave it alone. Cigarettes and booze were already more than I could handle.

Spike and Bob told me they had already seen the stoned janitors many times, but Frankie and I were still new to Vietnam, and thought it was funny as hell. "His feet weren't even touching the dang floor when he left," Frankie drawled.

Frankie Turner was a baby-faced version of James Dean. He dressed like Spike, his hair styled in a tall, greasy pompadour, his unbuttoned shirttail hanging out, with a smooth, white chest to match his hairless face. To reinforce this tough-guy façade, Frankie liked to turn up the back of his shirt collar and shove his hands into his blue jean pockets while his cigarette dangled from his lips.

But Frankie was nothing like Spike on the inside. Between bouts of drinking, smoking, fighting, and trips to the cathouse, Spike had shed most of his innocence and could claim credibility as a streetwise roughneck. But the gentle, good-natured look in Frankie's eyes betrayed his best efforts to appear dangerous and rebellious. He looked as tough as spring flowers.

Frankie and his older sister Joyce had come to Viet Nam from Beaufort, South Carolina. Their Southern drawls were as thick as honey. Hearing Joyce berate her little brother—as she often did—was a nostalgic experience for me: "Ah told yew tah meet me riot heyah after school, did'n ah? Daddy's gonna be pee-issed." It was like being in Florida again.

That summer, Frankie and Harry Stuart's brother Mac joined Spike and me in spending the night at Bob's to sneak out late and wander the streets of Saigon. Marie and Beverly had become best friends, so when we told them about our exploits, they began sneaking out of Marie's house to meet us. Occasionally, Bob would tell his mother he was staying with me or Spike, knowing she wouldn't call our parents to check. Likewise, Spike and I would tell our parents that we were staying at Bob's. On those nights, we roamed the streets without having to worry about sneaking back into Bob's house.

After one long night on the streets, we returned to Marie's house instead. "You can sleep in the garage or under my beds," she told us. Bob and Frankie were small enough to squeeze under the twin beds, so they crawled through her bedroom window and stayed in the house with Marie and Beverly. Mac walked home. Spike and I were relegated to a spot on the floor of the garage. Marie's family had no car, so we were sure we'd be safe sleeping on an old blanket with the door closed.

A few hours later, I felt someone tugging on my pants leg. I opened my eyes and looked up into the angry red face of Marie's dad, a middle-aged Frenchman with thinning white hair. Although it was Saturday morning, he was wearing a khaki suit over a white shirt and tie. He must've been getting ready for work when he discovered us.

I elbowed Spike awake and we stood up, dragging our tired bodies into the driveway as we groggily squinted into the sun. I steeled myself, preparing to withstand a barrage of hot, fast questions and accusations, all delivered with a French accent. I was sure he intended to call our parents (once he found out who we were), but I was too sleepy to try to think up an excuse. He hadn't asked for our names yet, but that would be next. As angry as he may have been at Spike and me, I knew it was nothing compared to the way he would feel if he discovered Bob and Frankie in Marie's room.

He told us to wait and went inside, I suspected, to fetch Marie and ask her what the hell was going on. I glanced at Spike, raising my eyebrows as if to ask, "What now?"

Spike looked around warily. "Can you see him?" he whispered.

I stood on my tiptoes, trying to look into the house. "No."

"Let's get the fuck out of here."

We took off like track stars, bound for glory. I was halfway home before I looked behind me.

Fortunately, Marie's dad never found Bob and Frankie. From their hiding spot under the beds, the two of them had listened as Marie denied any knowledge of the boys in the garage. "I thought I was gonna start laughing my ass off, and then he'd catch us," Frankie told us later. It was months before we went near her house again. Marie's dad supposedly had been assigned to Saigon to train the Vietnamese police, so it would have been a simple matter for him to call a couple of white mice to haul us off to jail for a while. Years later, and long after his death, Marie discovered that her father was known by the East German Secret Police as an American Central Intelligence Agency operative.

Chapter Fifteen

A Cinder in a Bonfire

As a soon-to-be-fourteen-year-old, I had little interest in politics, government, or Buddhism. The only news I received was when I read one of the military newspapers, *The Observer* or the *Stars and Stripes*, or heard a snippet in passing from the radio or my parents' conversations. But I found it impossible to ignore the political situation and the protest demonstrations that were a prominent feature of daily life, blocking city streets, causing traffic jams and massive detours.

I first became aware of the rapidly increasing level of Buddhist discontent in Viet Nam when I noticed that the telephone poles and trees lining the streets downtown had begun to sprout banners. On our block alone there were at least seven, mostly hand-lettered in red ink on yellow or white cloth, about two feet wide and long enough to span our two-lane street.

I asked Thi Hai to explain the writing on them, but our language barrier was too great. "Diem no good," she said, wringing her hands as she stumbled through what little English she knew, seeking words to describe the situation. Her eyes welled up and I thought she might cry. My Vietnamese wasn't even as good as her English. I gave up and called Bob to translate.

"Put her on the phone for a minute," he said.

Thi Hai took the phone and spoke to Bob in Vietnamese. She seemed agitated, as if the writing on the banners concerned her directly. When she was finished, I thanked her for her help and took the phone.

"Sounds like the same stuff that's in front of my house," Bob said. "The banners are demanding that the government punish the people responsible for the massacre of Buddhists in Hue. They want compensation for the victims."

Bob explained that after the killings, Buddhist leaders had presented a list of grievances to the Diem government, including demands for compensation. They also requested that laws prohibiting the free expression and practice of Buddhism—such as the celebration of Wesak—be lifted. But Ngo Dinh Diem was intractable, and their demands were quickly rejected. As the situation continued to deteriorate, Henry Cabot Lodge, Jr., the U.S. ambassador to Viet Nam pressed Diem for reforms, but with no success. In our neighborhood, and elsewhere, the demonstrations were becoming more frequent and more angry.

A week or two before school let out for the summer, Spike and I hired a motor-cyclo for a ride home from the bowling alley. It was a typical sweltering spring day, birds flitting from one tall tree to the next, bicycle vendors jingling bells as they pedaled slowly by the curbs, taxis honking their way through the heavy traffic. The sun was blazing above the patchy cover of leaves over our heads. We jerked the raggedy canopy open for shade and slouched down in the seat, pulling heavily on our last smokes before getting home.

I directed the driver to turn down *Duong Phan Thanh Gian,* a pleasant residential neighborhood with stately pastel townhouses several blocks away from the crowded commercial zones. This route would take us by the Xa Loi temple, not far from my house. But as we approached the temple, we were halted by wooden police barriers. On the other side of the barriers, a huge crowd filled the street. Bicycles, cyclos, Jeeps, and police wagons were jammed between the temple's outer walls and the trees along the sidewalk. A couple of motor-cyclos idled in front of the barriers, their drivers watching with interest. On the opposite side of the street, dozens of journalists, a few squads of white mice, and several MPs paced restlessly, their attention focused on the group of protesters.

Dozens of orange-robed Buddhist monks sat in the middle of Phan Thanh Gian, patiently listening as one of their leaders stood in front of the group addressing the crowd through a megaphone. The monk wore scholarly-looking wire-rimmed glasses and spoke excitedly, occasionally sharing the megaphone with another monk. A throng of Vietnamese men in short-sleeved white shirts and beautiful Vietnamese girls wearing ao dai clustered around the two, watching attentively; student supporters from the local colleges, I figured.

Reporters carrying cameras wandered the perimeter of the crowd, speaking into tape recorders or taking notes, their flashbulbs popping like little suns. The voice on the megaphone blared stridently above the dull buzz of orders shouted from cop to cop and the sounds of cameras clicking.

Spike suggested we take a closer look, so we paid off the driver and moved toward the crowd. As we walked into their ranks from behind, a few of the monks nodded to us and smiled. Encouraged, we found a space and sat down cross-legged among the shaved heads and orange tunics. I was sympathetic to their cause, but I couldn't have told you why I was sitting there. It seemed like a good idea at the time.

Spike and I quickly became the focus of several camera crews. They circled behind us, and one of them paused for a close-up of Spike's sleeveless sweatshirt. The shirt was covered with hand-lettered graffiti (surfers rule!), but the dominant feature was in the center of the back: an eight-inch-high, crudely drawn black swastika, a popular symbol among young Southern California surfers who intended nothing more than to piss off their parents and teachers. The cameras swept past our faces, then returned to filming the monk with the megaphone.

From time to time, different monks and students took up the megaphone, droning on and on in Vietnamese. We lost interest and left. I forgot all about it.

But the next day, as I came through the front door at dinnertime, Doc closed his newspaper and stood up from the couch, his eyes zeroing in on me like a hawk following a mouse.

"What the hell were you doing yesterday?' he demanded.

I'd heard this tone of voice from Doc much too often. I could feel a chewing-out coming on, but I had no idea what I'd done. I hemmed and hawed for a moment, then put on a confused expression. "What do you mean?"

"I got called on the carpet by my CO this morning, and he told me you were in a goddamn Buddhist demonstration!" Doc waved the paper in the air. "You were on the goddamn CBS Evening News!" He began pacing back and forth, alternately rolling and crushing the newspaper in his hand. "What the hell do you think you're doing?"

For a second, I thought he was going to swat my nose with the paper, like a disobedient dog. "We were just watching! We weren't making trouble."

I was unaware that the demonstration had been closely monitored by the international media plus undercover Vietnamese and American intelligence agents, not just local news and radio outlets. I shoved my hands in my pockets and stared at the floor.

"Well, you sure as hell made trouble for me. I felt like a fool, standing there while he tells me my kid was on TV." He slapped the paper down on the bar and poured a shot of Scotch. "Then he asks me what it means! How the hell should I know what it means, for crying out loud!"

"We were just sitting there," I pleaded. "We didn't do anything!"

"From now on, just stay the hell away from them!" He picked up the newspaper, poking it at me with an angry stab. "And if you see anything going on, *anywhere*, you get the hell out of there!"

"We didn't know it was going to be on the news."

"Well, you do now!"

Mother must have heard the shouting, because a moment later she was at the bottom of the stairs. Doc had already filled her in on my escapade. I think she could tell how I felt.

"Leslie," she said, patiently. "Your dad works hard all day, and then he has to hear about you and Spike from the people he works with. They could put this in his permanent file, you know." She paused, her lips tight, as she stared at me. I knew that enlisted personnel had sometimes been transferred because of the misdeeds of their Brats. "You have to be careful around here," she continued, "because everybody sees what you do, being American and all. I know you didn't mean to do anything wrong, but you have to be careful. What if shooting or a riot broke out?"

"All right, all right," I said, exasperated. I hadn't thought even for a second that the demonstration would turn violent, but I knew better than to try to argue that point with my parents. I'm sure Doc would have cited the disastrous events in Hue as proof of how wrong I was. Then I would be forced to admit he was right—an unbearably vile option.

I adopted a suitably ashamed pose, slithered into the dining room, and dragged the phone as far out of earshot as possible. I called Spike. He was surprised to hear we had been on the evening news in the States, but unlike my father, Spike's dad hadn't been reprimanded. I never figured out who had fingered me as one of the Brats in the demonstration. Spike, even with his swastika-covered sweatshirt, apparently went unnoticed, proof to me that he led a charmed life.

It wasn't long until school let out for the summer. It was a season of freedom for most kids, but for military Brats, summer often meant the beginning of the relocation process. During the month of June, a ritual of sorts took place at Ton Son Nhut Airport. Once or twice a week, a line of cabs, motorbikes, and motor-cyclos rolled into the airport and headed for the main terminal. The vehicles were filled with kids from ACS who had come to say goodbye to those friends who were unlucky enough to be moving on to the next assignment with their families. No Brat I knew wanted to come to Vietnam, but once they got a taste of life in Saigon, most didn't want to leave.

Inside the terminal, they exchanged addresses and promised to stay in touch. When the time came, the departee walked across the tarmac with their family and ascended the steel stairs into the plane. They smiled and waved, looking as cheerful as if they were going on vacation in Hong Kong or Nha Trang.

As the plane climbed, they all waved goodbye, laughing and joking, knowing that one day it would be their turn to leave Saigon, and their friends, forever. For the Brats of ACS, the American community in Saigon was a home to which they could never return.

June in Viet Nam was also monsoon season, and drenching rains fell daily. While running for cover, splashing through puddles in a mad dash for dryness, I noticed that the Vietnamese had the monsoon problem solved.

Hidden in every Vietnamese pocket, purse, or bicycle pouch was a six-by-six plastic package containing a paper-thin plastic raincoat, complete with hood. The raincoats had been folded by diabolical geniuses so as to be impossible to replace in their plastic envelopes except by devoted acolytes of this dark art. When a few raindrops signaled the imminent onset of a downpour—what Mother called a "frog-strangler"—the raincoats materialized as if by magic, and the locals went about their business in the torrential rains. Americans, who were mostly monsoon-ignorant, struggled with umbrellas, ran for cover, or got soaked. Once the rain stopped, the natives folded the raincoats back into their neat little plastic bags until the next rainstorm.

Rain or shine, the dingy sweetness of Saigon was multiplied for me now that school was out. With Spike's new moped, we could explore the city freely for just a few piasters' worth of gas. Our spirits were unchained from the mind-numbing routine of classes, free from homework and the soul-crushing frowns of Principal Rehnquist. Although by this time I had been in Saigon for six months, I still had plenty to see and do. Shopping at the markets, going to Cho Lon for Chinese food, patronizing brothels, or playing billiards in strange new parlors were all worth experiencing again and again.

Spike and I began to feel as though Saigon was our city, our home. It didn't matter that two million Vietnamese felt the same way. We were young; we would live forever, and each day would be better than the last as we cruised our city, high on life, unbound, unstoppable.

Spike's moped didn't have a radio, so we frequently broke into song while weaving through the crowded streets. A life as cool as ours needed a soundtrack, so we sang as only we could sing, with the manic sparkle of youth, uncorrupted by fear or insecurity, with voices yodeling from adolescence to manhood and back, often within the same phrase. We sang in harmony; we sang in unison. We sang songs by the Beach Boys as if they had erupted spontaneously from the depths of our teenage souls. We sang of our love for cars, girls, and surf; for life itself. The Vietnamese must have thought us a strange pair of Americans.

On June 11th, the first weekday of summer break, I woke late and went downstairs to grab a bite to eat. The house was empty, but a note on the dining room table told me that Lynn and Lowell were at the PX with Mother, and Doc was at work. I listened to the radio for a few minutes, then tried to call Spike to make plans for the day. The phone didn't have a dial tone—a common occurrence—so I walked out to the curb and hailed a motor-cyclo. I decided to swing by the bowling alley to see whether I could find Spike or Bob.

The humidity was around ninety percent, so I was sweating profusely by the time I arrived. Even my feet were wet, the rash between my toes starting to itch as the sun baked my constantly damp sneakers. It was a relief to step into the air conditioning of the bowling alley, but except for the hired help and a couple of GIs tossing balls, the place was empty. After a few minutes, I went back out into the sticky heat and hired another motor-cyclo for a trip to the central market, where I could buy some weeds and have a look around.

The market was swarming with people, warm, pungent smog resting like a blanket on the crowd as they haggled over prices or hustled past the kiosks. Squatting on the pavement in front of charcoal fires, skinny old women wearing cai non and black pajamas gossiped through betel-chew-orange teeth, watching as the meat they stirred sizzled and popped in the hot grease of black steel woks. Pushcarts slowly rolled by, their drivers keeping up a loud, steady chant to compete with the kiosk vendors. Beggars, mostly children with smiles frozen in place, wandered aimlessly through the shoppers, holding their hands out as they approached anyone they thought might be inclined to give up a few piasters.

I bought some smokes, lit up, and elbowed my way through the crowd for a little while, expecting to run into Spike, Frankie, Bob, or one of the other kids from school. It wasn't long before my feet were itching like mad. The constant rain and heat had given me a nasty case of athlete's foot. When I couldn't take the itch anymore, I caught a motor-cyclo and headed for home to deal with the raw, cracked skin between my toes.

I pointed the driver toward Phan Dinh Phoung Street. A few blocks later, I spotted a huge crowd in the street ahead, surging and shouting as a thick column of smoke rose into the humid midday air. Taxis and motor-cyclos were wedged around the outside of the mob at a distance of around thirty or forty yards away. I pushed the motor-cyclo's canopy back and stood up. As we neared the back of the crowd, I held my hand up, motioning for the driver to pull to the side. Whatever was going on, I wanted a look.

In the center of the throng was a large clearing, the inner part of the circle consisting mostly of orange-robed monks and nuns. At first I thought a car had blown up or the VC had thrown a grenade. I stepped up onto the seat, stretching my neck to see over the crush of onlookers.

The crowd was milling around the smoke, but giving it a wide berth. What appeared to be a dummy sat in the lotus position in the center of the circle, hands together as if in prayer. Fire leapt from his blackened body, spewing black ash into the air. It can't be a real person, I thought, it must be a dummy of Ngo Dinh Diem, burnt in protest.

I watched as the flames crackled and sizzled. But as I scanned the faces of people in the crowd, I saw they revealed not anger, but horror and sadness. Some of the men and women had fallen to their knees in prayer, rocking back and forth, crying and wailing; others stared numbly at the flames, mesmerized by the inferno. A few Saigon policemen roamed the inside of the circle, pushing the crowd away from the fire.

The smell of gasoline stung my nostrils as the charred statue slowly fell over in the flames. But as the figure gave way, falling backwards, I saw a leg move and thought it *was* a human being.

My mind said this was impossible, ridiculous even, but my eyes told me it was true. In front of me, a man was on fire, burning to death. Yet, he made no sound, no movement or gesture except the ultimate collapse, like a cinder in a bonfire.

I heard someone yell. Shaken from my trance, I turned around and saw the motor-cyclo driver wave at me to step off the seat. He seemed agitated, angry. Suddenly, he pulled the cyclo backwards, jumping on the kick-starter as we cleared the crowd. I wasn't sure whether he was angry at me for making him stop or because of the immolation and its implications, but I reluctantly tore my eyes from the scene and rode home, still unsure of what I'd seen. I knew I'd be hearing about it on the AFRS news.

When I walked in, Mother was standing at the bar in the living room, pouring a Hamm's into a glass. She looked up as I passed. "Where have you been? A Buddhist monk just burned himself to death right down the street."

"I was at the bowling alley," I said, innocently. I was amazed at how quickly the news had spread. It hadn't been more than five minutes since I saw what I now knew to be a burning monk. With Doc's admonition still fresh in my mind, I was praying that no one had snapped my picture. I didn't want to be caught screwing up again. Fortunately, she didn't doubt my answer. The phones were finally working, so I called Spike and told him what I'd seen. He'd heard about the immolation on the AFRS news.

"Was that the guy from the demonstration?" Spike asked.

"I couldn't tell." I dropped my voice to a whisper. "I saw the smoke and thought it was a dummy! Doc still hasn't forgotten about the demonstration, so I hope no one saw me."

The monk who had burned himself to death was 67-year-old Thich Quang Duc, from the northern city of Hue. He'd been preparing for the event for weeks—actually, his entire life—and was the first of several monks who would eventually make the ultimate sacrifice for the Buddhist cause. Two days later, I bought a picture-postcard of Thich Quang Duc engulfed in flames. The cards were being sold on a street corner less than fifty yards from where the immolation occurred.

The second immolation, October, 1963

Years later, the smiling image of Quang Duc began to haunt my sleep. It only happened when I was tired or worried, but the dreams had a vivid, nightmarish quality that was hard to forget. The dreams were always the same.

In my dreams, his skin is smooth, unmarked, his orange robe untouched by the flames and soot that engulf him. Smiling beatifically, he floats above the ground in lotus position, rising slowly, following the smoke billowing to the heavens. The crowd kneels in a circle around him, moaning and crying. They raise their palms to the sky, then throw them back to the ground, shouting in reverence: "Quang Duc! Quang Duc!" He sits motionless. The atmosphere pulsates like a beating heart. My eyes follow the gray smoke skyward.

Chapter Sixteen

Catholics and
Buddhists

O n several occasions, I'd rubbed elbows with Buddhist monks while shopping in the markets around Saigon. They exuded an aura of gentleness and good humor, as if they might at any moment erupt into laughter at some cosmic joke. They never seemed loud or boisterous, and went about their business with a quiet patience. But in spite of what I had experienced, Buddhists, like girls, were still a mystery to me.

I had yet to see the inside of a Buddhist temple, so a week after the self-immolation of Quang Duc, Spike and I returned to the Xa Loi temple. We locked his motorbike to a tree by the curb and knocked on the front door. While we waited, I thought about my experiences with religion.

The only reason my family converted to Catholicism was because my twelve-year-old brother Lee and his friend had been caught red-handed stealing a case of Coca-Cola from a grocery store in Mission, Texas. When Doc found out about Lee's crime, he unstrapped his leather belt, sent him into my grandma's bedroom, and told him to lie face down on the bed. It was whipping time.

Doc leaned into the whipping with evangelical zeal. The silence between Lee's agonized screaming and the sharp thwacking of leather on denim was broken only by the cutting whisper of the belt streaking through the air as Doc beat the devil's poison out of him. Lynn and I, not yet of school age, listened with fascination and more than a little fear, poking our heads in for a look when we dared. I can't remember a time when I feared my father as much as I did in that moment.

Later, I was standing near the kitchen sink while Grandma Davis spoke to Mother. Lee was Grandma's favorite, and hearing the thwack of that belt must have been torture for her. Mother listened anxiously while Grandma made her points.

"You just tell him he can't hit your kids," Grandma said. "You tell him or I will."

The next day, Mother insisted that Doc never whip any of her children again. He never did, but seeing Lee screaming in pain instilled in our young minds a fear of Doc that would last for many years.

"Send 'em to Catholic school," my Aunt Jean advised. "It straightened out my kids."

Mother was raised as a Southern Baptist, but Doc's stepmother was Catholic, so to achieve religious unity and obedient kids, Mother converted to Catholicism. Doc, never particularly religious, reluctantly renewed his commitment to his given religion, and every Sunday we all put on our best clothes and went to Mass. A couple of months later, Mother enrolled Lee and me in the local Catholic school—first grade for me, sixth grade for Lee.

Having never attended kindergarten, I was unprepared for my first day at the aptly named Our Lady of Sorrows Catholic School. Mother was late for work, so she dropped off my older brother and me, and we lingered near the schoolyard flagpole for a while, watching the other kids. I wasn't sure what came next. When the bell rang, Lee pointed and said, "Your classroom is over there." Then he ran toward his sixth-grade classroom at the opposite end of the school.

Effectively abandoned, I stood paralyzed for a moment, then grabbed the flagpole and hung on as the other kids filed into their assigned rooms. I knew exactly where my classroom was, but I sure as hell wasn't going to march into a room full of total strangers and introduce myself. Instead, I played with the flagpole, swinging around and around, pulling on the rope and watching the flag blow in the breeze until my first-grade teacher, Sister Kenneth Regan, pried me away and escorted me to class.

Sister Kenneth and I quickly developed a routine of sorts. When the first bell rang, she'd take attendance and then go to the playground, peel me away from the flagpole—my security blanket—and lead me to my seat.

"Take out a clean sheet of paper," she'd say, and I'd sit quietly, scribbling in my Dick and Jane reader. "Get out your Dick and Jane reader," she'd say, and I'd take out a sheet of paper and try to draw a jet or a ship. She quickly caught on to my attitude and kept me after school every day for the entire year.

After school, the other kids went home, but I remained alone in the classroom with Sister Kenneth. At her insistence, I practiced cursive writing, making my Os perfect and round, my Ls in lowercase and uppercase, extending each the full length of the ruled lines, while she checked papers and carefully watched me. We read from Dick and Jane, and she listened closely, correcting me when I stumbled, always patient, but firm and unyielding. After reading, we passed on to math, adding and subtracting, then reciting numbers backwards and forwards, endlessly. That I can read or write at all is a miracle for which Sister Kenneth alone is responsible.

I was too young to know that my resistance to her discipline was a clumsy and childish way to get her attention. I was fortunate, though. She knew me better than I knew myself. Under her tutelage, I made my First Communion with (what they told me was) my Lord and Savior, Jesus Christ. When first grade was over, we moved from Texas to Hawaii, and after two years attending Pearl Harbor Kai elementary school, to Philadelphia, PA. When I was nine, I was confirmed at Saint Richard's School in South Philadelphia, and correctly recited the Act of Contrition for the Bishop when he picked me out of the crowd. The nuns and priests in attendance gave an almost audible sigh of relief when I finished. They had never expected the Bishop to choose me, the most mediocre of students.

I'd never feared the firm but gentle Sister Kenneth, but the nuns at St. Richard's put the fear of God into me. Those hardscrabble Irish nuns were less inclined to put up with nonsense than any of my second or third-grade teachers in the Hawaiian public schools. The nuns patrolled our classrooms, usually with a ruler in hand, dishing out discipline without hesitation. I earned my fair share of welts.

It was easy to imagine what they might be thinking: "Do ya think our good Lord is goin' ta let a backslider inta heaven, Mr. Arbuckle? A crack on the knuckles is nothin' like the fires of hell, now."

As harsh as the nuns were, the thought of facing an angry priest made my heart race with fear. They seemed to be in charge of everyone, and I reasoned that if the nuns were mean, the priests must be worse than Doc on a bad day.

But one day, on the way home from school, Lynn and I threw rocks at a billboard. We only wanted to see if we could hit the big picture of the man with a cigarette in his hand. We took great pride in nailing it. Unfortunately, a St. Richard's nun who was marching some of the smaller kids home witnessed the amazing accuracy of our throws and chased us down. She took our names and told us we would be seeing the principal, who I'll call Father Dougherty, the next morning.

The next day, I heard my name called over the P.A. system. The disembodied voice told me to report to the principal's office. I took my time walking downstairs. When I arrived, Lynn was waiting just outside Father Dougherty's cramped little room. Lynn looked as scared as I felt, and I quickly developed a sinking feeling in my stomach. I took a deep breath and tried to look as meek and innocent as possible, figuring Father Dougherty might go easy on me if he thought I was a nice kid.

The office door was open, and crusty old Father Dougherty was sitting behind an ancient wooden desk strewn with papers and prayer books. His black smock was a little too tight where the little white band contacted his neck, turning his face a dark shade of pink. He waved us in.

"So ye've been throwin' rocks, I understand."

I assumed the pose of a penitent, hanging my head in shame as I prayed for the type of punishment doled out at confession every week: Our Fathers and Hail Marys by the dozen. "Yes, Father."

He tapped on the desk with his pencil, examining us carefully. After a tense moment, he sat back in his chair. "Well, ye're not known troublemakers, so I'll give ya a choice. I can call ye're parents or ya can take two whacks from paddy." He pointed and our eyes followed his arm. On the floor next to his desk sat a half inch thick slab of oak shaped like a squash racket, but riddled with six quarter-sized holes.

I looked at Lynn. Two whacks wasn't so bad. We knew Doc was capable of much worse. "We'll take the paddy."

The heartfelt compassion of Father Dougherty quickly brought a tear to my eye—or maybe it was the paddy, I don't remember—but we resolved never again to commit sins against billboards.

Now, as I stood outside the Buddhist temple in Saigon, I wondered whether going inside would bring back the emotions I had experienced in Catholic church services: a suffocating feeling of sadness, fear, and guilt that made me short of breath as soon as I sat down in the pews. On those doleful Sundays, when the leaden air of the church closed in on me, I prayed only that the Mass be over as quickly as possible.

Finally, a monk opened the door, and when we said we wanted to see the temple, he invited us in. I commented on his fluent English, and he explained that he had attended a private boarding school in the U.S. years before.

We stepped through the entrance into the spotlessly clean temple, cool in spite of the midday heat. He closed the door behind us, and we passed into a large, open room with a high ceiling and finely detailed, polished tile floors.

The room was decorated to the point of opulence, as if the monks and priests had replaced their personalities and material desires with the veneration of Buddha and the temples dedicated to him. On the far side, ornately carved wooden altars were spread with elaborately wrought vases of green, red, and gold, filled with fresh orchids, carnations, or lilies, each vase echoing the intricate patterns and hues of the glazed floor tiles. Dazzling enameled dragons, elephants, and ceramic temple dogs with fierce teeth and curly tails stood guard, protecting the rooms and halls (as he explained) from evil spirits. The altars also supported half a dozen ceramic and bronze statues of Buddha sitting serenely next to yard-high brass candlesticks. The air was redolent with the smell of incense, the sticks smoking gently at the ends of lacquered wood incense-holders, creating an atmosphere of contemplation and the stillness of eternity

In a smaller room nearby, several tables covered in yellow silk were arranged against the walls. Each table held several foot-high ancestor tablets on wooden pedestals. Incense, flowers, and small bowls of fruit had been placed before the tablets—a more elegant version of the setup I had seen in the brothel. Deceased monks, local citizens, and their relatives stared at us from the framed portraits scattered around the altar.

The South Vietnamese practice a form of Mahayana Buddhism that incorporates elements of Taoism, Chinese Confucianism (particularly ancestor worship or *hieu*), and elements of the Cao Dai religion. The tablets were evidence of the influence of Confucianism on Vietnamese Buddhists.

The room also contained a low shelf where three bronze statues of Buddha were seated in lotus position. I'd seen this triumvirate of Buddhas in some of the antique shops around Saigon. Never were there two statues or four statues; always one or three. "Why three Buddhas?" I asked.

"These represent the Buddha of the past," the monk replied, "the historic Buddha, Gautama, and the Buddha of the future."

He told us that in Buddhism, anyone may become a Buddha or enlightened one. Mahayana Buddhism has many of these Buddhas, represented by the first statue of the triumvirate. The historic Buddha is Siddhartha Gautama, the central figure of the three. The third statue pays homage to those who may someday become enlightened: the Buddhas of the future. I figured Quang Duc to be in the first category.

At the end of our tour, the monk led us into one of the larger rooms near the entrance. We entered the empty room, and the sound of our footsteps echoed off the walls. We paused in front of the only decor, an altar at eye-level. On the altar, a green vase containing a single white lotus flower had been placed next to sticks of burning incense and a framed, life-sized headshot of one of the monks who'd wielded the megaphone at the demonstration Spike and I had attended. A clear glass vase about ten inches high stood between the flower and the photo.

"What's that?" I pointed to the vase and the reddish object floating inside.

"The picture is Thich Quang Duc," the monk said. "In the vase is his heart."

The hair on the back of my neck stood up. "Why is it here?" I stammered.

He bowed slightly and lowered his eyes. "It proves that his intent was pure."

The heart was unburned. Later, I learned that shortly after Quang Duc's death, the monks of the Xa Loi temple had made three attempts to cremate his heart (so the legend goes), but it wouldn't ignite. Thich Quang Duc's body was pitch-black when I saw him fall to the pavement that day, but the heart in the vase showed no evidence that it had been engulfed in flames either on the day of the immolation, or at any time thereafter. This was understood by Buddhists to be absolute proof that his spirit had triumphed over the forces of adversity.

I had gotten not much more than a good quick glance at Quang Duc in flames on that day. But at the temple, I was able to stand quietly and fully contemplate for the first time the enormity of his sacrifice, as his eyes stared at me from the mantel, demanding that I never forget.

Today, Quang Duc's heart is preserved in a vault at the Reserve Bank of Viet Nam in Ho Chi Minh City, as Saigon is now known.

Spike and I left the temple in silence. As we walked down the steps, the cool sensation of spirituality I felt in the temple evaporated in the hot sun, replaced by the hectic, confusing pace of modern life in Saigon. Catholicism had never created much of a stir in me, but the sight of Thich Quang Duc's heart was like being plunged naked into ice water. It was then that I first began to feel that Buddhism was a philosophy with traditions and practices surpassing anything the Catholic Church had shown me.

Although the Ngo Dinh Diem government claimed the immolation was an attempt to incite the crowd to violence, Quang Duc had issued a written statement before he died that said, "I respectfully plead to President Ngo Dinh Diem to take a mind of compassion towards the people of the nation and implement religious equality..."

In the weeks that followed the immolation, the Diem regime continued to claim that his death was a sham, a publicity stunt, and made every effort to discredit Quang Duc's sacrifice. But their words only strengthened the resolve of the Buddhists. Madame Nhu called it a "barbecue," a word she used frequently when commenting on the thirty-six immolations that occurred during the course of the Viet Nam War. She told one journalist, "Let them burn, and we shall clap our hands." In a televised interview, she haughtily dismissed Quang Duc's immolation: "Even that barbecuing was done, not even with self-sufficient means, because they used imported gasoline." During a disastrous tour of the United States during which she defended her craven comments, her father, the Vietnamese Ambassador to the U.S., disowned her and resigned his post in protest.

Saigon had its own Marie Antoinette.

Madame Nhu's infamy was well established by the time I arrived in Saigon, though. She had already banned contraceptives, abortion, beauty contests, boxing matches, and dancing. She also closed dozens of nightclubs and the traditional French taxi-dance ballrooms, but she allowed cafés and bars to remain open if the girls, many of whom were prostitutes, wore a traditional white ao dai. Somehow, the logic went, wearing white would ensure their chastity.

My first experience with Madame Nhu's sanctions occurred when I was in Brodard's eating ice cream with Bob. He pointed discreetly toward a group of local teens sitting in a booth near the jukebox and told me to watch them. Bob walked to the jukebox, dropped a coin in, then rejoined me at our table. When the jukebox began blaring "The Twist," the Vietnamese kids began shimmying from the waist up, bobbing their heads and rocking their shoulders. Occasionally, they would pause and nervously look around the room to make sure they weren't being watched by the white mice.

Their faux dancing was a symptom of the absurdity and decay of the Ngo Dinh Diem government in general and Madame Nhu in particular. Of course, Madame Nhu's prohibitions didn't apply to Americans holding parties in their homes or elsewhere. While the Vietnamese citizens chafed under the rule of Madame Nhu and Ngo Dinh Diem, American kids and adults danced, boxed, held beauty contests, and used contraceptives with joyful abandon.

Had Ngo Dinh Diem focused on the more obvious threat posed by the North Vietnamese, the fight against the Viet Cong might have eventually attained a higher level of sustainability. But it seemed that Diem's first priority was to wage a war of religion and culture against his own people. The lack of national unity and the inability of the government to inspire its citizens to fight against the North would someday lead to the downfall of South Vietnam. If Madame Nhu was Marie Antoinette, Ngo Dinh Diem was Nero, fiddling while Rome burned.

Chapter Seventeen

Go-Carts

B efore Bob's older brother had been shipped off to boarding school in the States, he'd taken Bob to a go-cart track on the outskirts of town, past Cho Lon. When Bob told our group about the track, we couldn't wait to go.

"The carts haul ass because they don't have a governor on the engine," Bob said. A governor was a device that controlled how high the engine could rev, and therefore, the top speed a go-cart could ultimately attain. All the carts I had ridden in the States were hobbled by these thrill-killers, so I was excited by the prospect of driving a cart without one.

"You guys stay at my place," he said, "and I'll tell my mom we're getting up early to go to the track. That way we can stay out all night and not worry about sneaking back in."

"Ain't that Cong territory?" Frankie drawled.

"No," Bob said, "but Americans aren't supposed to go out that far. We just have to be careful."

Other than not going, I wasn't sure how we could be careful. I doubted the Viet Cong would warn us if they were going to attack, but I had yet to hear of an incident involving American civilians, so I didn't really expect the trip to be dangerous.

"Sounds cool to me," Mac said, looking at Beverly and Marie. "You guys going to come?"

Beverly looked at Marie. "I'll go if you will." Beverly's bedroom was on the second floor of her house, so sneaking out that window wasn't an option. Marie's bedroom was on the first floor, so she could open the window and easily climb to the ground unnoticed, just as we did at Bob's.

"Let me see if Beverly can stay over," Marie said.

"Why don't we just meet you guys at the corner at two o'clock?" Spike said. "If you want to chicken out, you can tell us then."

"We're not going to chicken out," Beverly said, directing an offended glare at Spike.

When 1:30 am rolled around, we slipped out of Bob's window on cat-feet and crept single file along the wall of the house, staying in the shadows until we tiptoed onto the grass at the side of the driveway. At the end of the driveway, Bob pushed open the gate, and we hurried down the street, walking quietly until we were safely away from the house.

After a block or so, we hailed a cab and the five of us crammed inside. We got out at the corner near Marie's house, and waited under the streetlight for Beverly and Marie. It was almost two o'clock, and the neighborhood was empty and quiet.

Spike always seemed incapable of doing nothing, even for a few minutes. In spite of the streetlamp that shone down on us like a spotlight, he leaned against a nearby stone wall, unzipped his pants, and began to masturbate. He didn't even bother to take his cigarette out of his mouth.

He'd done this type of thing before when we were smoking in the alley near home, but I was never sure what bizarre impulse motivated him. Most teenage boys are prolific masturbators, capable of multiple orgasms daily after a peek at something as benign as a bra in a Sears catalog. Beating off in groups in Bob's dark bedroom was something we'd done before, but only Spike was bold enough, or horny enough, to do it on the street.

He was in mid-stroke when Marie and Beverly bounded around the corner, breathless from the exertion of climbing out Marie's bedroom window and running down the street. Suddenly, they came face to face with Spike, who quickly spun away from them, shoved it in his pants, and pulled up his zipper.

Beverly asked, "What's up?"

"Nothing," he said, with an embarrassed grin. "We were just fooling around." His cigarette hung from his mouth like an erection gone limp.

We fell into hysterics as the girls stared at us, perplexed. "Spike was being a jerk," Mac said.

"A jerk-off is more like it," I added.

"Screw you, motherfuckers," Spike grumbled, adjusting his shirttail.

"What was he doing?" Beverly asked, doe-eyed and innocent. I think she was trying to figure out who, exactly, we were laughing at.

"I was taking a leak, ok?" Spike blurted.

"We should get out of here," Marie said. "Before you decide to mark any more territory."

Spike walked up close behind Mac and me and whispered, "I'm going to get you assholes."

We hailed a couple of cabs and headed for the bars downtown, the only area where cigarette vendors would still be hawking their wares at this time of night. We bought weeds and walked two blocks to the front gate of the Cercle Sportif Club. Marie asked us to pose for pictures, so we mugged for the camera like juvenile delinquents in a police lineup.

When she finished, Bob began climbing the main gate. Because guards were (allegedly) always on duty, this may have been the only gate in Saigon that wasn't topped with several rows of nasty barbed wire. I had no idea why Bob wanted to go in, but it seemed like a mischievous thing to do, and for that I didn't need a reason. The rest of us followed, but Beverly and Marie hung back.

"You guys are out of your mind," Beverly said. "I'm staying here."

"We'll only be a minute," I said.

"If the MPs show up," Marie warned, "we don't know you."

"Yeah, sure," Mac said. "Like you guys always hang around here at night."

Everyone else's parents were Cercle Sportif members, but Spike and I had never been inside the club. We dropped to the ground and moved into the shadows of the tall bushes lining the inner wall. I could see the outline of the guardhouse fifty yards away, a small light above the door burning dimly. We moved to the right, following the wall and the bushes until the guardhouse was out of sight.

"Let's go to the pool," Bob whispered.

The hub of social life at the Cercle Sportif, the swimming pool, sat atop the roof of the central building. On the first level were restrooms, lockers, and maintenance equipment. A spacious open veranda, ringed by doric columns connected at the top by a lintel, surrounded the pool. A tall diving board graced one end, and off to one side stood a bar where Saigon's most privileged citizens could quench their thirst with citron presses or sodas.

Bob led the way, creeping up the steps past the bar. By now it was four o'clock. We flopped down on the deck chairs and rested, wondering what to do next. I saw Spike climbing over the bar, then I heard a metallic rattling as he jiggled the locks on the coolers in back. "Damn things're locked up tight," Spike said, frustrated. "There ain't shit to drink."

The calm water of the pool reflected the red dots on the end of our cigarettes as we nonchalantly dropped our ashes into the water. "Beverly and Marie are waiting," Mac said. "Let's go."

Bob flicked his cigarette high in the air. The butt hit the water, and hissed out. He picked up his aluminum deck chair and held it above his head. "Okay, but first. . ." He threw the chair into the water with a big splash. Spike grabbed another chair, hurling it into the middle of the pool. We laughed like fools as we lifted chair after chair, heaving them into the water. The deck chairs were still bobbing and sinking when Bob whispered loudly, "I hear a guard! Run!"

We bolted down the stairs in a mad dash for the front gate. A sleepy-looking guard stepped around the corner and paused.

"It's the fuzz!" Spike yelled.

The startled guard suddenly raised his nightstick and ran toward us, screaming for us to stop. We rushed the fence, scrambling over like frightened monkeys. "Go!" Mac shouted. "Get out of here!"

Marie and Beverly looked surprised, then began sprinting down the street. "What'd you guys do now?" Beverly asked.

"We threw all the deck chairs in the pool," I said, looking over my shoulder to see whether the guard was following. "The guard is pissed."

"You idiots are going to get us killed," Marie said. I could see she was laughing, though. "What if he had a gun?"

We turned the first corner and slowed down. The guard wouldn't be all that upset until he discovered the chairs on the bottom of the pool. By then, we would be long gone.

"The guards don't carry guns," Bob said, trying to catch his breath. "but they might have gotten a look at me." He smiled. "I'd better stay away for a while."

Once we were far enough from the Cercle Sportif to avoid capture, we relaxed and wandered along Duong Le Van Duyet, waiting for dawn. The shops were silent, steel shutters drawn tight and locked. An occasional lonely cyclo driver pedaled down the street for home. In a dark alley, rats crawled over a mishmash of garbage. A scruffy beggar shooed them away as he picked through a trashcan. The bars were closed. Saigon was a ghost town.

As the first pink light of dawn appeared in the eastern sky, we walked to the Caravelle Hotel and waved down a couple of cabs. Bob sat in the lead cab, directing the drivers to the cart track.

My parents had always told me not to cross any bridges in Saigon; they all led out of the city into questionable territory, Viet Cong territory. But our cabs had passed over a river, and now a bridge was behind us. We were farther outside the city than I'd ever been.

It was common knowledge among Americans that Viet Cong agents had long ago infiltrated Saigon and the surrounding towns and hamlets. Because the VC dressed like the local working-class people, they were virtually undetectable. In theory, they could strike at a moment's notice. I prayed that we weren't on their hit list today.

After a ten-minute ride, I figured us to be about ten klicks (kilometers) outside the city. The asphalt road had turned into an obstacle course of potholes and crumbling ledges, the asphalt collapsing as the dirt beneath washed away with each monsoon. A few women, men, and children walked along the side of the road past a ragtag collection of shops and shacks separated by open space. We passed a man on a bicycle with a wicker birdcage in back, the tiny birds chirping energetically in the morning heat. For the poor Vietnamese who lived here, another day of struggling had begun.

Bob directed our two-cab convoy to a stop at an industrial office park near a small airstrip. When he got out, we followed him across the street, stepping into an alleyway that ended at a courtyard surrounded by more faded stucco office buildings and decrepit yellowing warehouses. Then I saw the go-cart track.

The go-carts were unlocked, sitting in the open as if guarded by invisible hands. Bob was right: these six carts were the real deal, European racing carts, nothing like the dumpy ones I had driven at the fairs and carnivals in Florida. The carts were spare, light, and built for speed. They had no bumpers and the engines had no governors. The track had neither tires nor fences around the edges for safety. It was a flat, asphalt oval about a quarter-mile long featuring a nasty hairpin turn that wound around a stand of small trees. No barriers, and no banked turns. There wasn't even a curb.

The carts were lined up in a row, so each of us boys picked one and sat down to wait. The owners were nowhere to be seen, and I thought it strange they would leave the carts unattended.

One cart remained empty. Beverly and Marie were still standing, watching. "Who's going to take the other cart?" I asked.

"Come on," Mac said. "We won't go too fast."

Beverly gave us a cynical look. "I don't think so. We just came along to take pictures until the ambulance arrives."

"They're safer than a motor-cyclo," Spike said, leaning over the steering wheel, grinning like a lunatic.

"Not with you driving," Marie said, raising her camera. "Say *Choi oi.*" (*Choi oi* is a catchall Vietnamese phrase akin to "Oh my God!" or "Holy cow!")

Around eight o'clock, two young Frenchmen in khaki pants and t-shirts walked into the courtyard. One was clean-shaven, but the other had several days' growth of beard. They seemed surprised by our presence, pausing to consult with each other before approaching us. I assumed they were the owners.

Even though we all could understand a few words from any conversation conducted in French (thanks to the required courses at ACS), only Bob could keep up when the language started flying thick and fast. We scrambled out of the carts, and gave him an encouraging shove towards the cart-owners.

Bob greeted them with a hearty "Bonjour!" and we listened closely as the bargaining began. But Bob's cheerful demeanor soon changed to heartfelt pleading as the owners considered his request. At first the Frenchmen seemed skeptical, shaking their heads and eyeballing us doubtfully. After a moment, the two stepped aside and talked privately, occasionally throwing glances at the girls.

We gathered around Bob. "What are they saying?" Mac asked.

"One of the guys doesn't want to do it, but the other one says they need the money. I think they're going to give in."

"Cool!" Spike said.

"Quiet," Bob said. "Here they come."

The bearded one spoke as he took a few steps toward us, but the only words I understood were "cent piasters."

"One hundred piasters?" Bob said, turning to us. "We can do a hundred Ps each."

"A hundred Ps!" Spike protested. "The cathouse is only fifty!"

"Yeah, but you can get that anywhere," Bob said. "Fork it over." He stuck his hand out. "Everybody." Bob collected a bundle of wrinkled bills.

In thickly accented English, the bearded Frenchman asked, "The girls won't race?"

Bob smirked at Beverly and Marie as he handed over our money. "No, they're afraid." The other Frenchman began explaining the rules, and Bob translated for us: "He said you can drive until you run out of gas or he tells you to stop. Stay on the track, and don't go too fast. And no bumping."

We each settled into a cart. The bearded owner jerked the pull-cord on Spike's cart, adjusting the throttle for smooth running. Spike yelled, "See you suckers at the finish line!" and pulled away.

In less than a minute, the owners had all of the carts buzzing. I hit the gas and took off around the track. The bottom of the cart was only a few inches from the ground, and I felt like I was really hauling ass, just as Bob had promised. The steering wheel was small and tight, wrapped in soft vinyl fastened by a thin leather band. My cart responded instantly to the slightest hand movements. The brakes were so tight, I thought if I stomped on them hard enough, the cart would jerk my brain loose. I gave the gas pedal a light touch, and a sudden burst of speed sent me careening down the course. I struggled for control, one eye on the track, one on the trees.

I went as fast as I could, passing Frankie, then Bob. I soon found myself locked into the pack, watching helplessly as Mac zipped by. Frustrated, I took my foot off the gas to slow a little, intending to drop back and move to a better position on the outside. I thought that if I pressed the chase hard enough, my maneuver might allow me to catch up to Spike, the current leader.

After about three laps, Spike faded wide and slid around a curve, a small puff of dust rising from his wheels. The slide slowed him down, so before he could block me, I passed him and took the lead. Bob and Mac were on my right flank and Frankie last in line as I weaved back and forth to prevent Spike from getting by.

We were zooming toward the hairpin curve when Spike jerked his wheel hard and rolled onto the grass. He sped through the trees, missing several by inches, then exploded back onto the track a few feet ahead of me.

I could barely hear through the whine of the engines. Spike's crazy-ass maneuver had thrust him into the lead. I decided to try an illegal tactic of my own. I took aim, stomped on the gas pedal, and my cart bolted forward, bumping his rear tire. I felt my front tires wobble violently, nearly ripping the steering wheel from my hands. Spike veered to one side and I prepared to pass him on the upcoming curve.

But as we rounded the next turn, both owners hurried onto the track ahead, waving and shouting. We slowed down and pulled over while they continued their tirade, shaking their heads as they repossessed our carts. I wasn't sure what they were saying until they switched to English.

"No more! The race is over!" the clean-shaven one yelled. "You go too fast and almost hit the trees! You don't listen!"

Spike snickered, then thought better of it and assumed his most contrite expression. "Hey, c'mon! I'm sorry, guys. I'll be more careful."

But it was too late. The clean-shaven one switched back to French, dismissing us with an angry wave of the hand. I could tell by the grim expression on the face of the bearded Frenchmen that he agreed.

"They said we should leave and not come back," Bob complained. "Good going, Spike. We're banned forever."

"I knew you guys were going to screw it up," Beverly said. "Marie and I had a bet on it. She said, 'I bet they can't do ten laps,' and I said, 'I bet you're right.'"

We walked back toward the street, crestfallen about our ejection. "That was a fast hundred Ps," I said, emptying my pockets. "I've only got ten left."

"I hope we have enough to get back," Bob said. "It's a long walk."

The street was more crowded than it had been when we arrived, and I began to feel uneasy about being so far from downtown Saigon. No one paid any attention to us in the city, but here I could see that our presence was attracting stares from the locals. Blending in wasn't possible.

"Fuck, man," Frankie said, giving Spike a shove. "The only goddamn go-kart track in Viet Nam and we're banned forever."

Spike didn't even shove him back. "Well, at least I won."

"I would've won if you didn't cheat," I said.

"If you wouldn't have bumped my tire—"

"I think you all lost," Marie said. "Good thing we're taking a cab. You guys drive like maniacs."

We pooled our money, but had enough only for a couple of motor-cyclos, which were not meant to carry groups as large as ours. Spike, Frankie, and Marie took one cyclo, and Bob, Mac, Beverly, and I crowded into the other. Beverly sat on my right leg and Mac's left, but I would gladly have taken her entire weight on my lap. It was the closest I'd ever been to her.

I still had her smell in my head when I arrived home around 10:00 am. We'd been out all night with no sleep or food. I told Mother and Doc that I was going upstairs for a nap and slept till dinnertime.

My parents never questioned my habit of sleeping long hours at odd times of day. They probably chalked it up to the late-night talk marathons and goofing off which were typical of teens. But if Doc had found out what I was really up to, I would have been thrown in shackles, grounded for life and sent to bed without dinner—after a good beating. Staying out on the streets all night was far more dangerous than any of the escapades I'd been involved in previously, even the Buddhist demonstration. If the MPs had dragged me home at 4:00 am, Doc would have exploded.

Later that summer, Spike and I joined the American Boy Scout troop in Saigon. I wasn't too keen on the idea, but my parents thought it might keep me busy. Lynn was already a member. I had once been a Cub Scout, but Spike was unfamiliar with scouting, so I talked him into it.

Boy Scout Troop #1, Saigon, Viet Nam; The author being sworn in

"They get into some cool stuff, man," I told him. "You know, camping and tying knots and field trips. It'll be fun."

We took the oath together and signed up for a camping trip scheduled for the following weekend. The trip, it turned out, was nothing like I had imagined. Because of the constant danger of Viet Cong attacks, we couldn't set up camp in the jungle, where it might have been fun and challenging. Instead, the Scout troop took a bus to the Johnson, Drake, and Piper compound out by Ton Sohn Nhut airport. Johnson, Drake, and Piper was an American civil service construction company. The houses inside the compound had been built for their families in the style of a typical American suburb. I had been there many times because the school dances were held in a building inside the compound.

Our scout troop set up tents just outside the chain link fence, in full view of the houses. I could even see people in the homes looking out the windows, pointing at us. I felt ridiculous, like a little kid camping in a neighbor's backyard.

After a hard day of gathering wood for campfires, listening to fire safety monologues, and performing assorted drills meant to instill discipline, Spike and I retired to our pup tent and lit our first cigarettes of the day, sucking down the sweet smoke like thirsty sailors with a bottle of beer.

A few minutes later, I heard the Scoutmaster outside our tent. "Can you guys come out of there?"

I looked at Spike with dread and crushed my cigarette into the ground next to my sleeping bag. We stepped out of the tent. The Scoutmaster stood in front of us with his arms crossed on his chest. "The smokes," he said, sticking out his hand. "Let's have 'em."

I reluctantly pulled my near-full pack of Pall Malls from my pants and handed them over. When he had all our cigarettes, he squeezed the packs together and shoved them in his pocket. "You can stay tonight," he said, "but tomorrow morning you're going home. Is that understood?"

We looked suitably ashamed, said "Yes, sir," and returned to our tent. Once inside, we crawled into our sleeping bags, staring at the roof of the tent in the dark.

"It's a lousy camping trip, anyway," I said.

If we'd lit our cigarettes by rubbing two chopsticks together, maybe he would have awarded us a Smoking merit badge, or possibly Fire Awareness, commending us on our resourcefulness as the entire scout troop looked on enviously. For exhibiting common sense and using a condom at a whorehouse, we could have earned the Birth Control merit badge. Mastering advanced sexual positions would make me a shoo-in for the Kama Sutra merit badge, while my profitable currency exchanges on the black market would easily net me the Wall Street merit badge. If the Boy Scouts had offered merit badges to match the skills I was rapidly acquiring, I might even have been promoted to Life Scout like my brother, Lee.

When my parents found out that I had been thrown out of the Boy Scouts, they confined me to the house for the rest of the weekend. To kill time and earn a few points, I put a spit-shine on Doc's work shoes, polished his brass, and begged Thi Hai to let me help her with chores. I even worked on ship models with Lynn and played Monopoly and checkers with Lowell to break up the day. Spike's punishment was similar, except that he also lost the use of his moped for two weeks.

A few days later, Spike and I were cruising down Hai Ba Trung Street in a cab when a cowboy riding a moped next to the cab gave us what Spike thought was a dirty look. "You see that shit, man?" he asked. "The way he looked at me?"

I hadn't, but it was too late. Spike stuck his arm out the window, flicking his cigarette at the moped driver. I watched with dismay as Spike's cigarette whizzed by the cowboy's nose. The cowboy did a double-take and his eyes honed in on us. He began to follow our cab. He wasn't alone though. Slightly behind him, driving an identical moped, was his buddy. The cowboy shouted something to his pal. They both looked pissed.

I yelled to our cabbie. "*Di-di! Di-di mau!* (Go! Go fast!)" I thought we might be able to outrun them because they were driving Solex mopeds, the slowest of all motorized bicycle brands. Unfortunately, these cowboys had souped up their mopeds and were squeezing every bit of speed they could get out of the tiny engine above the front tire. They were catching up.

They looked to be about eighteen years old—much older than the kids we'd fought with on Chi Lang Street, and they were bigger, too. Their faces were burning with anger. If they didn't like us before, they certainly hated us now.

Spike's face lit up with a nervous smile. He leaned over the front seat to shout at the driver. "Taxi! *Tai mot!* (Turn right!) Di-di mau!"

The cabbie seemed alarmed too, as if he thought the cowboys might believe that he was in on Spike's prank. He turned the corner and hit the gas pedal, but the traffic ahead had stopped, the street blocked by a passing demonstration. Our cab immediately slowed to a halt.

"Oh, shit," I said. "Let's get out of here."

We opened our doors to jump out, but we were too late. The cowboys blocked the doors on both sides with their front tires. They cursed in Vietnamese as we feigned innocence. Spike was halfway out of the cab when one of the cowboys rammed his moped's wheel against the door, repeatedly slamming it against Spike's leg.

With my escape blocked by the other moped, I quickly closed the door and tried to roll up the window. I had barely begun to crank the window handle when the cowboy on my side reached in and slapped me in the mouth, shouting angrily. The cabbie leaned from one side to the other, yelling rapidly in Vietnamese at the cowboys.

After the first slap, I began ducking, as if Doc was in the front seat, swinging at me wildly. The cowboy's hand swirled around me like an angry bee as I scooted away, eventually bumping into Spike's back. The idea that these two might be carrying switchblades had entered my mind (knives were cheap; no self-respecting cowboy had to be without one) so I was afraid to put up a fight.

Spike finally managed to slam his door closed, pleading, *"Xin-loi, xin-loi!"* ("I'm sorry, I'm sorry!") while holding his hands up to block punches.

The cowboys mouthed a few angry du mamia's and backed away from the cab. Up ahead, traffic had begun to move. Our driver shouted, pointing his long fingernail at us, the cowboys, then back to us, waving his other hand like a frantic orchestra conductor. The cowboys restarted their bikes and rolled away, much to our relief.

You would think we would've learned our lesson, but a few minutes later we joked about it as we lit fresh cigarettes. "Good thing they didn't have knives, huh?" Spike said.

"Of course they had knives," I said. "They just didn't want to get them bloody."

Stilettos and switchblades were only a few hundred piasters at the central market. It was rare that anyone whipped one out, though. Only MPs, authorized GIs, Vietnamese police officers, and a few high-level gangsters carried handguns. They were much too expensive for the average teenage cowboy.

A few weeks later, I was sitting in the bowling alley with Bob and Spike when Beverly, Marie, and Mac walked in looking dead-serious. "You guys hear about Will Shaw?" Marie asked. "He got stabbed in a fight with some cowboys. He's in the intensive care unit at the hospital."

"No shit!" Spike said.

"He and Jim, Mark, and Fred were riding around last night and some cowboys tried to run them off the road. They chased the cowboys into an alley and got jumped."

Jim had told Mac that at least a dozen more cowboys were waiting for them in that alley. "Guys were leaping off rooftops onto them and blocking the way out," Mac told us. "It was a set-up."

The cowboys were armed with knives, clubs, and chains, well prepared for the ambush. They also had the advantage of greater numbers and the element of surprise. The battle raged in the alley until the Americans managed to fight their way out, taking their fallen comrade, Will, with them. It sounded like a scene from a Vietnamese version of West Side Story.

"You know how Will always looks red in the face?" Beverly said. "He was white as a ghost. If he wasn't so sick, I would've pinched his cheeks."

"Spike got some guys pissed at us a while back," I said. "But they didn't try to stab us." I shot him an incriminating look, as if to say "I told you so."

He glanced at me sheepishly, then smiled. "I guess we were lucky, huh?"

Chapter Eighteen

More Sex Education

N ear the end of my first summer in Saigon, Bob and I were hanging out at the Cafe "33" when Spike walked in. He seemed unusually happy.

"Check it out," Spike said, sitting down at our table. "I asked this GI if he'd buy me cigarettes. I got three packs of Marlboros for forty-five cents. He said if I needed more to let him know." He showed us the packs. "Now I have to figure out how I'm gonna hide 'em from my folks."

Fifteen cents a pack was a hell of a lot cheaper than the black market smokes, which usually sold for fifty Ps (around thirty-five cents) a pack. "Think he'll get some for us?" I asked.

"Probably. He's still at the bowling alley, if you want to try."

We walked to the bowling alley, where I saw a skinny white guy in a Hawaiian shirt and sunglasses leaning against the wall near the steps. Even in civvies (civilian clothes) his crew cut and shiny black shoes marked him as a GI.

"Hey, Steve," Spike greeted him. "These are my friends, Les and Bob. They were wondering if you could get them some weeds too."

Steve adjusted his shades and checked us out before he spoke. "Yeah, sure." He glanced around suspiciously, turning back to us. "It might not be cool to buy them here, right now. I'll get them at the PX. What brand?"

"Winston for me," Bob said.

"Pall Mall for me," I said. "Two packs if you can."

"No problem." He nodded to Bob. "Two packs for you, too?"

"Yeah, sure," Bob said, reaching in his pocket. "You want some money?"

Steve crossed his arms and shook his head. "No. We can settle up later. I live on the first floor of the white building right across from the entrance to the MAAG (Military Assistance Advisory Group) compound. You know where that is?"

"Yeah," Bob said.

"Come by around 3:30 then."

We bowled a few games to kill time. "Where'd you meet this guy?" I asked Spike. Getting weeds this cheap seemed too good to be true. There had to be a catch.

"I was standing in the food line and he just started talking to me. Asked me where I was from and stuff. I've asked GIs to buy me weeds before, but they always gave me a hard time about it. I asked him and he said, 'Okay, but be cool.'"

"Is he a soldier or what?"

"He said he's CID. I'm not sure what that is."

Bob knew. "Criminal Investigation Division. Like a military detective."

When Frankie showed up we explained what was going on. Like the rest of us, he became excited by the prospect of a source for cheap weeds.

The MAAG compound wasn't far from the bowling alley, so we arrived exactly at 3:30. Steve's place was on the ground floor of an old French apartment building, four stories high, with faded striped awnings over the windows. We walked past the chalky facade and shuttered balconies into the cool, dark foyer. It smelled musty and damp, as if the hallway hadn't seen the business end of a mop in years. Spike knocked on the first door on the left.

Steve opened the door, and we entered without a word. The shades were drawn against the afternoon heat, a lone lamp in the center of the room giving off little light. In spite of the dark, Steve was still wearing his sunglasses.

"Hope you don't mind if I brought somebody else," Spike said. "This is Frankie. He could use a few packs if you have any extra."

"I'll see what I've got. Have a seat."

We sat down on rattan chairs and a couch, and Steve turned on another lamp. A central coffee table was littered with men's magazines—True, Gent, Argosy, and Playboy. Against the far wall was a double bed, its matching, decrepit dresser being used as a makeshift bar a few feet away. I saw no military uniforms, but scattered around the room were a half-dozen cartons of cigarettes and several cases of liquor. From the looks of things, it seemed Steve might be a black-market trader. When I noticed several handguns lying on the bed I realized that whatever he was into was dangerous.

"I was just cleaning these," Steve said, gathering up the firearms. He holstered the guns, smiling as we stared silently. "You ever hold a gun?" He unloaded a silver one, dropping it in Bob's lap. "That's a Colt 1911. Forty-five caliber semi-auto. Blow a hole in you as big as a grapefruit."

Bob's eyes grew wide as he picked it up off his lap. "Damn, this thing's heavy."

"It's a lot heavier when it's loaded," Steve said.

Bob held it out, feeling its weight. "How do you cock it?"

Steve was eager to oblige, moving around to the right side of Bob's chair. "Grab it with your right hand, here." He held Bob's hand to the grips with his right hand. "Then hold it out in front, here, and grab the slide with your left hand." He put his left arm behind Bob's neck, moving around behind him before placing Bob's left hand on the slide. It seemed to me that he was getting a little too intimate, but I thought maybe this was the way shooting was taught.

"Now hold the slide tight and push your right arm away from you, hard. Like this." Steve held Bob's left hand in position and pushed his right hand away. The slide racked back with a metallic *ka-jink*. The gun was cocked. "If that was loaded, you'd be the most dangerous guy in the room. Good thing for us it's not, huh guys?"

Spike picked up one of the magazines on the coffee table. "Okay if we look at these?"

Steve nodded, and holstered the guns. I picked up a Playboy, quickly thumbing through it to the good part. While we leered at the naked girls in the magazines, he put the guns in his closet, then walked behind where I was sitting. He bent over. With his hands shaking ever so slightly, he opened the Playboy in my lap to Miss August. The strong, minty smell of his aftershave couldn't hide the reek of tobacco and whiskey on his breath. I began to feel like coming here wasn't such a good idea.

"Take a look at this one." He held the pages apart, pushing his left hand into my crotch. "Are those the best tits you've ever seen?"

I squirmed in my seat, recoiling. "Yeah, sure." He ignored my discomfort.

He turned to another page, repeating the crotch-push with his still quivering hands. "And look here."

I twisted away from him, and he straightened up. I tossed the Playboy on the coffee table and took out a smoke. "We have to get going, right Spike?"

But Spike, Frankie, and Bob apparently hadn't seen what happened. "What's the hurry, man? Look at her!" Spike held up the foldout, showing us the fully nude Playmate of the Month. "Choi Oi!"

Steve moved on to Frankie, saying, "Let me show you my favorite." As he flipped through the Gent, he pushed one hand into Frankie's crotch. Now that I knew what was going on, I could see the shock and surprise in Frankie's eyes as Steve repeated his trick. I was afraid to say anything, not knowing how this heavily armed weirdo might react.

When Steve passed on to Bob, Frankie shot me knowing looks, then Bob did the same when Steve switched to Spike. It seemed like we were there forever, but finally we paid him him for the weeds and left.

"Fucking guy's weird," I said, when we were outside. "You see the way he kept pushing the back of his hand down on my dick? He was shaking like a leaf, too."

"I couldn't see his eyes with those shades he had on," Frankie said. "Is he on dope or something?"

But Spike had Steve pegged. "He's queer."

"He sure was nervous," I said. Steve made me nervous, too. I had never been hit on by anyone before, much less a well-armed homosexual man.

"He's a nervous queer," Spike corrected.

"At least he came through with the weeds," Bob pointed out. "And cheap, too."

The strangeness of the situation didn't seem to bother Spike, especially when he listed the potential benefits for us. "Did you see all the bottles of whiskey he had? He said he'd get us some if we wanted. There must have been eight cartons of weeds, too."

"He even had Newports," Frankie said. "Nobody smokes Newports."

"Those are his," Bob said.

From that time on, I was careful to avoid Steve, even when we went to his place for cigarettes. He always seemed to have several cartons of our favorite brands, and made them available without a hassle. After that first visit, he never tried to get close to me, but I guess he'd figured out who was more likely to experiment and who wasn't. It could be that I had flunked his hard-on test.

A month later, I was walking near Saigon market with Spike. He seemed a little quiet, but eventually smiled and said, "I went over to Steve's last week, and he blew me."

"He what?" I didn't want to believe what I was hearing. Spike had finally gotten the blow job he wanted, but not like I had imagined.

"He sucked my dick, then gave me five dollars and told me to keep quiet."

"I knew he was weird." I had firmly believed that Spike would never give in to Steve's sexual advances, that his trips to Steve's were just the sort of flirtations with danger I had come to expect from him. I was wrong.

"Then yesterday, I went over and Doug and Ernie were there." Spike smiled broadly. "He blew all of us! Gave us money, too." He pulled out a big bundle of Ps and green, showing me his newly acquired wealth.

Doug and Ernie were a couple of the junior-class kids I'd seen around school. I'd never paid much attention to them, nor they to me, but I was surprised to find out that other Brats had been going to Steve's. I began to see Spike (and Doug and Ernie) in a different light, and wondered who else might be involved.

Spike thought the whole affair was amusing and didn't seem ashamed or reticent about it, at least not around me. By this time in our friendship, I'd realized that my best friend was hornier than a fleet of sailors after six months at sea. He was always the first to suggest a trip to a cathouse, and he was the only one of us who had ever dared to go alone. He'd been trying for a while, with no luck, to get a free blow job from the girls at the brothels. Now, with the extra cash, he could pay for it.

"He told us to stay away for a few days, but said we could come back if we needed cigarettes. You want to come with us?"

"I don't think so." I had no taste for that kind of escapade and wasn't flattered that Spike had asked me. I never needed or wanted money that badly, but I don't think it was the money Spike was after. Money was just a side benefit. The main attraction was his unrelenting fascination with sex—a trait I shared, like most fourteen-year-old boys, but to a much lesser degree. I don't know whether Doug or Ernie ever went back, but in the months that followed, Spike visited Steve dozens of times. Between easy money, cheap cigarettes, and a blow job, I guess he couldn't see a down side. At that age, many kids aren't quite sure which way they're going, and Spike certainly fit that description.

Spike had no external traits that might suggest he was homosexual, though. He was as "manly" as any fourteen-year-old I knew, and had a keen eye for women. When I once jokingly asked if he was going to give Steve a blow job, he got mad at me, saying, "I ain't no fucking queer." We almost got in a fight over my comment. It seemed that he just liked oral sex and didn't seem to care where it came from. I could easily cast him as the victim of a child molester, but as long as I knew Spike, he never showed any anxiety, regret, or sadness over what happened. If he was a victim, he was a willing one.

Chapter Nineteen

Mrs. Tyson

After nine months in Saigon, my mother grew tired of going to the market with Thi Hai during the day or searching for things to do around the house. We weren't members of the Cercle Sportif, so Mother didn't have the option of spending her afternoons getting massaged, drinking tea, and gossiping by the pool with the other military wives. When Mother heard about an available position teaching English at the Free Pacific Institute (a Chinese Catholic school in Cho Lon where film icon Oliver Stone would one day teach), she applied for the job and began immediately. With some of the extra money, my parents hired Cuc (pronounced "kook"), a friend of Thi Hai's, to help out with the chores.

Thi Hai was in her late thirties, the age when middle-class Vietnamese women begin to wear their hair in a tight bun, a sign of maturity and wisdom. When Thi wasn't working, she stayed in her room, listening to her transistor radio or reading the local papers. Occasionally, when I went into the kitchen, I'd walk by her door and spot her standing before her dresser, where she kept an altar like the others I'd seen, with tablets, flowers, and pictures of deceased relatives. Her palms were pressed together in prayer; her head bowed while her lips moved silently. It was proof to me that she had another life we knew nothing about.

Cuc was more than ten years younger than Thi Hai. She was short and sexy and went about her chores barefoot most of the time, her hair loose and wavy. She never wore a bra, and her breasts swung freely under her silk top as she went from room to room. I found it hard not to stare at her. When she smiled at me, I wondered whether she might be aware that I often fantasized about her, trying to imagine what her bare breasts would feel like against my bare chest.

My frequent trips to the cathouse had honed my sexual imagination to perfection, which often plunged me into a frenzy of burning adolescent lust. Sometimes, like when I saw Cuc squatting to wash vegetables, I remembered the smell of sex and the naked women at the cathouse, crouched over the washbasin that first time. With Cuc's image firmly in mind, I would calmly hurry into the upstairs bathroom and lock the door behind me. A few frantic minutes of mortal sin would quench my passion, at least for a while.

Thi Hai. We never knew her full name.

Sometimes, when Doc was at work, Spike would come by during the day and hang out for a few minutes to try to talk with Cuc. Unlike the gentle, matronly Thi Hai, Cuc was brassy and confident. When walking from one room to the next, she would often run her hands through her hair and give it a gentle toss as she pretended to ignore our stares. Whenever she preened for us like this, Spike teased her, saying, "Cuc pretty, very numba one," to which the smiling Cuc would reply, sassily, "Spike numba ten boy. Very dinky-dau." She drove us wild, but because of the difference in our languages and ages, there wasn't a damn thing we could do about it.

Mother still didn't feel comfortable taking a cab alone, so Doc bought her a huge black '49 Ford sedan so she could drive herself to work, making us one of the few American families who owned a car. With her own transportation, Mother didn't have to worry about Viet Cong cab drivers, but local traffic was another problem.

Mother was an unusually slow, careful driver, and the dense traffic in Saigon just made her slower. On her way home one day, while she was stopped at an intersection, an elderly Vietnamese man on a bike slammed into the rear of her car. He began yelling at her, shaking his fist, and cursing. Mother was terrified. Unable to understand him, she rolled up her window and drove home with the old man tailing her. Although he and his bike were apparently uninjured, he followed her all the way home. When mother got home, Thi Hai called the police, who took statements and drew diagrams of the accident. In spite of the police's involvement, the old man stayed outside our house for three days.

As Doc came to and from work each day, the old man would rise to his feet and begin complaining loudly, though he kept a respectful distance. Doc would nod pleasantly in his direction. Mother was afraid to leave the house using the front door, so Doc parked her car behind the house, and for three days she left for work and returned using the back alley.

This type of pressure was common in Saigon. It was usually successful because the perpetrators didn't demand a lot of money. Most Americans were happy to pay five hundred piasters (about four dollars) to a complainant just to be left alone. With the implied threat of violence, the ruse was mostly directed at women.

But Thi Hai had worked for many American and French women and was wise to the old guy. When Mother finally got up the nerve to offer the man money, Thi intervened. "He no good," she told Mother. "You pay, he come many more time." Finally, Thi had had enough. She and Cuc huffed out to the street and took up positions on either side of the old man.

I had never seen Thi or Cuc angry, so I was surprised and a little pleased by the intensity of their verbal attack. I watched as they took turns berating the old man for his attempted con, their hands waving in the air like a horse's tail swatting flies. The old man remained seated on the ground, stubbornly ignoring them. But when they told him that they were going to call the white mice, he mounted his bike and rode off.

"I say police come, he no come no more," Thi explained, her normally gentle face bent into a frown.

We never saw him again.

After ten months of delay, the white mice finally decided in favor of the old man and Doc paid a one thousand piaster settlement. We had moved away by then and had no desire to appeal.

The author, age 14

The Free Pacific Institute was populated mostly by well-to-do, Vietnam-born Chinese students. The staff consisted of holdovers—French nuns and priests—and a few bored housewives like Mother. But most of the boys in Mother's classes were older than you would expect to find in a twelfth-grade class. With the South Vietnamese draft in force, many had chosen to fail and be kept behind a grade to avoid having to serve in the military. "A bunch of spoiled brats," Mother complained. "They like living here, but they won't fight for their country."

Class was usually uneventful, but once when Mother turned her back briefly to write on the classroom blackboard, a student threw an open switchblade in her direction. It smacked the wall a few feet away from her head and fell to the floor. She put it in her purse and went to see Father Jaegher, the principal of the school.

Father Jaegher was a stern, rosary-swinging disciplinarian in the old Catholic style, much like the priests I'd feared when I was younger. He applied ancient techniques of parochial inquisition to the students and the knife-thrower was betrayed and expelled. The class returned to normal, but my mother never again turned her back to her students. Instead, she learned to write on the blackboard while facing them.

While Mother struggled at her school, I was having my own problems at ACS. As the fall semester got underway, I began experiencing a relentless, dull throb that grabbed me behind the eyeballs and squeezed hard. Every day at 10:00 am, a blinding, pounding ache began creeping into my forehead, threatening to crack my skull down the middle like a walnut.

After a week of suffering, I understood what my mother meant when she said she had a migraine. On several occasions, I had seen Thi Hai pressing her index finger and thumb against the bridge of her nose, a common local remedy for headaches. Doc called it "Vietnamese aspirin," but it didn't work for me. It could have been the oppressive heat and humidity or the stifling air of the classroom—or maybe Viet Nam had finally gotten to me.

My migraines lasted into October, fading away every day at precisely 11:00 am. I could set my watch by them. They began when I sat down in Mrs. Tyson's history class and vanished when class ended.

A thin, wiry woman in her mid-fifties, Mrs. Tyson was a career educator. Her thick brown hair was streaked with strands of gray, and her voice was husky, probably from too many years of smoking. She usually wore dark, knee-length dresses that were more common in cooler climates.

A class of teenagers is like a pack of wild dogs: when they sense fear in a teacher, the pack quickly zeroes in on the unsteady voice, the accommodating smile, the anxious gesture. If the students see a shred of weakness or compromise in a teacher's eyes, they recognize it instinctually.

Mrs. Tyson, however, exhibited no fear or weakness. Like the other Brats in the pack, I sensed that goofing off wouldn't be tolerated in her classroom.

Mother reading to her class at the Free Pacific Institute, 1964

Chad Taylor sat a few rows away from me in Mrs. Tyson's class. During the second or third week of the semester, he was dozing quietly in his seat while she lectured us on European history. The ceiling fans hummed hypnotically in the thick, muggy air. If not for my throbbing head, I could just as easily have gone to sleep.

Mrs. Tyson picked up a ruler from her desk and walked through the aisles, pausing in front of Chad. She brought the ruler down on the edge of his desk with a loud *thwack!* Chad jerked awake, confused.

"Mister Taylor," she said, casting a bemused stare at the groggy Chad. Her voice echoed in the silence.

Chad rubbed his eyes. "Huh?"

"The correct response is 'Yes, ma'am.'"

"Yes, ma'am." He straightened in his seat.

"While you've been asleep, we've been discussing the Norman Conquest of England. Did you have a good nap, and can you tell us when that conquest occurred?"

Chad squared his shoulders, fidgeting nervously. "Uh…no. I mean, yes… I mean …"

She returned to her desk, tapping the ruler on her open palm. "Mister Taylor, you may explain what you mean when class is over. Can anyone give Mister Taylor a clue as to when the Norman invasion of England occurred?"

A few hands went up, none of them mine.

"Miss Oldman?"

"Was it 1066?"

"Don't ask me, Miss Oldman. Tell me."

"Yes. It was 1066," Carrie responded.

"You are correct, Miss Oldman. And can someone tell us who did the conquering."

"Norman?" Chad blurted out.

"Very funny, Mister Taylor. Unfortunately for you, it is also incorrect, unless you meant to say the Normans, which you did not." She shot him a look that could have wilted lettuce. "You were doing better when you were asleep."

Dharma Ganesh held her hand up. "It was William the Conqueror."

"Thank you, Dharma. William the Conqueror, or as he was known before the Battle of Hastings," she said, staring at Chad, "William the Bastard."

The word brought a few chuckles, but not from me. I knew I could easily have been the one receiving Mrs. Tyson's ire. The week before, she had requested that I, too, stay for a talk after the bell rang. On that day, as the other students filed out, I waited by her desk, trying not to look too guilty.

I'd been late for class because I was catching a smoke in the bathroom with Spike. A moment after the bell rang, I slipped into Mrs. Tyson's class reeking of Pall Malls. I didn't think she had noticed, so I sailed through the hour without a worry. When the ending bell rang, however, she told me to stay, and I realized I hadn't gotten away with anything.

I waited while she finished erasing the blackboard and put the eraser in its tray. Finally, she sat down at her desk. "Well, Mister Arbuckle, you have managed to distinguish yourself as one of my worst students, and it took you only two weeks. Is there some compelling reason for this dismal performance?"

I held my books to my chest with one hand and stuffed the other into my pants pocket. I wanted to fold myself up and crawl in after it. "No, ma'am."

"I didn't think so. If I thought you were incapable of doing the work, I would just admonish you and send you home."

I stood there feeling like a fool, unable to look her in the eyes. Her stare bored a hole in my forehead, but I could think of nothing to say, no defense that she wouldn't see through. The concerned gaze of a woman like Mrs. Tyson always had that effect on me.

"You seem determined to fail," she said. "But I'm not going to let you do that. That would be too easy." She picked up a pencil and opened her class log. "On Mondays, I'll create an extra assignment for you. You will hand it in on the following Wednesday after class. If you don't hand in the assignment on Wednesday, I'll give you a new assignment to complete here in class, after school, while I do paperwork. And it won't be as easy as the Monday assignment." She looked up from the log. "Do we understand each other, Mr. Arbuckle?"

"Yes, ma'am." Even though she was loading me up with homework, I sensed that I was getting off easy.

"Excellent. See me after school today and I'll have your assignment waiting for you."

"Yes, ma'am," I said, relieved that at least this part was over.

After school that day, I took my place in the line outside Mrs. Tyson's door. Apparently, I wasn't the only student with an extra assignment. As Beverly and Marie walked by on the way out of school, Marie smiled at me. She had been in Mrs. Tyson's class briefly in the spring semester. "What did you do?" she asked.

"I was late to class."

"We're taking a cab to the bowling alley," Beverly said. "Want to come?"

"Sure," I said. "Just as soon as she lets me go." Like a multitude of students before me, I was learning that you never get away with anything in Mrs. Tyson's class.

Chapter Twenty

Flying Sandwiches

S nack time was the only break in our short school day at ACS. We had no cafeteria, so the hallways filled with kids eating whatever they had brought from home. I usually hung around the third-floor halls with the rest of our crowd.

On a hot September morning, Spike was standing in front of me eating his usual snack, a bologna sandwich. When I turned to talk to Beverly, he ripped the "fruit loop" (a small cloth loop above the pleat) off the back of my shirt.

"You asshole," I said.

"Here you go." Spike handed me the loop.

"He tore it off?" Beverly asked. I don't know why she seemed surprised. Nothing Spike did surprised me much anymore.

"Yeah, but that's okay," I said. I'd already plotted revenge.

A moment later he turned his back. I grabbed his fruit loop and pulled. "We're even now," I said. Beverly laughed as I held up my prize.

Spike felt the back of his shirt where the loop should have been. "You horny cob!" He spun around to face me and raised his hand over his head, cocked and loaded with the bologna sandwich. I knew I was one second away from wearing the sandwich, so I bolted down the hall. Spike took off after me, holding his ballistic lunch high in the air, an expression of manic joy on his face. I expected him to fire at any moment.

I reached the stairway, grabbed the rail, and veered onto the stairs. I bounded down the steps three at a time. Behind me, Spike was closing in.

Mrs. Delort, our dour, matronly French teacher, was on her way up, grasping the railing with her left hand. I swerved around her just as Spike launched the meat-missile. It zinged past my head and smacked Mrs. Delort squarely in the face.

Horrified, I slid to a stop and turned around. "Ohhh, shit," I muttered. "Are you okay?"

She stood on the steps in shock, wiping a glob of mustard from her eyelid with her middle finger. Her cheek and forehead were streaked with yellow. A slice of bologna adorned one side of her grey hair, a piece of lettuce the other, like an avante-garde French hat. With a soft sigh of resignation, she said, "Come with me," and walked toward the administration building.

She didn't bother to brush the bologna and lettuce from her neatly arranged hair. Instead, she wore it with the kind of solemn dignity usually reserved for hangings and funerals. Following her, I could see the bologna hat-sandwich sitting cockeyed atop her head and the absurdity of the situation slammed into my funny-bone. The long tile corridor resonated with our snickering as Spike and I marched to our fate. I knew our already shaky academic future was racing towards disaster, but I was still laughing when we entered Rehnquist's office.

When we walked in the door, Mrs. Rehnquist looked up from her paperwork and a dark frown settled on her face. The bologna hat was all she needed to see. "You two. *Again.*"

Mrs. Delort took a Kleenex from the desk and extracted bits of mustard-slathered food from her hair. "They were horsing around and this is what I get." She held out the incriminating food.

Rehnquist glared at us, her index finger wagging back and forth accusingly. "So you think this is funny?"

I had seen so many episodes of *The Three Stooges* that it wasn't possible for me to think of it as anything *but* funny. I took a deep breath and managed to put on a solemn expression, struggling to gain enough composure to make a credible excuse. Then Mrs. Delort plucked the last piece of lettuce from atop her head, and I exploded with laughter. Spike hadn't stopped laughing since we left the stairway.

Mrs. Rehnquist flushed beet-red. "I don't see anything to laugh about here! We'll see if your parents think it's funny." She stood up, slamming her chair backwards into the wall. "You're both suspended for the rest of the week! You jokers need to learn a lesson!" She paused and I sensed a reservoir of righteous anger bubbling up from some deep, dark place in her chest.

"This is a school!" she shouted. "Not a circus tent!" She put one hand on her hip and pointed the other at the door, like a fat teakettle threatening to boil over. "Get your books and go straight home!"

By the time I got home from school, my sense of humor had deserted me in favor of simmering regret. I'd never seen Mrs. Rehnquist angry enough to turn beet-red. She had told Mother that, "I wouldn't have suspended them if they would've shown a little remorse. I know they didn't mean to hit her, but they just wouldn't stop *laughing*."

Mother had already phoned Doc at work to tell him about the suspension. When he got home from work he came through the door with a surly look on his face, but before he could say anything I put up my best defense: "He didn't mean to hit her!" I argued.

"Yeah, but he *did* hit her, goddamn it," Doc yelled. "And *you* laughed about it!" He dropped his hat on the bar and fetched a cocktail glass from the cabinet. "Your mother and I are tired of this crap! Every time there's trouble, it's you and Spike. Your grades are lousy and you've been suspended twice, now. Twice!" He shook his head, sullenly dropping ice cubes into his glass. "I never got suspended in my whole goddamn life."

I stared at the floor and shuffled slowly toward the stairs to escape to my room.

"Keep screwing around," he called after me, "and you'll flunk the year, wise-guy."

Spike's folks locked up his bike and we both stayed home from school for the next three days. My parents swore that I wouldn't see the outside of the house that week, but they were pretty lax about enforcing their punishments. After three days of sulking in my room and arguing with Lynn about whose stuff went where, they caved in. They didn't want me hanging out with Spike, but once I left the house, I was on my own. What could they do? They knew that Spike was only one-half of a trouble-making equation.

Military tradition and protocol requires that officers and enlisted men not socialize with one another. I'd never paid much attention to this glaringly obvious class divide between officers and enlisted men because Doc never spoke of it. Like sex, it was one of the subjects that never came up during dinner.

Mother was keenly aware of the distinction, though. When I once asked her why Doc didn't become an officer, she said, "Well hon, he'd have to go to sea for two years. Plus we'd have to live in officer's housing, and you wouldn't be able to have the same friends."

Except for the part about replacing my friends, that didn't sound like such a bad deal to me. But then she told me that becoming an officer also meant that Doc would have to take a cut in pay when he moved from the top of the enlisted ranks to the bottom of the officer's ranks. I dropped the idea, figuring that my meager allowance was thin enough.

Bryant Joseph "Doc" Arbuckle was born in New York City in 1924 into circumstances that most people might consider ideal. But when he was five, his mother was killed in a midtown Manhattan car accident, cut to death by razor-sharp shards of broken windshield glass. Because his father, Joseph Arbuckle, had no one to take care of his only child while he worked, he placed Doc in an orphanage just before the stock market crash of October 1929. After several years, Joseph married my grandmother, Margaret (Morrisey) Arbuckle and brought his traumatized little boy home.

Doc rarely spoke of his time in the orphanage, but when he did it was with a reticence born of emotional suffering and bitterness. If one of us boys complained about what we were having for dinner, for instance, Doc would angrily declare: "You'll eat it, and you'll *like* it! When I was little, I would've given my *eyeteeth* to have food like this!"

I'm sure he was remembering the black days he'd spent in the orphanage. I'd hang my head in shame, imagining a tiny ragamuffin Doc begging for another bowl of gruel under the cold, heartless glare of the orphanage's cook.

After his father and his new stepmother brought him home, Doc resumed his position as the only son of a well-to-do Manhattan family. His family summered on Long Island, paid for him to attend Peekskill Military Academy, and taught him manners appropriate to every occasion. His stepmother, my Grandma Margaret, would have sat in a parked car until glaciers melted rather than open the door for herself. A former hand model for Elizabeth Arden, Grandma Margaret was a stickler for etiquette, especially when it involved Doc's four little barbarians and his wife from Hick-town, Texas. In the weeks before a visit from Grandma Margaret, Mother and Doc nagged us incessantly about our table manners in the hopes of avoiding one of her not-quite-sober lectures on the proper way to raise children.

Grandma Margaret's elitism and Doc's upbringing meant that my brothers and I rarely felt the sting of inferiority that other families of non-commissioned officers (NCOs) experienced. We had been taught to tilt soup dishes with the best of them.

On military bases around the world, children of enlisted men and women rarely socialized with the children of officers outside of school. Because most aspects of base life were segregated by rank, this was an easy situation to perpetuate. But Saigon had no official military base, so the norms were different. Given the small size of ACS and our collective alienation from the locals, students tended to choose friends with little regard for income or the class hierarchy imposed by the military. Our mini-culture wasn't classless, but for the kids of ACS, it was far more egalitarian than it would have been stateside or on a military base. Military Brats have to get used to being the new kid in school quite often, but our school was different—almost all of the students were military, civilian, or diplomatic Brats.

At ACS, social acceptance was quick and easy once you figured out which crowd suited your style. Whenever a new student showed up, word got around, and if the newcomer had an interesting background, he or she could achieve instant notoriety. This was the case with one new arrival at ACS, a guy named Scott Pettigrew.

Scott had a deep tan and long, brown hair, streaked blond from too many hours in the sun. It slanted across his forehead perfectly, shading his eyes the way I always wanted mine to do. He dressed like the quintessential California surfer: desert boots, blue jeans, and Dewey Weber Surfboards T-shirts with bold competition stripes. He was thin, quiet, and uninterested in school, Saigon, and us. He already knew he was leaving Saigon when school ended the following June.

Scott wasn't a real military Brat—he lived in Malibu with his mother after his parents divorced—but his dad worked with Bob's father at USIS. Scott had repeatedly been caught skipping school to go surfing, so his mom insisted that he move in with his dad and he was shipped off to Saigon for the school year.

Back in Malibu, Scott wouldn't have been seen hanging around with someone like Spike or Frankie. In the wake of WWII, the warm weather and sunshine of Southern California had generated two new and diametrically opposed sub-cultures: Ho-dads and Surfers. Spike and Frankie looked like ho-dads.

Ho-dads were motorcycle and hot-rod driving greasers, dedicated to living on the fringes of society. Pictures in magazines such as *Life* showed ho-dads in white T-shirts or black leather jackets, wearing sunglasses and heavy boots as they cruised the California highways on their "hogs" or in custom cars. Like Spike, their hair was slick with oil, holding their pompadours firmly in place. Surfers were the ho-dads' polar opposite: laid-back, sun-drenched rebels with a hedonistic beach-bum image that parents loved to hate. In the numerous Hollywood "beach" movies (spawned by the success of *Gidget*), surfers were usually portrayed as harmless, goofy, and grease-free outcasts, bronzed beatniks on surfboards who wanted nothing more than to ride waves and deflower the daughters of staid, respectable middle-class squares from the inland suburbs.

Each of these groups considered the beach to be their turf, although I suppose the surfers had the more valid claim. Unfortunately, ho-dads mistakenly considered surfers to be sissies, so gang fights between the two groups had become commonplace in the beach towns of Southern California.

Although Spike had embraced the ho-dad look, he hadn't adopted their attitude toward surfers, so Scott began to hang out on the periphery of our little group, probably more out of loneliness than any sense of camaraderie. When we could get him to talk, he spoke fluent Surferese, and we listened carefully, trying to pick up each nuance of the strange new lingo coming out of Southern California: "I had this bitchin' wave and was riding the nose when this kook dropped in on me," he'd say. "I did a go-behind, but my skeg dug his rail and I went over the falls. My board ended up on the fucking rocks. Then the kook says, 'Sorry, man,' like that's going to fix all the dings in my board." He pantomimed all the proper contortions to make sure we got the full mental image of him surfing at Malibu, poised on the nose of his board like a hood ornament.

Even though ACS was far from the States, we were inundated with magazine articles and radio features describing the explosion of Southern California beach culture, hot-rods, and surf music. Thanks to AFRS, the music of the Beach Boys, Jan and Dean, Dick Dale, and other Southern California bands had burned brilliantly in our isolated little community. Scott appeared at ACS at the perfect moment to stoke the flames of our interest. Thanks to Bob, talk of Scott's background spread quickly.

"A surfer?" guys said. "That's cool."

"I think he's cute," girls said.

The older kids ignored Scott, as they did the rest of the freshmen, so he usually kept to himself, but on the bus ride home from school each day, he would sit with us. One day, Spike, Bob, and I were in the back of the bus struggling to open the windows so we could smoke. Scott boarded the bus and sat down next to me. "Who's this guy getting on the bus here?" he whispered.

I glanced toward the front of the bus. "John Johnson," I said. "Mostly a jerk."

"He keeps on saying shit to me, like 'nice shirt,' but I can't tell if he's being an asshole or what."

Bob turned around and leaned over the seat. "I'll put money on asshole."

While the bus rumbled away from the school gate, John strolled lazily down the aisle to our section wearing his usual lopsided smirk. He sat down with his back to the window, putting his feet on the seat. His hair was a military-style crew cut held firm in front by a thick layer of Vaseline. It looked like arrowheads were jutting up from his forehead. After a few minutes of watching us furtively blow smoke out of the rear windows, he turned his attention to Scott. "Where you from?"

"California. Malibu."

"I hear you're a surfer."

"Yeah."

John paused for a moment, checking us out. His smile vanished. "You think you're cool, huh?"

"Not really."

John squinted at him, like a con man sizing up a rube. "I was thinking about learning to surf when I get back to San Diego," he said, relaxing into his just-one-of-the-guys mode.

"I don't think you'd like it," Scott said.

"Why not?"

Scott brushed his hair back and looked John in the eye. "'Cause oil and water don't mix."

John glared at Scott, unable to muster a witty comeback to silence our cackling. When the bus pulled up at John's stop, he stood up, still staring at Scott. "See ya later, surfer-boy."

"Bye-bye, ho-dad."

John swaggered up the aisle, giving us the finger behind his back. He whispered to the MP and got off. We were putting the windows up when the MP walked to the rear of the bus. "Okay, guys," he said. "Let's have some names."

We reflexively assumed the incredulous demeanor of the innocent. "What for?" Spike protested. "We didn't do nothing!"

"I saw you toss the cigarettes out the window."

We gave him our names and he turned us in to Mrs. Rehnquist. The next day at school, Rehnquist called us into her office to let us know she was calling our parents. The three of us—Spike, Bob, and I—were thrown off the bus for a week. (We made sure to tell Rehnquist that Scott wasn't a smoker so that he wouldn't have to share our fate). If not for the fact that our parents found out about the smoking, being ousted from the bus would've been a good thing—we could smoke in the motor-cyclo we'd have to take on the way to and from school.

I dreaded going home that day. I arrived in time to see my mother, still in her schoolteacher garb, replacing the phone receiver. She looked at me grimly.

Lynn had taken the bus right before mine and arrived home earlier. He was sitting on the couch. I dropped my books on the coffee table and plopped down next to him.

"Well?" she said.

"Well, what?" I demanded, angry that I had to go through another inquisition.

"You know what your father's going to say, don't you?"

"Yeah," I said, descending into my persecuted-teenager sulk.

"You know, Leslie, if you would just stay out of trouble and improve your grades, your father would do anything for you."

I didn't believe her. As far as I could tell, the only benefit to pleasing Doc was being ignored by him. Lee had been an honor student, bringing home straight As like clockwork, but Doc never congratulated him or made a fuss about it, at least not while I was around. He sure as hell wouldn't throw a party if I had somehow managed to squeak out straight Bs.

Lynn's head was buried in a Mad magazine, but I could see by his smile that my situation amused him. I didn't blame him, though. Had it happened to him, I would have been equally amused. I felt like giving him a shove, but I had enough problems.

When Doc arrived home, my mother filled him in on what happened, but he didn't explode as I had expected. He was quiet during dinner, and I thought that perhaps he had finally given up yelling at me. But when dinner ended, he stood to leave the table, staring at me intently. "I should make you walk to the goddamn school, every goddamn day. Maybe then you'd learn." As he shuffled toward the living room, he added, "If I had the money, I'd send you to military school."

I believed him, and thanked God we were poor.

Chapter Twenty-One

Coup

After the immolation of Thich Quang Duc, demonstrations and protests in Saigon increased dramatically. Students and Buddhists rushed into the streets, demonstrating almost daily against the regime. In late August 1963, Diem declared martial law and imposed a curfew. Armed South Vietnamese soldiers fanned out across the city, patrolling in Jeeps and standing guard around government facilities.

The Diem administration suspected that the Buddhists had Communist ties, so Diem allowed his brother and head of the secret police, Ngo Dinh Nhu, to begin a series of raids against Buddhist temples throughout South Vietnam. The Xa Loi temple was the first to be raided, and hundreds of monks and nuns were arrested and jailed. In a symbolic strike against the resistance, the heart of Thich Quang Duc, still sitting in a jar on an altar at the Xa Loi temple, was confiscated by the government. In other Vietnamese cities, thousands of people were imprisoned, mostly student activists and ordinary citizens involved in protests against the raids and the Diem regime's oppression of Buddhists.

After a week or so the demonstrations abated and martial law was lifted, but the frequent curfews continued. On the nights we stayed at Bob's, we knew better than to sneak out and roam the city, so our late-night adventures were put on hold for a while.

By October, a new phrase had begun to creep into American conversations: coup d'état. Doc uttered it quietly at home. Teachers and kids at school discussed what it meant. But hordes of traffic still crowded through the intersections, the markets still buzzed with commerce, and students still idly sipped noodle soup at the Howard Johnson's when they weren't busy protesting. Then, on October 5, another Buddhist monk followed Thich Quang Duc into history, immolating himself near Saigon's central market. Demonstrations flared with bitter intensity.

A newspaper sympathetic to the government was sacked by protesters, its papers piled high on the sidewalk and set on fire. One of the smaller government offices near my house got the same treatment. When I returned home from school that day, I saw typewriters, paper, and mimeograph machines strewn across Phan Dinh Phoung Street like so much spilled garbage. An angry crowd stood near the front door of the government building listening to a man shouting what I assumed were anti-government slogans through a megaphone. Across the street, a Jeep with two well-armed American MPs sat in front of my home, guarding us from the turmoil. It seemed as if Saigon itself was ripping apart.

"I've been hearing a lot of talk at the station," Doc said, during dinner that evening. "Things aren't looking good for Diem and Nhu, so if shooting starts, get your butt off the street and into an American house or facility."

"What am I supposed to do if I'm out in Cho Lon at school?" Mother asked nervously.

"Stay there and call me at the station. If the phones aren't working, just stay there. You don't want to be driving around if tanks are rolling. That goes for you guys, too."

I wasn't concerned about a coup. I assumed the Vietnamese soldiers would understand that I had no stake in this conflict and ignore me. I stood up and put my napkin next to my plate. "Can I have some green?"

"Did you ask to be excused?" Doc said. Grandma Margaret would have been proud of him.

"Can I be excused? And can I have some green?"

"Yes and no."

"Oh, come on," I whined. "Just a couple of dollars."

"What for?"

"I was going to meet Bob and Frankie at the bowling alley, then go to a movie."

Doc paused, then fixed me in his glare. "After the movie, you come straight home, you got it?" He waited for my response. "I'm not kidding."

"*All right*! I promise."

"Get my wallet."

It was never easy squeezing money out of Doc, but he knew no jobs were available for American teens in Saigon. Well, *almost* no jobs. A few of the seniors were lucky enough to land a job bagging groceries at the PX, but for kids my age, unemployment was the normal state of affairs. Americans were prohibited from competing with the locals, so I couldn't cut lawns or deliver magazines like I had in Florida, and Thi Hai and Cuc protested whenever we tried to lift a finger around the house. My group of friends had other ways to make money, though.

I took a motor-cyclo to the bowling alley, where I found Bob, Spike, Frankie, and Mac huddled at a table in the corner of the cafeteria. I sat down and pulled out my wallet.

"How much have you got?" Bob asked.

"Four dollars." I gave it to him.

"That makes a total of thirty dollars." He penciled my donation on a small scrap of paper and put it in his pocket. "I can get a twenty and a ten, or three tens."

"You sure your pa's gonna do this?" Frankie asked.

"If he hasn't got it, I'll go to the exchange window at the PX. I'm going there with my mom tomorrow anyway."

The money exchange window at the PX was one of the few places where Americans could exchange a limited amount of piasters for American dollars. Smugglers and refugees could hide a thin pile of American twenties and fifties more easily than a thick stack of ones and fives, so we were shooting for a slightly different angle on the black market: capitalizing on the need for large denominations of American currency.

Our plan for a big score had hatched a few days earlier, after Bob overheard a conversation while visiting his father's office. "The guy was telling my dad they were paying top price for dollars on Tu Do Street," Bob said. "Especially the big bills. If we pool our money, we should be able to get more than five times the PX rate."

For two days, I had begged and borrowed to accumulate as much American cash as I could. I combed couches, chairs, and car seats for coins and gambled at Monopoly with my brothers, trading every piaster I could find for American greenbacks or silver.

A jump in the price of dollars on the black market meant that someone was feeling the need for the security of American currency and was buying up as many dollars as possible. I figured it was the political players in Diem's government, usually as skittish as wild horses. With rumors of a coup d'état circulating, they must have been preparing for the worst. A sudden rise in the price of dollars was common, but rarely lasted for more than a few days, so we hurried to make the most of it.

When school let out the next day, Spike, Frankie, Mac and I met at Bob's house. He showed us the crisp, new ten-dollar bills his mom brought home. "When we get to Tu Do Street, I'll check the rate at a few different stores. You guys wait outside."

"Why can't I come in?" Frankie protested.

Spike shoved Frankie and said, "It ain't a gang bang, stupid."

"They get nervous if too many people are watching," Bob explained. "This shit's still illegal, you know."

On Tu Do Street, we followed Bob as he visited several jewelers, checking for the best rate. He emerged from the last store holding up a thick wad of piasters. Bob fanned out the cash like a deck of cards. "Twenty-one thousand piasters. Seven hundred to the dollar. The guy didn't even blink when I told him what I wanted."

We walked up the street to Brodard's to divide our booty. My four dollars would net me 2,800 piasters. If I could exchange it back to American money at the legal rate, I would have more than thirty-eight dollars. I had to be careful to do it slowly, though; my parents would get suspicious if they knew I had that much cash.

At Brodard's, we sat in a corner booth a few feet from the front door. Bob pulled the money out of his pocket and counted it under the table. While Bob dealt our shares, Mac pointed out a couple of locals who were staring at us. "Keep it down, man," he said. "Those cowboys are watching."

"I'm gonna have a good time tonight," Spike declared as he folded his share into his wallet. "Anybody up for some tail?"

"Maybe," Mac said. "I have to give my brother his share first. Who's coming to the bowling alley?"

Spike glanced at the cowboys, then turned back to us, speaking softly. "Don't anybody look now, but those fuckers are still checking us out."

We stood up and began to file out. I was last in line. As I passed through the door, I noticed the cowboys getting up from their table. A couple of thugs with knives could easily strong-arm a group like ours. The money we'd inadvertently flashed was a tidy sum by local standards, and it looked as if they might want a cut.

I pushed Spike from behind. "Here they come!"

We bolted into the street, ran to the first cab we saw and crammed ourselves inside. The cab pulled away just as the cowboys reached the street. One of them pointed in our direction.

"Them cowboys is shit outta luck," Frankie said, unrolling a pack of Winston from his shirtsleeve.

Spike nudged me. "Take a peek at the fucker on the left there. I think he's the one that was trying to hit me that time in the cab."

Through the rear window, I saw the cowboy raise his middle finger in recognition. "You think he saw the money or just wanted to punch you again?"

Spike grinned. "Probably both."

Bob turned around in the front seat and asked, "You guys want to play golf?"

"I was thinking more along the lines of a trip to the cathouse," Spike said.

"Is that all you ever think about?" Bob asked, frowning.

Mac was dividing his cash into two wads: one for him, one for his brother. "I have to go by the bowling alley first or Harry will kill me."

After Mac gave Harry his share of the booty, we splurged for a couple of cabs and went to a golf course and country club out by Ton Son Nhut Airport. Originally built by the French, the club had a wide second-floor veranda where golfers could relax under the ceiling fans and get soused while they lied about their scores. Locker rooms and equipment rentals were on the first floor. Like the Cercle Sportif, the club was staffed exclusively by Vietnamese locals.

At the golf course, we each rented a set of clubs, but instead of hiring caddies to carry our golf bags around the course, we did it ourselves. After just a few holes, the mid-day heat scorched the he-man right out of us, so we turned in our clubs and went upstairs to the veranda bar for a Grenadine and Coke. One of the kids from school, Chuck Novick, was sitting at the bar. Bob knew his family; they'd been in Viet Nam for years.

"You guys should see the monkey cage Chuck has," Bob said. "More monkeys than you've ever seen."

"What for?" Frankie asked.

"My dad sells them to zoos and restaurants," Chuck explained. "We've got about thirty right now. You can come see if you want."

We walked the half-mile to Chuck's home, a large compound with high walls, a two-story house, and several rusted tin outbuildings. In the center of the compound, a steel cage about twenty-five feet long by ten feet wide and high enough for a tall man to stand in sat atop a concrete slab. Several wretched-looking leafless trees and a few upside-down water dishes were scattered inside. The cage was jammed with dozens of spider monkeys, including a couple of dead combatants sprawled on the dirty cement floor.

Some of the monkeys had recent bite wounds: sharp red crescents carved deep into the flesh on their shoulders, legs, sides, or head. At one end of the cage, a disembodied arm lay a few feet from its dead owner. Blood oozed from the dead monkey's shoulder, glazing the cement floor. When we approached, the monkeys erupted into a shrill chorus of howling and screeching, baring their teeth at us and swinging across the steel bars with furious abandon. These were not the kind of docile primates I had grown accustomed to seeing at every zoo. These monkeys were fresh from the wild. Their hostility and instinctual desire to survive had been compressed, with violent results, into a small, tight space.

Bob threw his cigarette in the cage. When several monkeys began fighting over the smoking butt, Bob grinned and said, "It's a jungle in there."

We strolled around the cage, tossing them whatever we could find—bugs, leaves, sticks, rocks. They hissed and shrieked as they snatched our gifts, leaping from the trees to the bars, throwing anything inedible back at us, including the still-lit cigarette butt Bob had thrown in. I'd heard that a spider monkey can strangle a person to death with its tail, so I kept my distance from the hairy arms and grasping hands that shot through the bars.

We'd only been there a few minutes when a black Mercedes rolled into the compound and stopped in front of one of the tin outbuildings. A tall

American man in a khaki suit emerged from the driver's seat and walked quickly over to the cage. He seemed tense. "Listen up, guys. I want you all to get a cab and go home right now. Go *straight* home. Don't go anywhere else. This isn't a joke."

"What's going on, Dad?" Chuck asked.

"Something's happening with the government," he said, sternly. "You all need to be at home when it does. Now go!"

Spike, Frankie, and Mac took the first cab we hailed. Bob and I took the next, but were stopped near Bob's house at the corner of Le Qui Don Street. A long column of troop carriers, tanks, and half-tracks had blocked the road leading toward the palace, which also happened to be the road to my home. Unable to continue by cab, I said goodbye to Bob and started walking the four blocks from Bob's place to mine. The palace was just two blocks beyond my house.

The Vietnamese army, with the support of the Kennedy administration, had finally rebelled against Ngo Dinh Diem's regime. Now the rebel troops were surrounding the presidential palace. Just minutes later, the bombing began, and I ran like hell for home, accompanied by a chorus of mortars exploding, thunderous volleys from tanks and Howitzers, and the incessant chattering of machine guns. My family and I could do nothing but wait and hope that the fighting wouldn't escalate into total civil war. I'm sure many other American families—as well as Vietnamese and Chinese families—felt the same fear we did during that long night.

By morning the battle was over. AFRS and several Vietnamese stations reported that when capture was imminent, Ngo Dinh Diem and Ngo Dinh Nhu had committed suicide. But a few days later I learned the truth: As the battle raged around the palace, Diem and Nhu had fled through a secret tunnel and escaped to Cho Lon, seeking asylum at the St. Francis Xavier Cathedral. They were holed up in the cathedral when the rebel army surrounded them. The rebels guaranteed the pair's safety if they cooperated, so Diem and Nhu surrendered and were taken into custody. The way the events were related on the AFRS news broadcasts, Diem and Nhu had allegedly been shot while resisting arrest. But the inside scoop (from Marie's father) was that a rebel commander, Major Nguyen Van

Nhung, had executed both of them gangster-style, with a bullet to the head in the back of a van, their hands bound behind them.

Days before the coup, Madame Nhu had fled Viet Nam for Italy and the safety of family connections. She eventually moved to France, where she lived in exile. The new government, with the tacit approval of Washington, quickly swept aside rumors of Diem's assassination and announced a renewed effort against the Viet Cong.

The Diem regime had been destroyed and the hated Madame Nhu was gone, so South Vietnamese bars and nightclubs began to operate with few restrictions. Nightlife in Saigon resumed with fervor, the bar girls quickly shedding their white ao dai in favor of American-style short skirts and low-cut blouses.

The day after the coup, I met up with Spike and Bob to have a smoke. Lynn had other plans, however. For months, he'd been trying to assemble an authentic military first aid kit, begging most of his stuff from American soldiers he encountered around Saigon. He figured that if he had something to trade with the Vietnamese soldiers, they might give him some bandages or other first aid goodies (Morphine!). He knew I occasionally lifted cigarettes from my parents, so he followed my example and swiped a couple of packs from Doc, then headed for the palace with Lowell in tow.

The badly damaged presidential palace had yet to be sealed off, so when my brothers arrived, they slipped past the barricades and gun emplacements and went inside, dealing directly with soldiers who had been involved in the fighting.

"They were pretty grim," Lynn told me later. "They looked like they'd had a rough night and would just as soon shoot you as look at you. They all had the thousand-mile-stare in their eyes. I found a couple of guys that weren't too shell-shocked and they were happy to trade some of their first aid gear for the cigarettes."

One of the soldiers gave Lynn and Lowell a guided tour of the abandoned palace, which had been looted twice, first by the Diem loyalists and again by rebel troops when Diem's Presidential Guards high-tailed it or surrendered. My brothers even ventured into the basement, where several windowless rooms had been constructed, each equipped only with a couple of chairs, a table, and a bare ceiling light—much like the interrogation rooms you might see in prisoner-of-war or detective movies. It was in these rooms that Buddhist monks had been detained, questioned, and tortured. "It was creepy down there," Lowell said.

On the way home, they spotted an abandoned machine gun nest at a corner near our house. They picked up a string of M-50 machine gun bullets and a live grenade that was still in its cardboard container.

"Mother's eyes popped out of her head when she saw the grenade," Lynn told me. "I thought she was going to faint."

She gave the grenade to Doc to turn over to the MPs, but Lynn didn't show her the string of .50-caliber bullets he'd stuffed into his Army pack.

The following day, Lynn and Lowell sneaked into the musty hall closet under the stairway. By the glow of Doc's flashlight, they pried the bullets out of the brass and emptied the gunpowder into a pile. Next, they cut one of Thi Hai's old newspapers into wide strips and created homemade firecrackers, complete with crude hand-rolled fuses. It was a feat of daring and imagination equal to any of my most foolish stunts.

The Presidential Palace after the coup.

But when they set them off in the alley next door, the ear-shattering explosions immediately attracted the white mice and two MPs who confiscated the rest of their batch of firecrackers. "It's a miracle you didn't blow your hands off," one of the MPs told them.

I have to admit I was totally impressed and more than a little proud of my brothers.

After the coup, Saigon settled down quickly, and our group resumed staying out all night on weekends. About three weeks after the coup, late in November 1963, Spike, Bob, Frankie, Mac, and I headed to Steve's apartment to buy some smokes and get some rest after a long night of wandering the streets. Going to Steve's in a group was relatively safe now; he'd ceased being aggressive when all five of us were together. He'd also moved into a nicer apartment, in a residency hotel down the street from the Caravelle—away from the prying eyes of the MPs around the MAAG compound.

Even though it was barely 6:00 am, Steve didn't seem to mind playing host. He made coffee for himself while we smoked and looked at girlie magazines for a while. I had finally figured out that the magazines weren't for Steve; they were for us. I wondered how many other kids had thumbed through the pages of the *Playboy* that lay spread out in my lap.

Around 7:00 am, I looked at my watch. "I'm tired as hell, guys."

Bob yawned. "Me, too."

"Let's get out of here," Mac said, rising. "I can't keep my eyes open much longer."

When I got up to leave, Spike looked up from his *Playboy*. For a second, I thought he might stay.

He dropped the magazine on the table. "Okay, okay, I'm coming."

One by one, we left and walked downstairs to the lobby. The radio at the front desk was tuned to AFRS, cranked up as loud as possible so that everyone could hear. ". . . Kennedy has died at Parkland Memorial Hospital in Dallas, Texas, at one pm, shot by a sniper as his motorcade passed through downtown. . ."

"Holy shit!" Mac said. "Did you hear that?"

Spike and Frankie were the last two down the stairs, still smiling as they entered the lobby. Our faces of stone were hovering around the radio.

"Hear what?" Spike asked.

"President Kennedy's been assassinated." Bob's voice broke with emotion. Spike and Frankie stopped smiling and came closer.

"We have to go," Bob said, walking toward the door. "My folks will get up as soon as they get the call from USIS. They'll go to wake me and see I'm not there." He put his hands over his face, rubbing his tired eyes. "I can't fucking *believe* it."

I was choked up, too. We were stranded 9,000 miles from home, watching helplessly as the world went mad. It mattered not one bit to me when Vietnam's president was assassinated, but this was different.

"I'm going home," Frankie said.

Even Spike had a somber look. "I think we all should." It was the first time I'd heard him suggest doing something responsible.

We stepped out of the lobby into the soft light of a beautiful morning. Monsoon season had ended, leaving Saigon calm, relatively cool and dry. We hailed cabs, riding home in silence, our mood deflated by the news from the other side of the world.

Things were sad at home, too. Doc had gone to AFRS to deal with the inevitable mountain of information coming in over the wires. Mother sat on the couch in the living room, her eyes red and bleary, her hanky crumpled and wet. Lynn and Lowell stood close to the radio, listening to the most recent news. I hoped that someone had misread the information, gotten a detail wrong, but every report contained the same bad news.

"Are we gonna have to move again?" Lowell asked me.

"I hope not." The last thing I wanted was to leave Saigon and my friends.

In the weeks since the coup, the new Vietnamese government had proved itself no more effective than the old one against the Viet Cong. If the events of the past were any indicator of the course the future would take, I reasoned, then having a new president in the United States could only make the situation in Saigon deteriorate.

After the fall of the Diem regime, the incompetent General Minh, or "Big Minh" as he was known, had become chairman of the ruling military council. But in spite of the guidance and prodding of U.S. diplomats and military officials, the political intrigue and convulsions continued unabated. Catholics (most of whom were loyal to the old Diem regime), Buddhists, and students continued to demonstrate, sometimes violently, upset at any advantage the new junta granted to one group over another. The Viet Cong were making crucial advances in the rural areas of the country, winning the "cooperation" of the peasants through a well-executed program of fear and intimidation. In Saigon, the threat of terrorism had become a constant companion for soldiers and civilians, Americans, Vietnamese, Chinese, and French. And now President Kennedy was dead. Things couldn't get worse, I thought.

But in Saigon, things could always get worse.

Chapter Twenty-Two

Masters of the Night

AMERICAN COMMUNITY TEEN CLUB

After the assassination of President Kennedy, Saigon's American community grieved, but without a constant barrage of television and print media discussing his death endlessly, our lives returned rather quickly to what passed for normal. The news we received came mostly from our one radio station (AFRS) and two weekly military newspapers, the *Stars and Stripes* and *The Observer*. The PX stocked a limited number of magazines featuring stories about the assassination, but they usually took anywhere from a couple of weeks to a month to reach Saigon. We discussed the assassination at school, we talked about it at the dinner table, but for the Brats of the American Community School, when Saturday night rolled around, life went on.

It seemed like every weekend, ACS held a dance at a large Quonset hut inside the Johnson, Drake, and Piper (JDP) compound, an area of single-family homes enclosed by a high chain-link fence. JDP's employees were civilian contractors working in Vietnam; the houses were built for their families, modeled after antiseptic, cookie-cutter American housing developments such as Levittown, NY. The JDP compound was as neat and clean as a bottle of bleach—and about as pretty.

Except for the kids who lived at the compound, ACS students could attend the dance only by riding in on one of the American school buses that were permitted access through the guarded entrance. The bus made a scheduled stop at the corner near my house. One night, I boarded the half-full bus and spotted Beverly sitting alone. I squeezed my way through the crowd in front and sat next to her. "Hey, Beverly."

"Hi." She gave me a winsome smile. "Going alone?"

"I'm supposed to meet Spike, but he's not sure he can make it. I didn't think I was going, either, but my parents got tired of me hanging around."

As the bus pulled away from the curb, she looked out the window. Her face was framed by the street lamps: light, then dark, then light again. She was wearing silver earrings and a matching, frosty-looking shade of lipstick. She seemed a little sad, and I wanted to comfort her, cheer her up. But I wasn't sure how she felt about me, so I played it cool. I was no longer a virgin, but when it came to girls, I was still a complete coward.

John Johnson boarded at the next stop and I looked away from him, hoping he wouldn't notice us. He paused, standing in the aisle next to me, holding the overhead handrail. "Where's your little friends?" he asked me.

"What d'you care?" I replied, turning my cynical eyes to Beverly. John sometimes acted as if he wanted to be your pal, but most of the time he was just looking for someone he could screw with, someone smaller or younger. Either way, I didn't trust him.

"Have you seen Phil?" John asked. "He usually gets on at your stop."

I saw Phil a lot because he lived two doors away from me. "His parents are in Hong Kong, so he's going to stay home and have Minnie over."

John plopped down in the seat across the aisle. He played outfield for the ACS softball team, but they had no one to play against except the older, more experienced GI teams. Even though the ACS team played hard, they lost most of their games.

"So," I asked, "has the softball team won a game yet?"

Beverly giggled, which was all I needed to hear.

"Maybe you could play the cheerleaders," Beverly teased.

"Or find a Vietnamese team to play," I added.

"Maybe you guys could fuck off." John was still smiling a little. He slid over to the window and turned away. He could easily kick my ass, but with Beverly watching, I had to put up a good front and pretend to be brave. I was relieved when he backed off.

The bus turned down Truong Minh Giang Street, where Amy Rome boarded with Jim Carr, Mark Hutchinson, and Harry and Mac Stuart. The bus was nearly full by now, so it looked as if there was going to be a big crowd for the dance.

The next stop was near Bob's house, and to my surprise, he and Spike were both waiting on the corner. They squeezed their way down the aisle and stood next to me. "I didn't think you were going to make it," I said.

"He wasn't, but I talked his mom into it," Bob said.

Spike was obviously pleased by his unexpected good fortune. "He asked her if I could stay over and help with his history project . . . and she bought it!"

Bob smiled. "She thinks I'm a nice boy because I say 'yes ma'am' and 'no ma'am.' If you want, I'll call your mom and see if you can stay over, too."

"Sure, but let's wait a while until my dad heads for his gig. He can't say no if I don't ask him." The Men of Note had become the top American combo in Saigon. With Doc playing every Friday and Saturday night, the authority to grant me permission to stay at Bob's usually fell to Mother, and she could rarely resist my persistent bellyaching.

The bus passed into the JDP compound and stopped in front of the dance hall. As we filed off the bus, I heard the record player blasting away. Inside, red, white, and blue streamers had been draped from the ceiling, signifying that tonight the Quonset hut was reserved for the use of the American Community Teen Club. The ACS senior class members, every one of whom seemed as mature as any adult, were in charge of everything, including decorations, music, and punks like me.

We couldn't smoke inside, so Bob, Spike, and I hung around outside, blowing smoke at the bugs buzzing around the streetlight. A brilliant full moon bathed the Quonset huts and two-story houses in an eerie glow. The stark outline of the homes and the well-paved streets without trees, shrubs, or bushes made the JDP compound look like an island that had drifted over from America and anchored itself to this country. Nothing around me looked or sounded Vietnamese, and for a while I felt like a teenager at a dance in Anytown, U.S.A, courtesy of the Johnson, Drake, and Piper Corporation, and by extension, the U.S. government.

Bob and Spike eventually went inside, but I stayed behind, thinking about the conversation I'd had earlier that day with Marie. I had been sitting on one of the twin beds in her room as we compared the classes we'd taken with Mrs. Tyson. Then she changed the subject.

"Beverly says she's going to try out for the cheerleaders in the spring," she said.

"Really? I thought she didn't like that rah-rah stuff."

"She doesn't, but I think her parents are bugging her to get involved in something extracurricular. She's a little embarrassed by it, so don't tell her I told you."

"Are you sure she doesn't like one of the jocks?" It would be helpful to know if I had competition, although I wasn't sure what I could do about it.

"If she does, she hasn't said anything."

Outside the Teen Club, I stood alone for a while, imagining her dating Ron Trump or John Johnson or one of the other meatheads. My reluctance to make a move, to let her know I liked her as more than a friend, made me wonder whether other guys were as overcome with doubts and insecurity as I. Above me, the man in the moon smiled benevolently, as if amused by my deep-seated fear that, when it came to girls, the universe was a limitless and unknowable place. I tossed my cigarette and went inside.

Entering the hall, I scanned the crowd for Beverly, Marie, Spike, or Bob. The dance was in full swing, with kids twisting, strolling, clapping, and shuffling to "Surfin' U.S.A." The Senior and Junior classmen were in control of the dance floor at the front of the hall, closest to the record player. Freshmen and Sophomores congregated in the center, so I edged my way through the crowd of Ivy League shirts and bushy-bushy-blonde hairdos, moving toward the back. I passed several tables spread with trays of cookies, chips, and assorted snacks, and at the last table, I saw Spike talking to Brigitte Welch, a girl from my class. Her hair was the lightest shade of blonde I had ever seen, but dark roots gave away her secret: peroxide.

Brigitte suddenly walked away, leaving Spike standing alone by the punch bowl. "You see that?" he asked. "Brigitte asked *me* to dance."

"I thought she hated you." She had always brushed him off when he asked her to dance, before.

"Yeah, me, too. I told her maybe later."

Spike and Brigitte were opposites in many ways. Unlike Spike, Brigitte seemed sensitive and troubled, and she rarely smiled. I'd never seen her hanging around with the other girls in school, only with Charlie Greenwood and his friend Dave Hicks. In class, she usually had one hand in her hair, idly twisting it around a finger before breaking off a few strands. It was a hairdresser's nightmare.

Laura, as Brigitte had been called in her former life, was in the process of reinventing herself as a steaming-hot sex bomb. By changing her name and bleaching her hair platinum blonde, she may have figured we'd all think she was a sexy French celebrity instead of an insecure American teenager. We sometimes made fun of her—although not to her face—but I think we felt a little sorry for her, too.

I spied Beverly, Marie, and Beverly's friend Eileen standing in a corner with Bob and Scott Pettigrew. Spike and I joined them and watched the dancers. As a new tune started spinning, Eileen raised her voice over the music to speak to Scott. "It's not a dance if you just *stand* there the whole time."

He ignored her, so Spike said, "Come on," and latched onto her wrist, leading her into the throng of dancers. Brigitte had managed to rope Charlie Greenwood into a dance and was already on the dance floor. Spike led Eileen into a gap in the crowd next to Brigitte and started dancing to "Big Girls Don't Cry." It seemed to me that he just wanted to irritate Brigitte for refusing him so many times.

Beverly was almost shoulder-to-shoulder with me, so I composed myself and unsheathed my silver tongue. "Want to dance?"

"Yeah, sure." She actually seemed to brighten at my invitation.

I swung into action, then Marie and Bob joined in, and soon we were all in a circle, free-dancing. We moved easily from one dance to another—not that style mattered. All you had to do was find the beat and shake something and you were good enough.

I twisted, mashed pounds of potatoes, and locomotioned as if Dick Clark's American Bandstand cameras were zeroed in on me, but when I heard the first bars of the Beach Boy's "In My Room," I did the Chicken Dance: I excused myself to go out for a smoke. I was dying to slow-dance with Beverly, but I didn't know how. I hung around outside until the tempo of the music picked up to a safe pace.

Later, I suggested to Bob and Spike that we ask Beverly and Marie if they wanted to sneak out, but when I asked Beverly, she came up with a better idea. "My parents are in Bangkok 'til tomorrow night," she said. "Come on over."

"Great!" Mac said. "Party at Beverly's house!"

"No party!" she protested. "My sister and the maids will be there, so we can't be making a lot of noise."

A little while later, the seniors began pulling decorative ribbons off the walls and packing up the records. The dance was over, but the night had barely begun. Outside, I told Marie and Beverly we'd come by at about 1:30 p.m. or so.

The bus loaded up and headed slowly for the compound's gate, the portal that reconnected us to Vietnam. We'd had our brief taste of American culture and music.

One of the seniors, Jim Carr, walked to the front of the bus and addressed the MP as if they were old pals. "Mind if we have a smoke?" He offered the driver and the MP a Winston.

"If it's all right with him," the MP said, pointing to the Vietnamese driver.

Jim produced a couple of cigarettes and put them in the driver's shirt pocket. "Cigarette okay, everybody?"

"OK," the driver consented. "Everybody OK."

Jim turned to face the rest of us, raising his hands like a king bestowing favors on his subjects. "The smoking lamp is lit."

Without being too obvious, I had managed to squeeze into a seat with Beverly. She didn't smoke, so I restrained my desire to break out the weeds. It wouldn't be gentlemanly to be blowing smoke in her face. I knew that Grandma Margaret would condemn such behavior.

I tried not to focus on Beverly too much and instead watched Amy Rome, one of the seniors who seemed as comfortable around the guys as she did with her girlfriends. I had always thought of Amy as a "bad girl," the kind that might go farther than just smoking cigarettes or necking on her parent's couch. She was standing in the aisle facing the rear of the bus, talking between drags on a Marlboro. Her silver Capri pants were painted-on tight, and the collared blouse she wore was hanging out, greaser-style. She wore some old pumps and held the handrail above with one hand, leaning against the side of a seat, crossing and uncrossing her legs as the bus swayed back and forth. She had a few pimples and a huge gap between her front teeth, but was still as sexy as hell.

Two of the prettiest girls in the school, Carrie Oldman and Joanne Brown, sat across the aisle, and a group of ACS upperclassmen squeezed into the seats around them. Marie and Eileen were behind me talking to Spike and Bob, but in spite of my efforts to do otherwise, the only girl I could think about was Beverly.

Beverly and Marie got off at Beverly's house. The bus continued rumbling through the streets to drop off passengers until it was almost empty. When the bus let us off at the corner near Bob's house, we slipped through his gate and clomped onto the porch and through the front door. In the living room, Bob's mother was curled up on a chair in the golden glow of a cloth-fringed lamp, a glass of bourbon in one hand and a book in the other. She was usually asleep when we returned from dances or movies, but her being awake wasn't a problem. We could outlast her. We were masters of the night.

She looked up. "You boys getting up early or sleeping in again?"

I stuffed my hands in my pockets, leaving it up to Bob to come up with the correct response.

"I'm all for sleeping," he said. "What do you guys think?"

Spike appeared suitably tired. "Sleep."

"Me, too," I said.

Satisfied by our answers, she closed the book on her lap. "Well, I won't wake you in the morning, then."

A few minutes after we retreated to Bob's room, I heard her bedroom door close. We waited a half-hour to make sure she was asleep, then climbed out Bob's bedroom window. On the ground below, we listened to be sure we hadn't aroused the servants. Their quarters were only a few yards away. All I could hear was the chirping of a cricket. Even Bob's monkey was silent.

With the practiced stealth of cat burglars, we tiptoed to the front gate, and soon we were crammed into a cab, smoking and joking. The night was ours. A block before Beverly's, we let the cab go and walked the rest of the way.

Her home was a tall, boxy townhouse with a flat roof, one of the newer homes built since the French had given up Vietnam. Surrounding the three-story, bone-white stucco home was one of the highest walls I had ever seen, complete with barbed wire and broken glass on top. We slipped through the gate and up the cement steps. I knocked softly on the front door.

Marie opened the door and said, "Come on in, but keep it down." We sat down in the living room, sprawling over the modern sofas and chairs. Beverly had already placed sodas on the glass coffee table for us.

"Got any food?" Spike asked, reaching for a drink.

"Did you just come over here to eat?" Beverly asked, with an annoyed glance.

"It was here or the chicken house," Spike said.

Beverly laughed. "I guess I should feel honored, huh?" Spike had long ago told her and Marie about our trips to the brothels.

The gossip quickly turned to the evening's events at the dance.

"Did that surfer guy—Scott—actually dance with anyone tonight?" Marie asked.

"No." Bob said. "I even invited him here, but he said he was only at the dance because his dad wanted to bring a girl over for a while."

"Did you see Brigitte's hair?" Beverly said, to no one in particular. "It's going to fall out if she bleaches it any more."

"She's blonde anyway," I replied. "Why does she need to bleach it?"

"How do you know it's blonde?" Beverly asked.

I started to answer, but Spike cut me off. "'Cause Charlie Greenwood and Dave Hicks told us about her." He shifted forward, leaning on the coffee table, his face lighting up with a suggestive leer. "They was at her house, and Charlie was trying to get her to let them feel her up, and she finally said okay. She lay down on the bed buck naked, and let Charlie feel her up, but she wouldn't let Dave do anything but watch." He looked from Beverly to Marie and back. "They said her hair was blonde . . . but not as blonde as the hair on her head."

Beverly put her hand over her eyes, her face flushing with color. Marie looked shocked, but began laughing, quietly.

"She must buy peroxide by the gallon," I joked.

I briefly tried to imagine Beverly naked, lying on a bed in front of me like Brigitte did with Dave and Charlie, but I couldn't. The feelings I had for her were too pure and wholesome to be sullied by the baser instincts erupting from my hormone-drenched body, currently mired in the Prince Valiant stage of adolescent male development. I dreamed only of the most chivalrous aspects of romance, like those I saw in the movies: "Get the door for you there, ma'am?" "Here's looking at you, kid." "You should be kissed, and often. By someone who knows how." If I'd had a coat, I would have gladly thrown it across the warm Vietnamese mud for her.

As far as I could tell, sex was something naughty, a pleasurable fascination to be hidden from the adults who went to great lengths to conceal it from us. As a result, I could only fantasize about sex with girls I thought to be loose, bad girls, Amy Rome types: girls I had no emotional stake in.

I had occasionally thought about holding hands with Beverly, kissing her, maybe even going a little farther, but sex? Sex was the kind of cheap, guilty fun we indulged in with prostitutes, not something I expected from girls as impossibly virtuous and beautiful as Beverly, who I was certain was saving herself for marriage the way any impossibly virtuous girl would. But sometimes when I was near her, I felt a strong physical desire, an aching I didn't understand. It felt wrong to even think of her while masturbating, but once in a while, like when I was sitting in class or riding around town, I'd imagine her face, the smell of her hair, and the curve of her hips, and suddenly I couldn't stand up because the front of my pants had formed a tent just below my belt buckle. I didn't know why, but seeing her blush at Spike's comment made me catch my breath.

Chapter Twenty-Three

New Year's Eve

B y December 1963, I had lived in Saigon for almost a year and knew my way around. I was fourteen-and-a-half years old, but so far, I had spent every New Year's Eve at home with my family, watching TV and making popcorn until the ball fell. I was ready for one of those wild New Year's bashes I'd heard about.

As usual, Spike had ideas. "I told my folks we're going to the party at Sam Andrews' house," he said over the phone. "But if it sucks we can head downtown."

After we hung up, I threw on a clean shirt and got the okay from my parents. Lowell was staying at his friend Ray's house, and Lynn was going to the home of his schoolmate David Phu, whose father owned the My Canh Restaurant.

When Spike came over, I called upstairs and told Mother that I was leaving. She walked down and turned her back to me. "Zip me up," she said. She was wearing a shiny red-and-white dress that flared from her waist to her knees. Tilting her head to the side, she attached an earring. "Where did you say you two are going?"

I stood behind her, tugging at her zipper. She couldn't see me exchange looks with Spike. "There's a party at General Andrews' place."

"Well, you be home by one o'clock. No later. Your father and I will be at the AFRS party at the Continental, if you need us." She gave Spike an incriminating stare. "You're not taking your motorbike, are you?"

"No," Spike said. "My dad said if I took it out on New Year's Eve, I'd end up getting killed. Then he'd have to give it to my brother."

"Well, you boys be careful."

"Okay. We're leaving." I wanted to get out of the house as soon as possible. Doc was still upstairs getting dressed, and I knew he'd start asking questions if he saw me with Spike.

As soon as we were outside, Spike whispered, "Got any?"

"Yeah. Wait till we get around the corner."

I gave Spike one of my Pall Malls and we lit up.

"God, these things are strong," he protested.

"Did Steve run out or something?" I asked. Spike had been going to Steve's at least once a week since last summer. He was never without weeds until tonight.

"He told me not to be coming around for a while. He says they're screwing with him at work, but I think they might be watching him because of all the shit he buys at the PX. Nobody could smoke or drink *that* much." He raised his hand and waved. "Let's grab this *cyclo* and I'll get some now."

After Spike bought his Marlboros, we directed the driver to the Andrews' house. Sam Andrews was a good natured, roly-poly kid who looked as if he'd stepped out of an ad in an Ivy League clothing catalog. When we pulled up, he was sitting on the front steps, guarding the entrance as guests arrived. Like Scott Pettigrew, his hair hung perfectly over his forehead, a trick that I could never manage with my own. Tonight, though, he didn't look like his usual happy self.

"It's New Year's, man," Spike said, as we walked through the front door. "Cheer up."

"Jeff's being an asshole again." He mocked his brother, Jeff: "'When can we have a party without all your little friends hanging around?' Fuck him. It's my house, too." He stood up, a frustrated look crossing his face.

I looked inside and saw that only a few of our crowd were there. Most of the people were his brother's high school friends, including the entire softball team. With so many kids decked out in button-down Madras shirts, penny loafers, and chinos, it looked like an Ivy League frat house.

We left Sam on the steps and went inside. Beyond the foyer, a glass chandelier hung above an oak parquet floor. The windows stretched from floor to ceiling. This was the biggest house that I had seen from the inside in Saigon. For a while, we hovered near the door, watching, waiting for something or someone to inspire a plan of action and provide direction. Then I accidentally locked eyes with John Johnson, who was standing on the other side of the room.

"Shit," I whispered to Spike. "Here he comes."

John had peeled away from his crowd and was sauntering over. "You little bastards got any cigarettes?"

"You don't smoke," Spike said, "And we haven't got any, anyway."

John edged in closer, like he was going to chest-bump Spike. "Yeah? I bet. You better not be smoking in here."

"Doesn't your girlfriend smoke?" I asked.

"I don't have a—" John stopped smirking. "Fuck you. Where's your little red-headed friend, shithead?"

I sniggered a bit, trying to hide my surprise that John could see through the casual indifference I tried to show toward Beverly when people were around. I wondered if my crush was obvious to anyone else or if he had just made a lucky guess.

Spike gave me a shove to get us moving away. "We'll see you around!"

"See you little bastards later." John shot us the finger and turned away.

Mac stood near the tall windows and must have been watching us deal with John. "Johnson giving you guys shit again?" he asked.

"Yeah, at least once a week," I said. "How come he never picks on you?"

"'Cause I have an older brother to kick his ass."

We looked up when a large group of motorbikes roared into the driveway. Spike and I hurried out back to watch as they pulled into the courtyard by the garage.

Phil Boyd was driving Fred Hibbard's bike, a red Honda 55. He killed the engine and lowered the kickstand. Phil sported a decidedly un—Ivy League shirt with vertical dark purple and black stripes, its tail trailing outside the waist of his jeans. The top two buttons were undone, the collar turned up in back. His pompadour, a mature version of Spike's, sat atop a narrow, ruggedly handsome face. He was taller than most 16-year-olds, well-muscled, with broad, square shoulders. He was also the only guy I knew who had his parents' permission to smoke, a rare liberty in my experience.

Spike had told me that Phil was the guy he had overheard talking about going to brothels. "He used to get laid in the cathouses in Tijuana," Spike had said. "I even heard him say that the ones here are better."

Phil's father, like mine, was a lowly enlisted man, but Phil possessed a personality that demanded acceptance without regard to his daddy's rank. Phil was cool.

"I think I've got my dad sold on buying me a Honda," he told Fred. "But my old lady won't like it."

"Tell her you'll take her for a ride, too," Spike chimed in.

Phil smiled and winked at us. "That might work."

About half the guys in the courtyard had arrived with a girl on the back of their bikes. The idea that owning a motorbike was a ticket to more and better opportunities with the opposite sex renewed my desire to possess one of these heavenly vehicles. It hadn't occurred to me that Spike wasn't doing any better with girls since he'd gotten his moped.

"Let's go around the side of the house," Spike said. "I want to crack this pack of weeds."

We had just started to light up when John Johnson showed up again. "I thought you didn't have any cigarettes, assholes."

Spike said, "I didn't know cigarettes *had* assholes."

John was still grinning, but his eyes narrowed. "If I didn't know better, I'd think you little bastards were trying to fuck with me." He stared at us and pounded his fist into one hand, as if he were softening up a catcher's mitt.

I knew he wanted to see if he could shake us up, so I remained calm, wondering how far he was willing to go. "You can't take both of us, you know." Things must be pretty dull inside the house, I thought. Why else would he want to be out here, screwing with us?

He backed up and thrust his fists and arms in front of his chest, forming a semicircle. "C'mon." Crouching low, he shuffled from side to side like a crab. "You little bastards might win, but I'll get a couple of licks in first."

Spike blew a cloud of smoke high in the air. "Nah. We don't want to hurt you."

"Come on, chicken-shit. I'll even put one arm behind my back."

John put his left arm behind his back and raised his right fist.

Suddenly, Phil Boyd strolled around the corner. He frowned and asked, "Who's got a cigarette?"

I pulled out one of my Pall Malls.

John put his hands down. "They didn't have any for me!"

Phil glared at him and feigned surprise. "You *'ath-leets'* don't smoke, do you?"

"No, no, I was only kidding." John stuck his hands in his back pockets, looking at us expectantly, as if we might bail him out. "See you guys inside." I think he had enough sense to know that Phil wouldn't let him get away with bullying us.

Phil flicked his lighter and watched as John walked away. "Tell me if he gives you any more shit."

I was surprised and more than a little pleased that Phil might intervene on our behalf. Spike and I had enough muscle to handle John if things got nasty, but what the two of us might accomplish with fists, Phil could do with a few well-chosen words and a hard stare.

"You going to kick his ass?" Spike asked.

"No," Phil said. "I'll just give him a talking to, you know?"

Through the fence, I saw Frankie and his sister Joyce get out of a cab. We thanked Phil, ditched our cigarettes, and went into the house. We caught up to Frankie near the stereo, where Joyce stood shuffling through the 45's, picking out her favorite tunes. I pulled him away, out of his sister's hearing. "If the party sucks, we're getting out of here," I said. "Want to come?"

"Yeah," he said, glumly. "But my dad told her to make sure I stay here. I'm fucked."

Mac walked through the front door and stood with us near the record player.

"There's Jane Moore," I said, nudging him to look. None of us wanted to be caught gaping at her, but she was so sweetly sexy our hormones insisted we take notice. She was fourteen years old, and much to our delight, had yet to master the wearing of the bra.

Mac passed a comb through his hair. "I'm going to go ask her to dance."

But before he could put his comb back in his pocket, one of the older guys approached Jane, slipped his hand around her waist, and in one smooth motion, swung her onto the dance floor.

"Too late, man," Spike said.

"Shit." Mac's hopeful smile faded. "Now he's going to be after her all night. I haven't got a chance."

Spike went back to the record player, bugging Joyce to play some hot-rod songs. At his insistence, she put on "Little Deuce Coupe" and we stood around staring at the crowd, watching the fun like a bunch of wall-weeds. The older guys had snatched up all the girls our age, and no girls younger than us were there. Marie and Beverly were babysitting Beverly's sister. We had no idea where Bob was. The wild New Year's bash I had imagined wasn't happening for us. This party belonged to the older kids. New Year's was starting to suck.

Someone yelled, "Play 'Louie, Louie'!" and the energy ratcheted up a notch as the more adventurous boys made an all-out effort to impress the girls with a little dirty dancing. While Twisting feverishly on the floor in front of me, one guy suddenly squatted low, then leaped to his feet, into a brazen pelvic thrust aimed directly at his partner. She smiled sweetly and rolled her eyes. Once the dirty dancing got started, any boy not willing to be outdone by the others performed a similarly suggestive move until all the girls were, apparently, charmed right out of their panties. For shy boys like me, these overtly sexual overtures were much too aggressive to be anything but embarrassing.

Finally, Spike came over, shouting in my ear for us to leave. I scanned the room for reinforcements, but it looked like it was going be just Spike and me tonight.

"Is Mac coming?" he asked.

"No. He's still eyeballing Jane. He can't get away from his brother anyway."

"What the hell. Let's go."

Outside, Phil was leaning against the wall of the compound with his girlfriend, Minnie. Her arms were around his waist, her chest pressed tight against his. Her freckled face was inches from his nose. The look of love was in her eyes. Like so many of the military-Brat girls I knew, Minnie was gorgeous, a trophy girlfriend from a high-ranking officer's family.

Phil looked our way, lifted a hand, and waved at us. Minnie's unfocused gaze followed his, her smooth-as-corn-silk hair swishing against his shirt.

We walked out the gate, past two MPs who were sitting on their Jeep, guarding the party. A few minutes later, we caught a motor-cyclo and headed toward the Caravelle Hotel. At the rotary near the hotel, we let the driver go and walked across the square and up the block.

It was a warm, dry night, and the sidewalks were as jammed with people as the street was with cars, bicycles, and motorbikes. Above every bar, signs ablaze with red, yellow, and green neon lights lit up the sidewalks. Leftover Christmas tinsel and Chinese lanterns hung prominently in windows and doors. Near each bar or nightclub entrance, bar-girls paced the street, elbowing their way into passing groups of soldiers, trying to snag one for the evening.

Since Madame Nhu's hasty departure from the country, the bar-girls were dressing in a more sexually suggestive manner. Hemlines were mid-thigh and skirts were tight, with shapely legs shining in freshly purchased black-market nylons. Their blouses had low, loose necklines, showing just enough cleavage to make a GI's heart race. The girls' fingernails were lacquered bright red, their makeup caked-on to slutty perfection. Tonight, Tu Do Street would once again earn its reputation as the Street of Sin.

As we passed a hole-in-the-wall saloon at the end of the first block, two girls in short skirts and filmy silk blouses emerged and quickly latched onto our arms, dragging us up the stairs into a bar. I was an easy catch, flattered as I was that they thought we were old enough. Inside, there was no room for tables; the barstools were only a couple feet from the back wall. I nervously scanned the room for MPs, but the only Americans there were a couple of GIs who seemed intent on ignoring us. We sat down with the girls to order beers.

The girls who dragged us in were talking to each other, but I figured it was only a matter of minutes before they asked us to buy them Saigon Tea, a popular (with the bar girls only) weak tea the bars sold for "many, many Piaster."

At the other end of the bar, a carefully groomed bar-girl casually put her arm around the soldier next to her. In the hand she placed around his shoulders, she held a glass of Saigon Tea. She smiled and leaned towards him and her blouse curved open in front, allowing the soldier an eye-popping view of her cleavage. When he looked, she "accidentally" spilled the Saigon Tea on the floor behind his back, then pouted and said, "Oh no! I spill! You buy me more Saigon Tea?" The bars raked in bookoo piasters on Saigon Tea.

When Spike and I chuckled at the spilled tea, the soldier glared at us and we looked away, fearing that eye contact might invite him to ask what the hell we thought we were doing there. I put a cigarette in my mouth and snapped my new Zippo smartly. Assuming a serious expression, I concentrated on looking older than my fourteen years. I thought if I could do the cigarette-hanging-out-of-your-mouth trick that Spike managed so convincingly, I might be able to pull it off. I let my cigarette hang from my lips, but the smoke stung my eyes and nose and I had to snatch it out to avoid the sneeze that would mark me as a kid.

The middle-aged woman behind the bar strolled over. I thought she was going to take our order, but instead she leaned over for a better look. Suddenly her calm, Buddha-face turned into a scowl. "You *baby*! No drink!" She dismissed us with a wave. "You go now!"

"Shit," Spike said.

We got up, and I shrugged at the bar girls.

"You no come here!" the woman added, pointing at the door.

A rotund Vietnamese man hurried over and stood behind us, looking pugnacious and threatening. As I stepped off my stool he put a hand on my shoulder and I pulled away from him. The bar girls clucked and frowned, arguing with the bartender. Apparently, the girls thought they'd rounded up a couple of young soldiers new to Vietnam—easy money.

As we strolled to the door the bouncer put his hand on my shoulder. Angrily, I spun to face him down. I wasn't going to let him push me out.

Surprised, he backed away, poking his finger at me accusingly. "You *numba 10*! No come back!"

Spike said, "Don't worry grandpa; we won't."

For the second time tonight, our plans for a wild New Year's Eve had been shot down. We let the door slam behind us.

As we went through the door onto the street, a couple of sailors were passing in front of the bar, watching as the bouncer stood in the doorway ranting in Vietnamese. I was worried that they might think we had been tossed out like a couple of bums. When they walked by, we fell in behind them.

Spike and I noticed that the sailors were taking turns swigging from a bottle of booze they had hidden in a brown paper bag. We slowed briefly when they stepped into the alcove of a closed jewelry store, then picked up our pace, pretending we weren't following them. When we passed the alcove, one of the sailors said, "They giving y'all a hard time tonight?"

"Yeah," Spike said, without hesitation. I could see him eyeballing the bag in the sailor's hand. "What're you guys drinking?"

"Wild Turkey. Good stuff." The sailor held out the bag. "Y'all want some?

I didn't have the nerve to say yes, but Spike did. "Sure," he said, taking the bag. He took a sip, wiped his mouth with the back of his hand, and gave it to me.

I put it to my lips and took a gulp. The sailors grinned when they saw the shock on my face as the whiskey burned its way down my throat. It tasted horrible, like gasoline, but Spike seemed to like it.

"One more sip," he said, taking the bottle. He took a mouthful and handed it back to me.

"Take it easy, fellas," the second sailor advised. "That stuff'll fuck y'all up real good. See that turkey?" He reached out, pulled the bottle out of the bag, and tapped the picture on the front. "That's what y'all are gonna look like if you drink too much."

I looked at the turkey, put the bag back around the bottle, and took an even bigger gulp, then handed the bottle back. Every taste was as bad as the first, but I didn't want to wimp out. Besides, it was New Year's Eve.

As awful as it tasted, the whiskey (unlike beer) made me feel like a lamp had been lit in my chest. I was glowing on the inside, the warmth spreading through my body like a gentle fire. I'd never understood how Doc could drink something that tasted so awful, but tonight I began to comprehend the allure of hard liquor. After just a few gulps, the bar girls seemed demure and charming, Spike and I were handsome and strong, the sounds of the night mellow and round. Everyone on Tu Do Street was a good friend. It was a happy place to be. Maybe booze wasn't so bad after all?

We stepped out of the alcove into the flow of revelers, following the sailors as they teased the bar girls. Every now and then they turned around to hand the bottle to us for another taste. Before long, Spike and I were stumbling down the street, laughing at nothing. Spike hitched one arm around my neck for support as I held his shoulder, leaning against him. We swayed across the sidewalk toward the street and back again.

All of a sudden, a crescendo of honking horns and cheers filled the air. We opened our throats, baying like dogs—really drunk dogs. It was midnight, and the New Year, 1964, had arrived. This called for a drink.

"One more, guys," the first sailor said. "Then we're going in this here bar and find us some girls and stay there till they throw us out." He gave me the bottle. I tried to take a sip, but couldn't. Something was wrong.

"Take the cigarette out of your mouth," Spike snorted.

"What the hell. . ." I snatched the cigarette from my lips and took a long pull on the bottle, probably longer than I should have.

Spike took a gulp, then handed it back to the sailors. "Thanks for the booze, man." He leaned back against a light pole, smiling like a Cheshire cat.

"We'll see you later," I said, wobbling away, ignoring Spike. My legs didn't seem so light anymore.

"Wait up." Spike jerked himself upright, running clumsily after me.

One of the sailors said, "Damn," then they disappeared into the bar. We staggered down the sidewalk, finding amusement in everything and everyone. Tonight, all of Tu Do Street was a party. The whole world was invited.

"We should go back to Sam's place," Spike drawled.

"We're too drunk, man," I said. "The MPs'll throw us in the fucking brig."

"Fuck it, then. Buncha shitheads there, anyway. Johnson and the rest of 'em can kiss my ass. You see the way he shut up when Phil came around?"

"Yeah, man. He's scared of Phil, but if you were a little bigger and a little stronger and a little faster and a little smarter . . ." I paused to burp. "You could kick his butt, too."

"Hey, I know!" Spike stopped. His bleary eyes grew wide. "Let's get laid!" His voice was full of surprise, his face animated as if he had thought of this for the first time.

I swerved to a halt and faced Spike, trying to hold his gaze. "How am I gonna get laid? I can fucking barely see."

"I'll help you, man."

I believed he would, and gladly, too. "No, we gotta get out of here," I said. As we drew near the end of the block, I saw the Caravelle Hotel just across the street. "If I don't get home before Doc, he'll give me shit. Besides, I'm too drunk to screw."

"The ground won't stop moving," Spike complained. "And I've got booze on my breath. If my dad smells it, he'll take my bike. I need a Coke or something to kill the smell."

"I betcha they're drunk, too," I reassured him. "Just don't breathe on anybody. You'll be OK."

We threaded our way through the crowds, back to the Caravelle Hotel and waved down a motor-cyclo. We took turns giving drunken directions, instructing our patient driver to take the long way home, past Saigon market. We doubled back around the palace, past Notre Dame Cathedral, out to the zoo, and finally to my home on Phan Dinh Phung Street. Spike still lived out in the Gia Dinh neighborhood, so he dropped me off and continued on in the motor-cyclo.

The cool air didn't help. I was still drunk as I staggered on rubber legs to the front of the house, slipped, and fell against the screen door. I lay on the front steps for a moment feeling the ground spin, confused. I got up and tottered inside.

I retrieved a can of Coke from the kitchen and gulped it in the desperate hope that it would relieve the dizziness, straighten out the world that had become an un-navigable nightmare of harsh angles and hostile objects assaulting me from all sides. The next step was getting upstairs to the bathroom, but the room wouldn't hold still. I set the Coke on the dining room table and lurched from the chairs to the wall, struggling to stay on my feet. Nausea had taken control. I breathed deeply, trying to calm myself. Climbing the stairs in the dark, I clutched the railing like a lifeline. I banged my way into the bathroom, closed the door, and sat down on the edge of the bathtub, my shirt clinging to my body from the sweat oozing from every pore.

Then my saliva started squirting, and that rush of vertigo you get just before your stomach turns inside-out whirled through my head. I fell to my knees, hugged the rim of the toilet bowl, and sucked wind. I stuck my head in and gushed, over and over, until my stomach squeezed out a thin line of dark yellow bile, trickling down my chin into the toilet.

I weakly raised myself off my knees and stood, shaking. I leaned on the sink and put my head under the faucet, splashing water on my face. I looked in the mirror, wondering who the idiot was with the bloodshot eyes.

As hard as I tried, I couldn't spit the funky taste of bile and whisky out of my mouth. With my stomach empty of its contents, a cool wave of relief settled on me—but then the room started spinning again. I heard a knock.

"Leslie?" It was Mother. "What are you doing in there?"

I could barely talk. "I threw up," I mumbled.

"Threw up? What's wrong? Are you sick?" She pushed the door open and came in with that High-Strung look in her eyes. "Are you okay?"

"I'm drunk."

Doc appeared in the doorway behind my mother and he didn't look happy. Or sober. His tie hung loosely around his neck beneath his open collar. His eyes were red and watery. "What'd you mean you're drunk?" Doc said.

"Me and Spike were following two sailors and they gave us some whiskey."

"What the hell did you do that for?" Doc said.

Mother rushed to my defense. "Bryant, calm down."

But it was too late. Doc had his hackles up. "Where the hell were you?"

"Bryant, will you leave him alone? He's sick."

"What the hell are *you* drinking for?" Doc said. "You got a goddamn problem or something?" He moved toward me. "Why the hell . . . I *told* you to stay away from Spike, goddamn it!"

The room was rocking like my brain was seasick. "Well, who else am I going to hang around with?"

"Why don't you get some real friends instead of those goddamn delinquents you're always screwing up with?"

"Stop now, Bryant!"

Doc had pushed his way in until we were face to face. Mother wedged her way between us, trying to keep us apart with her arms. This bathroom wasn't made for three. It felt like a steam room. As she tried to separate us, the thought of having guys like John Johnson as friends came to my addled mind. I blurted out the first thing I could think of.

"Yeah," I sneered. "Gotta stay away from those little bastards, huh?"

Doc cupped his right hand and swung hard. He caught me on the ear, knocking me onto the toilet. As I rose, dizzy from the slap, he strained to elbow Mother aside. His eyes were flashing with an anger that I'd never seen before. This wasn't going to be the same kind of thrashing he dished out when he was upset at my brothers and me.

He grabbed at me with his left hand but missed, probably because Mother was beating on his shoulders, yelling at him to get out. As furious as he was, I knew he would never hit her, even though she might slap him silly. She pushed her way forward, twisted him around and shoved him into the hall.

"Go to bed!" She screamed, slamming the door.

I sat down on the edge of the bathtub again. My skull was throbbing and my left ear was buzzing like a smoke alarm. Crappy Booze Year.

Mother put the lid down on the toilet seat and sat down to examine the side of my head. "Are you all right?"

"I guess so."

She wet a washcloth and wrung it out in the sink. "You shouldn't have said that to your father. You know how he feels about that." She pressed the cool, wet cloth against my forehead. Drops ran down my cheek.

"Said what? What are you talking about?"

"Calling him a little bastard. You know he was in an orphanage when he was little."

Then I realized that the only word he heard me say was "bastard." He may have been as drunk as I was. "I didn't call *him* that. I was talking about this jerk at school."

"Well, you need to go to bed and sleep it off. You'll feel better in the morning. Stay here. I'll go to the kitchen and get you some water."

"Okay, but I didn't call him a bastard." God, I feel like shit, I thought. Why would anyone ever want to get drunk?

I awoke the next morning with a pounding headache to match the nasty sink-hole in my stomach, but at least the bells had stopped ringing and the room wasn't spinning. The fuzzy but ominous image of a bottle and a turkey floated up from the mysterious depths of my hangover, it's meaning unknown. I reluctantly went downstairs, sure that whatever happened next, it couldn't be as ugly as the scene in the bathroom last night. I felt like a slug, but I moved quickly toward the kitchen, trying to avoid another confrontation with Doc.

He was in the living room sitting by the radio, a newspaper in his lap. He turned off the radio and folded his paper. "Hold on just a minute, buster." He looked at me accusingly.

Here it comes, I thought.

"Where did you and Spike get the booze?" Doc's tone was short and clipped. There would be no cozy, how-are-you-feeling questions today.

"These sailors we met."

"What sailors?" He listened as I explained the whole sordid night.

"What the hell were you doing on Tu Do Street?" he said. "You were supposed to be going to a party at the Andrews' house!"

"We did, but none of our friends were there, so we left." I wanted to yell, "I screwed up, already! I puked my guts out and now I feel like shit! Okay?"

"What were the sailors' names?"

"I don't know. It wasn't their fault." I backed away and started for the kitchen. "They didn't make us drink."

"Stop right there, damn it." He tossed the paper on the table. "Next time you say you're going somewhere, you better goddamn well *be* there. And I don't want you hanging around with Spike anymore. All you two ever do is get in trouble." He gave me a threatening stare. "You got it?"

"Yeah, okay." I would have agreed to anything to get this inquisition over with. By now, Doc should have known that I wasn't going to dump my best friend, no matter what I might promise while in the throes of a hangover.

Mother had been watching us from the dining room. "We worry about you, Leslie, what with your grades and all."

"I know," I whined. "But it's not Spike's fault. His parents are probably saying the same thing about me."

"Well, it wouldn't hurt you to listen to your father."

The new semester began a few days later. I hadn't tried to call Spike after New Year's, figuring that his parents were pissed off too, but I was wrong. I saw him heading down the walkway at school and caught up. "Hey man, you get home okay the other night?" I asked.

"Yeah. My parents were up and they still had people over. I thought I was screwed when my mom came up to me and said, 'Let me smell your breath.'" He gave me a toothy grin. "So, she smells it and then starts giggling and says, 'You've been *smoking!*' I almost cracked up."

"My folks came home and found me in the bathroom, puking my guts out. My dad was pissed and wanted to know who the sailors were so he could report them. It's a good thing I didn't know their names. I barely knew my own."

"When I tried to go to sleep, the room was spinning so much I thought I was gonna fall off my bed, so I slept on the floor," Spike said. "Then my sister got up and stepped on my face."

In the weeks and months that followed my wild New Year's Eve outing, nothing in my relationship with Doc changed. That I had the power to alter this situation never occurred to me. I couldn't imagine a world where Doc and I were not at odds with each other, a state of affairs that had been in effect as long as I could remember. I didn't understand that my good behavior might hold rewards other than paternal affection. But had anyone taken the trouble to explain that to me, I wouldn't have listened because I didn't trust most of the adults I knew. What I trusted was my burning desire to grow up as quickly as possible, a desire that I shared with more than a few of my peers. Like many teenagers, we mistakenly thought the adults were the ones having all the fun.

Chapter Twenty-Four

The Substitute

During the last month of the fall semester, Mrs. Tyson had given our class bad news.

"As of next Monday," she had said, "You will have substitute teachers for the rest of the year. My doctor has requested that I take a trip to Clark Air Force base for a medical procedure and a little R & R." She paused, then said with a wan smile, "I am looking forward to the R & R."

I'd heard rumors that Mrs. Tyson had lung cancer. Now I was sure they weren't just rumors.

"I trust," she continued, "that you will afford my substitutes the same respect that you have shown me."

At the time, only a few days remained in the fall semester, so I figured that when the spring semester arrived, class would return to normal with Mrs. Tyson at the helm. On the first day of school in January, I sat in class expecting her to come through the door. Instead, jowly old Principal Rehnquist waddled in with a short, frumpy middle-aged woman at her side. The woman seemed uncomfortable with the heat and was pulling on the front of her blouse, fanning her chest. I thought she might be Mrs. Rehnquist's assistant.

Mrs. Rehnquist waited for us to settle in before she spoke. "As some of you may know, Mrs. Tyson will not be returning to ACS. During her operation, there were complications . . . and . . . she passed away on the operating table."

By the looks on my classmate's faces, I realized that none of us had known until now. Mrs. Tyson had no children in school, so the news hadn't traveled the grapevine.

The words were a slap in the face. I sat in shock, glancing up only when several of the girls broke into sobs and ran from the room. They gathered in the hall, crowding together as they wept. The guys around me stared at their desks. I could see them struggling to restrain their emotions, but it didn't work. Like me, their best efforts couldn't hold back the tears running down their cheeks.

Mrs. Rehnquist used the handkerchief in her hand to blow her nose, glancing at the new teacher on her left, the first of several substitutes. I don't remember their names, so I'll just assign them names according to the personality traits they exhibited in our class.

"Mrs. Nerves will be filling in for a few days," Mrs. Rehnquist said, "until the regular teacher gets here." She left the room, still wiping tears away. On the way out, she paused to comfort the girls in the hall.

Mrs. Nerves looked at our distraught class. "Why don't we sit at our desks and read today instead of having a regular class?"

But I knew that without Mrs. Tyson, we could never again have a regular class.

Mrs. Nerves managed to keep us under control for the few days she was there, but the class was surly and resentful, like a spoiled stepchild waiting for a chance to misbehave. We tortured her often, playing games like "Stupid Questions." Whenever someone got such nonsense under way, the rest of us were quick to take up the game.

"When the Constitution was ratified in Philadelphia..." Mrs. Nerves began one day.

Dave Hicks interrupted immediately. "What does ratified mean?"

"It means it was approved by all the delegates," she said.

"How many delegates were there?" Charlie Greenwood asked.

"There were, let's see, fifty-five, I believe."

"So ratified doesn't have anything to do with rats, does it?" Chad Taylor asked.

"No, of course not." She looked confused. "It—"

"How did they all get there?" Carrie Oldman interrupted.

"Did they stay at the Holiday Inn?"

"How long did it take?"

"What kind of clothes did they wear?"

"*Enough!*" Mrs. Nerves slapped her textbook down on her desk and put her fingertips to her temples. After a few more tense days, she turned the class over to Mrs. Happyheart.

Mrs. Happyheart was new to Saigon and to teaching in general. She was young and pretty, with curly light brown hair, and wore bright, flowery dresses that matched her sunny personality. She would have made a good kindergarten teacher.

Mrs. Happyheart couldn't fill Mrs. Tyson's shoes any more than Mrs. Nerves could. Class never started on time. Students, including me, wandered in whenever they felt like it, ignoring her as they gossiped freely. She quickly turned into a beggar—begging us to show up on time, begging us to stop talking, begging us to do our work. She was an annoyance at worst, but we tolerated it. For a while.

One day, halfway through a class made notable by Mrs. Happyheart's sincere pleading, a brilliantly loud lip-fart hit the air. It may have been the product of Charlie Greenwood's over-active mouth, or maybe his wise-ass pal, Dave Hicks. She stared at us blankly for a moment, and then, as she turned back to the chalkboard, a chorus of random lip-farts echoed around the room like popcorn popping.

Mrs. Happyheart spun around from the blackboard and chirped in her high-pitched voice, "We *will* have a quiet class today or I will see you *all* after school!" On the word *all,* she gave her right foot a pert stomp for emphasis. "Is that *understood*?"

But she'd said this many times before. We knew it to be an idle threat. The guys next to me straightened up in their seats, the expressions on their faces somber except for the barely noticeable smiles forming at the corners of their mouths. I felt momentarily guilty, but like my partners in crime, I quickly recovered.

"You, you, and you," she said, pointing to Charlie Greenwood, Dave Hicks, and me, "move up to these seats." She directed us to three desks at the front of the class. "You girls can move to their seats."

It was the old, Machiavellian, "Move 'em to the front of the class" trick: Keep your good students close; keep your bad students closer.

"I'm going to put a list of dates and names up here." She glared, tapping her chalk insistently against the blackboard. "And I don't want to hear so much as a *whisper* from anyone."

She had barely written three dates when a spitball whacked the blackboard on her left. She spun around and picked up the spitball without looking down. "Who threw it?"

No one spoke.

"You." She pointed to Roger Streep near the back of the class. "Go stand in the hall, right now."

"Me? I didn't do it!"

"Well, who did?"

Roger was one of the guilty, but he assumed an exasperated look as if he were completely innocent. "I don't know. I was just sitting here."

"You can stand out there anyway," she said. "Maybe you'll remember."

"Come on," he said. "That's not fair." He pushed his chair away from his desk and began to walk out.

"Take your books."

He took a step back to grab his books, then shuffled into the hall and sat down. With Roger gone and the Three Stooges up front where she could keep an eye on them, Mrs. Happyheart once again began to write on the blackboard. Three more spitballs hit the board.

Without turning around, she backed away from the board, lowered her head, and took a deep breath. She let out a soft sigh of resignation, slammed the chalk into the tray, gathered her purse and books, and hurried out of the class, stomping down the hall towards the administration building.

Roger stuck his grinning face in the room. "What did you animals do?"

"We didn't do nothing," Chad Taylor said in mock astonishment.

The bell rang. On the way out of the classroom, Dharma stopped in front of Chad's desk and gave him an annoyed look. "It's 'We didn't do *anything*,' stupid." She sneered at him and huffed out of the room.

When class began the next day, Mrs. Rehnquist was standing behind the desk, hands on her hips. Mrs. Happyheart was in the hall outside, pacing nervously.

The principal leaned over and clamped down on the teacher's chair with both hands. "Let me make this clear." She paused, scanning the class. "If I hear about any more trouble from this class, I . . . will . . . flunk . . . you . . . *all*." She gave us a tight-lipped, beady-eyed stare, trying to impress each perpetrator with the gravity of the situation. "No more spitballs. No more catcalls. If I have to come back here, there will be *hell* to pay." After a suitably intimidating pause, she released the chair from her death-grip and left the room.

Mrs. Happyheart took her place behind the desk. While Rehnquist's warning was fresh in our minds, history class was uneventful. After a week, however, the fear faded. It started off harmlessly with noise and talking as we settled in, but each day it took a little longer for Mrs. Happyheart to quiet us down. Finally, she started showing up late for class. We were wearing her down; crushing her will.

One morning, she hurried into the classroom, dropped her books on her desk, and left. She had begun delaying the start of class until well after the bell had rung, postponing her descent into the purgatory we had created.

A moment later, Chad Taylor appeared in the doorway, looking down the hall furtively. When he sat down, he was holding a brown paper bag in his hands. The girl next to him asked, "What's that?"

Instead of answering her, he got up, glanced at the door, then walked quickly to the front of the class. He hurriedly dug Mrs. Happyheart's class logbook out of her book pile and put it in the top front drawer. He emptied the contents of the bag into the drawer and carefully pushed it closed. He threw the bag in the trash next to the desk and dashed back to his seat, watching the windows onto the hall the whole time. He opened his history textbook, feigning studiousness.

A few minutes later, Mrs. Happyheart returned. She sat down and began searching for her logbook to record attendance. After a brief but futile search of the desktop, she opened the desk drawer. She threw her hands in the air, slammed her chair back, and let out a scream that could peel a banana.

Two huge geckos had leapt from the drawer onto her lap, then to the floor, before scurrying away and up the wall to safety.

The class sat frozen in silence. Mrs. Happyheart bounced to her feet, shaking with fury, tears in her eyes. I felt a stab of guilt for enjoying her misery. She gathered her books and hurried out, dropping everything onto the bench by the door as she sat down, her face in her hands, her shoulders sagging. Her gentle sobbing reverberated in the hall like a babbling brook. She could take no more. A degree in education didn't qualify anyone to handle Brats like us.

Mrs. Rehnquist must have heard the scream from her office, because a few minutes later she sat down next Mrs. Happyheart. She put her arm around her, offering words of comfort, but Mrs. Happyheart kept shaking her head as if to say, "No, I'm not going back in there, not ever."

Dave Hicks' eyes sparkled through his Coke-bottle glasses, making his grin seem even more impish. He turned around and whispered, "You really did it this time, Chad."

Surprisingly, Chad didn't look pleased. His prank might have gone off better than he expected. "Shut up. Here she comes."

Rehnquist stormed through the door looking like the top of her head was going to blow off and splatter on the ceiling. Hands to her hips, pacing the aisles, she dared any of us to look her in the eye. We stared at the floor, the window, anywhere but at her pudgy, purple, enraged face. I steeled myself for a blistering explosion of invective that would blow our hair back and singe our eyebrows.

But it never came. After a couple of tense minutes of looking us over, she left without a word. She gathered up Mrs. Happyheart, who was still dabbing at her eyes with a hanky, and returned to her office.

"You guys ought to be ashamed," Dharma said. A couple of Dharma's friends eyed Chad incriminatingly.

"It was just a joke," Chad whispered. "I didn't mean to hurt her or anything."

"Did you see the look on her face?" Dave said with glee. "I thought she was going to pee in her pants."

I never would have had the nerve to do what Chad did, but I could enjoy it, even if I did so with a fair amount of shame and guilt. I had nothing against Mrs. Happyheart, but she was trying to do something for which she was completely unqualified. She might as well have been a green cowboy attempting to ride the toughest bull in the rodeo.

The following Monday, I entered Mrs. Tyson's class (we still thought of it as her class) prepared for the worst: Mrs. Rehnquist teaching the class. But sitting at the desk was Mrs. Hardassus, a trim, dark-haired woman in her mid-thirties with a slight accent that I could never quite identify. Mrs.

Hardassus was the geography teacher many of us had had in eighth grade. She was a known quantity.

"Well, hello, again," she said, cheerily. "It's been a while since I've seen most of you, but I trust you all remember how I love to stay after school."

I remembered well. Spitballs and lizards wouldn't faze her. If she had a problem with a lizard-terrorist, she'd eat the lizard like a candy bar, then keep the entire class after school, the good with the bad, the innocent with the guilty. The jig was up.

She surveyed the room expectantly. "Chad, Dave, Roger?"

They looked up, nodding slightly.

Although discipline would never be as tight as it was under the firm hand of Mrs. Tyson, Mrs. Hardassus kept us in line. No one wanted to be responsible for having the entire class detained.

I flunked anyway.

I don't know how many other kids failed history class, but I'm sure most of the boys and a few of the girls shared my fate. It could have been that Rehnquist made good on her threat and flunked the whole class, but I think she knew that not everyone in the class was part of the problem.

In spite of the mayhem and chaos in the bigger world, Mrs. Tyson had given us an island of stability. Her class lasted only an hour a day, five days a week, but it was a time when order ruled. The entire class knew what to expect, and Mrs. Tyson never disappointed us. When she died, I slid into the type of behavior she wouldn't have tolerated for a minute. With Mrs. Tyson, I had grown used to a certain level of discourse, but none of the replacement teachers rose to that standard. Even though Mrs. Hardassus maintained order, I behaved out of fear of her—but without the respect that fear sometimes implies. My classmates and I weren't afraid of Mrs. Nerves and Mrs. Happyheart. Their distaste for our antics was obvious, and we returned that sentiment tenfold. Only a strong, confident hand can break a spirited horse.

The feelings I had for Mrs. Tyson were, at best, vaguely familiar to me, but at the time, I didn't recognize them. Only years later did I realize that Mrs. Tyson was much like my first-grade teacher, Sister Kenneth. Both women helped me understand that my limitations were mostly self-imposed. By the time I reached ACS, I had found a persona I could hide behind—the rebellious teenager—but Mrs. Tyson drew me out in spite of my alienation from the academic process. Facing her was like looking in a mirror.

I would attend thirteen schools before I received my high school diploma, and in all of those schools, the only teachers who made a positive, lasting impression on me were Mrs. Tyson, Sister Kenneth, and my band directors, Mrs. Schaffer, and in high school, Mr. Bailey.

Had Mrs. Tyson lived, I'm certain that the entire class would have earned passing grades. She wouldn't have let us slouch our way into failure.

Chapter Twenty-Five

The Capitol Kinh Do Theater

I n Saigon, I discovered that even going to the movies could be risky. Several months prior to my arrival in Saigon, the Viet Cong had detonated a bomb in the bathroom of the Rex Theater, the largest and most popular theater in the city. Although the explosion injured a couple of Vietnamese workers, none of the injuries were serious and no one was killed.

The movies shown at the Rex were usually dubbed in French with Chinese or Vietnamese sub-titles, but soon after the bombing, the Capitol Kinh Do Theater opened. The Kinh Do was the only theater run by and for Americans, and featured films exclusively in English. Like the nearby bowling alley, it was staffed mostly by Vietnamese, but the bright, cheery lobby smelled of popcorn and featured posters of movies like *Donovan's Reef, Follow the Boys,* and *Blue Hawaii,* just like the theaters in the U.S.. The Kinh Do was a focal point of American teen culture.

Although movies in 1963 delivered little in the way of sex, quite a bit of action could be observed by sitting in the back of the Kinh Do. The older kids who wanted to make out always sat in the dimmest rows of seats under the balcony, engaging in the kind of lust usually reserved for steaming up the windows of a car at a drive-in. Kids my age also congregated in the back, watching furtively in the dark whenever teenage lips crushed together during an ardent embrace, the boys' hands slipping beneath blouses while their girlfriends' passionately drawn breaths softly whispered through the aisles. Most of us younger teens were hoping to get involved in making out as soon as possible, so nothing on the screen was ever quite as exciting as the heavy petting usually going on a few seats away.

Sometimes, I actually went to the Kinh Do to watch the movie, but on a particularly hot day, I might go just to hang out and escape the heat. Sunday, February 16, 1964 was that kind of day. The movie playing was *The List of Adrian Messenger,* a mystery flick with a cast that included many of Hollywood's biggest stars.

"I thought you saw that movie last night, Leslie," Mother said, when I told her my plans.

"Yeah, but there's nothing else to do, and some of my friends are going." Earlier, I had told Marie that I would meet her and Beverly there. I needed to move quickly if I was going to escape a dull afternoon at home, so I hurried out the door.

"Well, I don't have any money, and your father's not home," she said, following me out to the street.

"That's okay, I have some Ps."

"Be home in time for dinner, then. You know how your father gets when you're late."

Mother was standing on the sidewalk a few feet away when a cab pulled over. I opened the door to get in.

"Leslie, hold on." Lowell walked up behind Mother and she took him by the hand, pushing him my way. "Drop Lowell off at General Oden's house."

"Oh, *God*," I moaned. "Do I have to?"

"It won't hurt you to do something nice for your brother for a change. It's on the way, and it'll save me a trip."

I started to reply, but was interrupted by the sound of a massive explosion coming from the direction of the Kinh Do Theater. It was over a mile away, but the ground trembled as if an earthquake had struck.

"What was *that*?" I asked.

Mother's eyes widened with fear, and I could see that her nerves were screwing up tight, just like during the initial tank blasts of the *coup d'état*. Lowell backed away from the cab.

"Maybe we should wait," I said. I watched Mother, as High-Strung as ever, going into full lockdown mode, grabbing Lowell firmly by the hand. She latched onto my sleeve, pulling me toward the house and safety. "Get back in here right now," she said. "I'm going to call your father and find out what the *hell* that was."

I sent the cabbie away, and we hurried through the front gate.

As we moved onto the front patio, Lynn opened the screen door, trying to come out to take a look. Mother pushed him back in.

"That was *huge*," he said. "What direction did it come from?"

"Somewhere downtown," I said. "Sounded too far away to be the Palace. You could feel the ground shake."

Just then, Doc rushed in. His driver was outside, idling the car at the curb. Mother stood by the bar with the phone in her hand and a frantic look on her face. "Bryant! Thank God! What was that sound?"

"I don't know," he said, looking as serious as I'd ever seen him. "Let me call the station." While Mother fretted, he dialed AFRS, talked for a few seconds and then hung up abruptly. "They blew up the Kinh Do Theater. I have to go back to the station."

"No!" she cried. Doc had turned to go, but Mother grabbed him by the sleeve. "Please, don't leave! What if there's another attack?"

For once, I didn't want Doc to leave either. I didn't feel up to being the man of the family if Viet Cong attacks started sprouting up in our neighborhood, a possibility I had never considered until now.

Doc stopped and gently put his hands on her shoulders, reassuring her that he had everything under control and that she had nothing to worry about, which I knew was a pack of hot lies. "Just stay here and don't go outside. The MPs will be patrolling the American housing."

"Was anybody killed?" I asked.

"I don't know. Medics are just getting in there now. I'll call you from the station." Doc shot me a poisonous stare. "And stay off the phone!"

I was desperate to find out whether Marie and Beverly were hurt, but I'd have to wait. I imagined them strewn across the destroyed theater, blood oozing from gaping wounds, the cries of the injured and dying rising from the dust and rubble.

Lynn and Lowell had been inside the Kinh Do just a few hours earlier. "They could've blown it up while we were *there!*" Lynn said, astounded by their proximity to the bombing. As soon as Doc walked out the door Mother dumped two aspirin into her hand and reached for a bottle of beer.

Until now, the Viet Cong's attacks had been limited to military and government personnel, but this bombing marked a change in strategy, and although we didn't know it then, a shift in the nature of the war. Now we were all fair game.

By early evening, the situation had calmed down and I was finally able to call Marie. She told me what I had missed by minutes: "Beverly and I were sitting about four rows from the lobby doors. It was getting close to the end of the movie when I heard some noise coming from the lobby near the candy counter. It didn't sound right, and I thought something strange was going to happen, and then a guy runs into the theater yelling, "Get out! There's a bomb!"

"All of a sudden," Marie continued, "the women sitting in front of us began screaming. People panicked and started pushing their way out of the rows, shoving and falling over each other to get to the doors. Somebody yelled 'Get down, get down!' and we dropped to the floor and covered our heads with our hands. A split-second later, the explosion ripped the lobby apart and sent debris flying. I thought we were all going to die."

Marie escaped unharmed, but Beverly received a deep gash on her head, her blood soaking the front of her blouse. They left the theater, dazed, and walked to the bowling alley where a triage unit was setting up. The medics helped Beverly with her cut, and a GI gave her a clean shirt. Once Beverly's head wound was under control, Marie hailed a cab, and the two of them went to the hospital. It took seven stitches to close Beverly's head wound. Marie's parents were attending a party when they received the news. Frantic, they hurried to the theater, but Marie had already gone to the hospital. "You should've seen the look on their face when they found me," she said.

Over the next day, more details trickled in. After killing the MP stationed outside (Pfc. Peter M. Feierabend), two Viet Cong operatives had dropped a crate-bomb rigged with twenty pounds of plastic explosive on the floor of the lobby by the candy counter. A Navy lieutenant and a Marine captain had just purchased tickets when they heard shots and saw the VC rush in with the explosives. Seconds before the blast, the captain and lieutenant ran into the theater shouting, "Get down!" Their warning undoubtedly saved many lives. The Marine, Donald E. Koelper, died from head injuries sustained in the blast. The other soldier (SP5 William A. Reid) who warned the audience was also killed in the blast. The explosion rocked the theater so hard that the air conditioning units fell out of their places in the walls onto the panicked crowd, causing many of the injuries.

All told, three Americans were killed: the captain, the MP outside the lobby, and an Army enlisted man. The bomb was so powerful a section of the tall iron grate protecting the entrance to the theater was hurled across the street by the force of the explosion, decapitating a Vietnamese pedal-cyclo driver. Forty-nine Americans were injured, seven severely enough to require hospitalization, one in critical condition.

If I had left home a few minutes earlier, I might have been in the lobby buying my ticket when the Viet Cong ran into the theater with the bomb. I realized that I was lucky to be alive. In the days that followed the bombing, school and the hassles of life didn't seem quite so pressing. My brush with death was not as intense as what Marie and Beverly experienced, but I felt as if a broom had swept away the cobwebs of my ordinary concerns and cleansed my mind, at least for a while.

At school, everyone seemed to be talking about the bombing, about who was there, who got hurt, who saw what. Marie and Beverly were at the center of the talk, Beverly showing off the white bandage on her head and an animated Marie relating the tale of danger again and again. I understood their joy. The thrill of survival has few peers.

The Front of the Kinh Do Theater, post-blast.

In spite of the bombing, life quickly returned to its normal state of chaos and turmoil. Like the coup and the Buddhist immolations, the bombing was a remarkable event, but life in Saigon was full of such events. In a letter to my parents, ACS officials informed us of the new precautions being taken, including an increase in the number of MPs and soldiers guarding the school and other American installations. Every afternoon, before Lynn, Lowell, and I boarded the school bus for home, we helped the MPs by checking underneath the vehicle for bombs, as if we would know what a bomb might look like.

Sometimes, I felt as if we were living in a Salvador Dali painting:, life warped into surreal abstractions, reality twisted and curved, familiar scenes and landscapes transfigured by unexpected and bizarre events. At the time, I didn't understand how much stress my parents must have felt living in that environment; if I had, I probably wouldn't have been so inclined to contribute to their anxiety with my antics.

Chapter Twenty-Six

Chapter Twenty-Six

Monkey Love

A while after the theater bombing, I was sitting in the bowling alley polishing off a plate of French fries when Spike walked in with his hands cupped around something.

"What's that?" I asked. He opened his hands and set the object on the table.

"A frog."

It hopped toward my fries. It was about the size of a toad, three inches long, but smoother and greener. I put my arm between the frog and my food to keep it from jumping onto my plate.

"I'm taking it to the monkey over at the stables," Spike said. "Wait'll you see what he does. Come on."

From the lurid grin on Spike's face, I knew something weird was up. Maybe the monkey would eat the frog, I thought, or strike up a conversation in French. We left the cool of the bowling alley and crossed the street to the *Cercle Sportif* stables, behind the club. Spike led me to a horse stall that had been converted to a cage. A large, brownish monkey with a prominent nose sat in one corner, legs spread, thin fingers picking at the hair on his arms.

"What kind of monkey is that?" I asked.

"I don't know." He tossed the frog into the cage. "But it's a lot bigger than Bob's."

Suddenly, the monkey hissed at us, leaping onto the bars. We backed away from the cage to avoid its grasp.

"Not too friendly, huh?" I said.

"Nah, but wait till he sees the frog," Spike said. "He'll get *real* friendly."

Once we had assumed a respectful distance, the monkey turned his attention to the frog which was hopping around the dirt floor, frantically seeking an escape, as if it knew what would happen next. The monkey pushed the frog with his foot, then picked it up, went to the corner, and sat down facing us. He contemplated it as a jeweler might inspect a rare gem, turning it over in his hairy hands, examining it from every angle. Once he had thoroughly inspected it, he tossed the poor frog gently against the concrete wall. It bounced into the dirt. He picked it up and threw it against the wall repeatedly, each time a little harder until the frog lay on its back dazed and confused, its mouth hanging open.

I pointed at the monkey's crotch. "Damn, look at that thing."

While I was watching the frog get his brain knocked loose, the monkey had popped an erection that stuck out from his crotch like a pink finger. He suddenly picked the frog out of the dirt and forced its slack jaws apart. He shoved his lumpy, pink hard-on down the poor frog's throat and began jerking it up and down, using it to masturbate.

The sight was disgustingly repellant, yet fascinating, like watching a python swallow a rabbit. Witnessing the hostility of the monkeys in the cage (on the day of the coup) was eye-opening, but this brutal scene suggested to me that monkeys were as capable of sexual violence as humans. I felt sorry for the frog, but it was too late to stop what was happening even if I had wanted to. "That's the *weirdest* thing I've ever seen," I said, gaping at the bizarre spectacle.

"A Vietnamese kid showed me this a couple of months ago," Spike said.

The monkey finished with a screech, throwing the frog in the dirt at our feet as if to say, "I'm done, thanks." The frog lay on its back, but I saw one of its legs shift, so I turned it right-side up to see whether it was still alive. It didn't move much, at least not yet, so I pushed it out of the monkey's reach into a nearby bush.

Spike said. "You really gotta be horny to want a piece of frog."

"That monkey's almost as horny as you."

"We should tell Beverly and Marie."

"Somehow, I don't think they'd like it."

"Yeah, I know. But I want to watch 'em turn red."

Had I mustered the nerve to say anything sexually provocative to Beverly, I probably would have been the one to blush. Since the Kinh Do bombing, I'd been thinking about asking her out, but I had never asked a girl on a date, and just the thought of doing so made my palms sweat. I decided to wait until I could take her to a party or a school dance—somewhere where a lot of people would be around. I was afraid that if we were alone all night, I might give away my true feelings. Plus, I had no idea what we'd talk about.

It turned out that I would have plenty of time to think it over, because Doc had decided to take our family to the Philippines for a vacation. The following week, the five of us boarded a military flight from Ton Son Nhut airport to Manila. In Manila, we transferred our bags to an old, gray American school bus and rode through tropical green hills into the mountains.

It didn't take long for us to notice that our Filipino bus driver was oblivious to the concept of safety on the roads. The narrow highway snaked along the side of the mountain, a rocky, brush-covered cliff on one side and a boulder-encrusted wall carved from the slope on the other. He swerved recklessly from one side of the road to the other, dodging potholes, motorcycles and oncoming cars, laughing at the fearful gasps of his terrified passengers like a man possessed. As we rounded each curve I fully expected our bus to careen off the road and tumble over the cliff, killing us all.

After several nerve-wracking hours of clutching the seats of the bus in abject terror, we arrived in the small village of Baguio. Like Saigon, Baguio was colorful and run-down; the only difference I noticed was that signs were in Spanish, a language (unlike Vietnamese and Chinese) that I felt comfortable not knowing.

We checked into the American "R and R" facility at Camp John Hay, a small military post with apartments for vacationing families and GIs living in the Southeast Asia theater of operations. For a week, I played golf, swam in the resort pool, went horseback riding, and forgot about the Viet Cong, the Buddhists' immolations, and the war. The older Filipinos I met seemed to love Americans—we had rescued them from the horrors of the Japanese occupation during World War II—and they always greeted us with smiles, upturned thumbs, and a "Hey Joe, OK." Even if we weren't buying anything.

The third day we were there, Lynn spotted a go-cart track in front of a strip of shops near the center of town. After quite a bit of inspired begging and whining, we convinced Doc to let us have a go at the track. The carts were old two-seaters painted to look like Le Mans race cars, with big tires, oversized steering wheels, and big numbers painted on the doors and hood. They lacked the power and speed of the French go-carts I'd driven in Saigon, but they were about as much fun as I could have with Lynn and Lowell around.

Lowell and me, Baguio, Philippines, Pre-crash

While the owner struggled to start my cart, Lynn began to drive away in his. Finally, my engine sputtered, coughed, and began buzzing. Then I saw Lowell standing next to my cart, his lower lip quivering. At ten years old, he was too young to drive alone, and Doc had already disappeared into the shops looking for Mother. "All right, all right," I said, irritated. "Get in." I knew I would never be able to catch Lynn if my cart was burdened with Lowell's extra weight. Then I saw that Lynn had stopped a few feet in front of us and was snapping our picture with the tiny Minolta camera he kept in his shirt pocket. He turned around and pulled away as I hit the gas.

We took off around the square, quarter-mile, black asphalt track that surrounded a grassy field. A modest cement curb separated the tall elm trees in the center from the cars speeding around the course. We wore no helmets or seatbelts, and there were no bumper tires or other protective features. Apparently, driver safety was not a concern in Southeast Asia.

I accelerated to a blistering pace, the wind whipping through my hair as I weaved back and forth. I pushed the gas pedal to the floor and kept it there. Brakes were for sissies. I did my best to catch Lynn, the old engine wheezing with fury, tires on the verge of squealing at each corner.

"Let me steer!" Lowell shouted.

"No way."

"Come on!"

"No."

"Lynn would."

"I'm not Lynn."

"Lynn's cooler."

"Is not. What if you wreck it?"

"I won't!"

I thought about it for a second. If Lynn suddenly appeared to be cooler than me, it could upset the delicate balance of power in our family. "You'd better not."

"I *won't*."

My desire to be a cool older brother shoved my common sense aside and I let Lowell take over. "Okay. But just the wheel."

I still had control of the brakes and gas, so nothing could happen, right? Lowell firmly grasped the steering wheel with both hands, focused intently on the road ahead. I held the gas pedal to the floor as we buzzed down the straightaway, heading for the first turn. As we pulled around the curve, Lowell tried to straighten out, but instead of letting the wheel spin straight naturally, he tried to turn it back, hand over hand. I grabbed the wheel and hit the brakes hard, but I was too late. The cart slammed into and over the curb and smashed head-on into the trunk of a huge tree. The crash threw us forward, then snapped us backward into our seats. The engine chugged and died.

I gripped the wheel with both hands and began bouncing my head against it, cursing my fate. "Fuck, fuck, *fuck*!" I looked at Lowell. "I *told* you...."

He lowered his head and his lip began quivering again. He wasn't hurt, but I could see that he was shaken up and, I hoped, consumed with the kind of guilt that would indebt him to me forever. The front right wheel of the cart was deflated, bent at an odd angle where it hit the tree. When I saw Doc hurrying over with the track owner, I climbed out of the wreck and slouched away from the cart in silence. When Doc realized that we weren't hurt, his eyes turned angry and locked onto us. I stared at the ground like a prisoner awaiting execution, dodging Doc's intermittent dirty looks as he negotiated with the cart owner for our damage.

Mother and Doc In Baguio, Philippines

Mother had followed Doc. She stood next to Lynn as he basked in the glow of my misery. Lynn smirked at me and said, "Nice driving, Les."

I wanted to tell him to shut up, but if Doc heard me, it would just make him angrier. I decided that silence was the only way to get through this nasty turn of luck.

Lowell put his hand next to his mouth and whispered, "You're not going to tell Doc I was steering, are you?"

"I should," I muttered.

"Please..."

When the owner left, Doc turned to us. He was angry with both of us, but because I was the older, supposedly more responsible one, he spoke only to me. "Now do you understand why I don't get you a motorbike?"

Chapter Twenty-Seven

Dating?

Until I met Beverly, I hadn't shown much interest in girls, preferring to adore them from a safe distance like Goddesses, or to accept the few girls I knew as the most casual of friends. A couple of girls in Florida had caught my eye, but we moved before I managed to give a thought to asking any of them out to a movie or elsewhere. I felt differently about Beverly, however. I thought about her night and day.

Dating is a difficult proposition for most budding teenagers, but for boys who are as shy as I was, asking a girl for a date is a daunting task, a minefield of real and imagined horrors. I was slowly working up the nerve to ask Beverly out, but the idea that she might turn me down cold was not nearly as frightening as the alternative. The pain of a resounding "No!" would end my crush with the speed and precision of a surgeon's scalpel, but the anxiety generated by a good-natured acceptance might fester unchecked, growing until the fateful day arrived, and the date—plus the blossoming hope that accompanies such excursions—was at hand.

If anyone had asked me what specific personality traits of Beverly's I found appealing, I might have told them I liked her sense of humor. Sure, I was also drawn by her good looks, but ACS was swarming with good-looking girls, as if a genetic experiment to produce beautiful females had been secretly tested on military families with stunning results. Other than that, my feelings were a mystery, even to myself. I rarely spoke to Beverly unless we were with a group of friends or in one of the classes we shared, so I really didn't know her very well. We'd never had an intimate conversation, but I talked to Marie one-on-one all the time. She was like the sister I never had, so one day, at her house, I decided to let her in on my clever plan.

"I'm going to ask Beverly out," I finally confessed.

"Really?" Marie asked. She seemed taken aback, as if this was outside my social experience (which it was), or maybe the idea that I had eyes for Beverly had caught her by surprise.

"Yeah," I defended. "Why not?"

"I don't know. Where?"

"I was thinking of Mac's party."

"But she was going there anyway."

"Yeah, I know, but I figured I could pick her up at her place, and we could go together."

"What then?"

"I don't know, usual stuff." I hadn't thought that far in advance. "You ever ask her who she likes?"

"Yeah, but she just says, 'Oh, I don't know' and smiles."

"Well, I'm going to ask her out anyway, so I guess it doesn't matter."

When I asked Marie whether she thought asking Beverly out was a good idea, she said, "What's the worst she could say? No?"

I always wondered why guys always had to do the asking anyway. I was sure the world would be a better, happier place if we men could simply flash a smile and wink at the girls, then sit back and let them approach us. As it is, when a guy gathers his resolve to make that lonely phone call, fear enters his mind like a thief, prepared to steal his confidence at the first hint of rejection.

Now that I had expressed my intentions to Marie, I decided to calm down, rehearse my lines, and pick up the phone. I refused to be paralyzed by my own fears, so I resolved that if Beverly said no or made up a transparently phony excuse, I'd chalk it up to experience and get over it.

At home that night, I dialed Beverly's number, and my palms immediately turned clammy. "Hello, Beverly?"

It was Beverly's mother. "Hold on, I'll get her."

I could still hang up, I thought. She doesn't know it's me.

"Hello?" Beverly said.

"Hi, this is Les."

"Oh, hi," she said, casually. "What's up?"

"Mac's having a party Saturday night and I was wondering if you wanted to go."

"Yeah, I heard. Sure, that'd be great."

"Cool," I said, trying to match her relaxed tone of voice. "I'll see you about eight."

As I hung up the phone, I noticed Lynn listening in on the conversation. Inside, my spirit was bounding like a baby kangaroo, but I maintained a blank expression. I knew that if he figured out what my phone call was about, I'd have to listen to multiple choruses of "Les has a girlfriend!" from him. I fetched my books, went upstairs, and sat at my desk. I struggled to concentrate on a math assignment as I fondled the silver identity bracelet in my pocket.

Because ACS had no class ring, when Brats went steady, a boy would give his girl a solid silver identity bracelet to wear instead. Identity bracelets were mostly just for giving to girlfriends, and it was rare to see a boy actually wearing one. Bob, Spike, and Mac each had a bracelet; it was a tradition. I still had money left from trading currency before the coup d'état, so I could easily afford one. I went alone to buy the bracelet on Tu Do Street and paid the jeweler to engrave my name in big swirly italics: LES.

On Saturday, I drove myself and everyone else in the house crazy trying to find the right outfit. Checking my clothes in Mother's bedroom mirror, I argued silently for and against each item: The Ban-Lon's too hot and looks stupid besides, I told myself. The pinstripe should do it. Girls go for that Ivy League style, and it makes my shoulders look more imposing.

But one look in the mirror convinced me otherwise: Too boring, I decided. I'll try the custom with the three-quarter-length sleeves. . . No. Too ho-dad. Let's try the Ban-Lon again.

I walked back into the bedroom and the shirt was gone. "Fuck! Lynn! What'd you do with my Ban-Lon shirt?"

He was sitting near the window at his desk, and didn't bother to look up from the model plane he was working on. "It was on my bed. Don't put it on my bed."

"I'm sorry, your majesty. Now where the hell is it?"

"I told Lowell to throw it in the dirty clothes."

"You . . . shit. I give up." I took two steps toward the clothes hamper and changed my mind. I didn't have time to fight with Lynn. These pants, that shirt, those socks. What felt right one minute looked like a clown suit the next. Finally, I donned the pinstripe shirt and went to the bathroom to obsess about my hair, teeth, pimples, pants, shoes, and socks: areas where immediate improvements could easily be made.

When I was finally ready, I went outside and flagged down a cab. Normally, I would have fired up a smoke as soon as the cab pulled away, but tonight I didn't want to kill the delicate manly scent of Doc's Aqua Velva aftershave. At Beverly's, I asked the cabbie to wait and went to the front door. She must have seen me coming, because before I could knock, the door opened and she walked out onto the veranda.

Beverly liked to wear tight clothes, and tonight she had worn her best: a sleek green skirt and matching blouse filled to overflowing with her feminine charm. Her red hair was carefully teased, and I marveled at the voluptuous, mature woman who stood before me. Not so she could see me marveling, of course, but one glance at her, and I knew I had my hands full.

"That was quick," I said.

"My little sister's getting too nosy for her own good."

I saw her sister's face and hands pressed against the window glass, her tongue sticking against the pane. She may have been a mature woman to me, but not, apparently, to her sister. Beverly threw her a disapproving scowl as we walked toward the street.

With Grandma Margaret's etiquette lessons resonating in my mind, I held Beverly's cab door open, then directed the driver to Mac's house while struggling to appear relaxed, a difficult task in the presence of such a radiant beauty. As the cab turned onto Cong Ly Street, I glanced at Beverly out of the corner of my eye. The setting sun lit her face, and each freckle glowed like an island of love, promising pleasures beyond compare.

On the ride to Mac's, I strained to think of something to say. It finally occurred to me that I'd never been alone with Beverly until now. Then I remembered something Bob had told me a few days before. "I hear you and Marie got caught by the white mice last week."

"It was my fault." She smiled a guilty smile. "I'm the one who brought the paint."

"Were you the one who decorated the street?" I asked.

She laughed with the squinty, almost bucktoothed smile she would sometimes get when embarrassed. I wanted to make her laugh all the time.

Late the previous Saturday night, she and Marie had slipped out of her house for a little nocturnal mischief. They hired a motor-cyclo and rode through the deserted streets of downtown Saigon, paying the driver to stop occasionally so they could spray-paint a tribute to Mrs. Rehnquist on the pavement in bright pink: "PINQ RIHNQ STINQ." They were urban graffiti innovators, decades ahead of the cultural curve. One of Saigon's finest white mice had broken up their late-night painting party and tried to arrest them.

"Yeah, but it was her idea," she confessed.

"You're lucky you had enough bribe money," I said. Saigon had the best police that money could buy. Marie's dad had trained them well.

"I was more worried about what Mrs. Rehnquist would do if she found out. I'd rather take my chances with the police."

We pulled up in front of Mac's house. On the sidewalk in front, Spike and Frankie were sitting against Spike's moped as if it were a park bench. Their shirts were unbuttoned to the middle of their chests, sleeves rolled up a couple of turns, cigarettes hanging from the corners of their mouths. Their tall, greasy pompadours were nearly identical.

"You two look like twin brothers," Beverly said.

Frankie jumped off the moped. "If he was my brother, I'd kill myself."

Spike pulled the cigarette from his mouth and threw him a derisive glare. "If you were my brother, I'd help you."

"Anybody inside?" I asked.

"A few people," Spike said. "Mostly Harry's friends." Spike arched his eyebrows, glancing quickly at Beverly and then at me. I had never let on to Spike that I liked her, so I wasn't surprised by his curiosity. I shrugged at Spike, and Beverly and I walked up the stairs.

Mac's home was a townhouse, but on a much grander scale than where I lived. The ceiling in the living room was two stories high, plus the home had a large garage with the servant's quarters above. The oriental rugs that usually graced the floors had been rolled up and put away, along with the Chinese ceramics and anything else breakable. The kitchen bustled with Vietnamese servants preparing snacks, filling coolers with ice, and arranging trays. The furniture in the living room had been pushed against the walls, and in one corner, the Esquires, the most exciting teenage American combo in Vietnam, were warming up. When I saw the band, I felt like kicking myself for not bringing my sax.

I knew I wasn't much of a catch for a girl as pretty as Beverly. I spoke with a slight lisp, was blessed with a bumper crop of pimples, and had a nose oily enough to grease a frying pan. My voice changed octaves at the most embarrassing times, such as every time I opened my mouth, and Lynn was always eager to remind me that my hairstyle was vaguely reminiscent of Julius Caesar.

But if I had brought my *horn* with me, I could've played a tune with the Esquires and captivated Beverly like a snake charmer coaxing a cobra from a basket. After all, what woman can resist a man with a sax in his hands and a song in his heart?

"Want something to drink?" I asked.

"Sure, a Coke would be nice." Beverly waved at the door. "There's Marie and Bob."

I went to get drinks as the band lit into their repertoire. The Esquires had a short list of songs and no singer, so I knew they'd blow through all their tunes in about fifteen minutes. When the Esquires finished their set, Eileen and Joyce would take over. They were standing in the corner next to the record player, sifting through stacks of 45s.

Mac and Harry were among the most popular kids in school, and all of their considerable charm had gone into making this a party to be remembered. It seemed as if every American kid in Saigon was there. When the record player took over from the band, the party started rocking out with a vengeance, as if we were collectively saying, *to hell with the Viet Cong!*

As I slipped through the crowd holding our drinks, I noticed John Johnson leaning over to talk to Beverly. He walked away before I arrived.

"What did *he* want?" I asked, handing Beverly her Coke.

"He was bugging me to dance, but I told him I was waiting for a drink."

I didn't know whether John had seen me show up with Beverly, but I figured that the best way to keep him at bay was to keep her busy. "C'mon, let's dance." I took her hand and we moved into the crowd. In a few minutes, Spike, Marie, and the rest of our group joined in. After three or four fast tunes, Beverly put her hand to her mouth and shouted to Marie, but I couldn't hear what she said. When the tune ended, they left the dance floor and went upstairs.

"Where are they going'?" I asked Spike.

"I don't know. Powder their noses, I guess."

The living room was oppressively hot, filled with the sweaty bodies of dozens of teenagers. I couldn't wait to get outside. "Well, I'm going to have a smoke."

Spike and Bob followed me down the front stairs to the sidewalk. Even at this hour, the air temperature on the street was hovering around 90 degrees, but it felt cooler than inside.

Spike pulled out a Marlboro and tapped the filter end on the pack. "What's up with you and Beverly?"

"Nothing," I lied. I retrieved a Pall Mall from my shirt pocket and put it to my lips. I snapped my lighter and waited for the questions I should have known were coming.

"You like her, don't you?"

I held the flame to his cigarette. "Sure, don't you?"

Bob poked his elbow in my ribs. "You know what he means."

I took a deep drag and exhaled. They were onto me, but I didn't want to admit to my crush without knowing whether Beverly and I had any chemistry. I always wanted to be like the guy in the Dion song "The Wanderer"—a cool guy, a dispassionate Romeo who could "love 'em and leave 'em" without a backward glance, but I wasn't feeling it. Now, as Spike stared at me pointedly, I knew I had to confess to something, some level of like. "Sure, she's all right," I said, without looking him in the eye. "Where'd Frankie go?"

"I saw him with his sister and she didn't look happy," Spike said. "I think he fucked up again. You going to ask her to slow dance?"

"I don't know." I flicked my ash and looked at the curb. "Maybe."

I wanted to, but I had never slow danced with anyone. I wasn't going to embarrass myself by asking Spike about the proper technique. I decided it might be best to secretly watch some of the older kids for a few pointers.

"You're going to have to stand three feet away if you do," Spike said.

Bob and I looked at each other, puzzled. "Huh?"

"Yeah man," he continued, "you won't be able to get very close with those big ol' boobs in the way."

I glared at Spike, then laughed. "You're such a motherfucker."

"You call me a motherfucker?" He raised his fists in mock anger, dancing like a boxer, a cigarette jutting out of his mouth. "You can't talk about my mama like that."

Bob raised his skinny fists, cutting in front of me to defend my honor. I watched them play-spar for a bit, then I took a last drag, threw my half-finished cigarette in the gutter, and returned to the party. It was time for a crash course in slow dancing. I needed to learn sooner or later, I thought. Might as well do it now.

I pushed through the crowd to the staircase on the far side of the room. I watched the dancers from the perimeter, hoping Eileen would spin a slow tune while Beverly was still with Marie, but, unfortunately, an up-tempo tune, "Surf City," was playing. Then, in one corner, I saw Phil Boyd and Minnie dancing close and tight, moving in a slow rubato to a song that apparently only they could hear. I found an empty chair nearby and sat down to watch on the sly.

This was a lesson from a master, and I, like a devoted disciple, paid attention to each detail: Phil's right hand on the small of Minnie's back, her right hand in his left, held near shoulder height, as they curved into each other like dozing cats. I watched his feet closely also—I was sure I had two of the left variety. Boyd moved with an easy, confident smoothness, as if he'd done this a thousand times, qualities I intended to acquire within the next few minutes. The song continued at a moderate tempo as the couple danced out of sync to Jan and Dean, but in perfect time to the internal jukebox spinning romantic ballads in their heads. Minnie laid her head on Phil's shoulder, closed her eyes, and sighed.

Instead of asking Beverly to slow dance, I decided to skip the awkward question, wait until we were already on the floor, then wordlessly segue from a fast tune to a slow one as if I knew what I was doing. I could have her slow dancing in my arms before she knew what had happened.

I saw Eileen at the record player choosing tunes, so I decided to help with some important musical decisions and stack the deck. I went over and sorted through the records until I found two special songs. A minute later I saw Beverly and Marie coming out of the kitchen.

"Will you play these two for me?" I asked Eileen.

"Sure. Now?"

"Yeah. Play this one first."

I squeezed my way to the other side of the room as the Beach Boys lit into "Barbara Ann." I picked a spot near the dance floor, one I knew Beverly would have to pass, and when our eyes met, I waved her onto the dance floor. Marie and Spike joined in, and soon the whole crew was clapping with the rhythm, pulsing with energy and intensity. The dance floor was packed with perspiring bodies, swaying in the thick heat.

As the song faded, I slid closer to Beverly. The crowd paused as the first strains of "Surfer Girl" filled the room. I took a deep breath, placed my hand on Beverly's waist, and turned towards her. I acted nonchalant, looking past her into the crowd. She raised her right hand, I took it in mine, and we began to sway.

I slipped my hand to the small of her back, as I had seen Phil do with Minnie. I was hoping Beverly would rest her head on my shoulder, but if she didn't, that was okay. Things were going much better than I had expected.

We danced ear to ear, and I could smell her hair, the sweet, intoxicating bouquet of her perfume mixing with the fragrance of Prell. Her breasts pressed gently against my chest. Someone dimmed the lights, and we moved in rhythm with the secret place in my heart.

When the song ended, I realized that my mouth was dry, and my palms weren't. I excused myself and went into the kitchen for a glass of water. I wanted to be alone for a moment so I could review our slow dance in my mind. I was giddy with relief that things had gone so well and pleased that I hadn't stepped on her feet. Slow dancing wasn't so hard after all, I told myself. I drank long and deep, savoring the fresh memory of her warm body flush against mine. I couldn't wait to feel that sensation again.

It wasn't long before one of the servants entered the kitchen and chased me out into the living room, back into the frenetic energy of the party. Spike and Bob were at the record player bugging Joyce and Eileen, and Frankie was dancing with one of the eighth-grade girls, but Beverly and Marie were nowhere in sight, so I elbowed my way through the crowd to go outside.

On my way down the front stairs, I saw Marie standing next to a taxi. It pulled away from the curb, and she stepped onto the sidewalk, turned, and seemed surprised to see me. Then her brow furrowed and a look of concern darkened her face.

"You feel all right?" I asked.

"Les—"

"Where'd Beverly go?" I thought she might be in the cab, but somehow it didn't seem right.

"That was her in the cab."

The cab disappeared around a corner one block away. "Is she okay?"

"I don't know how to tell you this."

"Tell me what?" It slowly dawned on me that I was asking questions that involved answers I didn't want to hear, but I couldn't stop myself. "What's going on?"

She walked away, but I followed her. "Come on, what's up?"

She turned. Her expression was gloomy. "She asked John to take her home."

I mentally sifted through a list of possible Johns. The only one I could think of was the worst one. "John Johnson?" I winced in disbelief.

"Yeah. Les—"

I stood glued to the sidewalk as her words settled on my mind. There *are* worse things than getting turned down for a date.

"Les, sometimes—"

"Did I do something? I don't get it."

"You didn't do anything wrong, Les. You were nice to her. Maybe too nice."

"How the fuck can you be too nice?"

"I think you scared her." She paused. "Les, try to understand..."

I shuffled away from the glare of the streetlight, into the shadows. "I understand. It's okay." I made a move and she didn't know how to tell me to fuck off, so she bolted. But it made no sense that she'd left with John Johnson, unless of course she had a crush I didn't know about.

Marie followed me. "If you want to talk, will you come by tomorrow?"

"Yeah, sure."

She flashed a faint smile, and walked toward the stairs. I think she knew I wouldn't be coming by.

The party was still going strong. I lit a cigarette and slouched the five blocks home.

Chapter Twenty-Eight

Down by the River

The next day, I didn't want to talk to Marie, Spike, or anyone else. I needed to settle into that most endearing and popular of the teenage arts, sulking. Why Beverly had asked John to take her home instead of, let's say, whacking me in the head with a shovel had me baffled. Given a choice, I would have taken the shovel. I stayed in bed until I couldn't take it anymore, then left the house without breakfast, desperate to get away from anyone who might start asking pointed questions about my sour demeanor. Alone, I might be able to rethink the previous night's events, maybe even convince myself that I still had a chance with Beverly or that things weren't as bad as they seemed.

The city was calm and cool, at least as calm as Saigon ever got. Dozens of motorbikes and cabs still commanded the streets, but because it was Sunday, the pace was rather slow and relatively peaceful.

I caught a motor-cyclo, lit the first in a long chain of cigarettes, and directed the driver to take me past Notre Dame Cathedral, where Mass was beginning. Neatly dressed Americans, French, and Vietnamese parishioners were filing into the cool of the nave. Had I been a devout Catholic, I might have sought answers there, but I had never accepted the Catholic Church's views on God or spirituality. I wouldn't have known what to pray for, anyway. Peace? Happiness? Beverly's affection? I was pretty sure that the God I didn't believe in had better things to do than grant wishes to lovesick teens.

I cruised down Doung Duy Tan for a few blocks past the bowling alley, but I couldn't stop there, because Spike or one of the crowd might show up, and I didn't want to face them. I continued downtown toward Tu Do Street. The air was fresh and crisp, so I let the motor-cyclo go at the Rex Hotel and sulked my way down Tu Do Street. The nightclubs were closed, but the stench of the previous night's business in the bales of trash outside the nightclubs and bars was unusually offensive. The sidewalks were nearly empty.

The more I thought about Beverly, the less I understood. The only thing worse than being a fool is finding out that you've been a fool. Why hadn't I seen it coming? What sort of blindness had led me to believe that she could see me as more than a friend? Her rejection cut me like a knife, but the worst part was that she knew damn well how I felt about John Johnson, but chose him to escort her home anyway. That was Olympic-level knife twisting.

I reached the end of Tu Do Street and passed the My Canh restaurant. A rusty old ferry was already moving across the Saigon River in the morning heat. Farther down, crude, thatched-roof boats were huddled at the docks between larger ships. I wandered along the riverbank, watching children play fisherman, dragging their hand lines up the stone launch ramps with glee, casting them into the murky water again and again. I'd never envied any Vietnamese person before today.

I wandered onto a dock and sat down on a piling next to an ancient tugboat. The river on the opposite shore was dotted with huts supported by waterlogged pilings, the lush jungle canopy dominating the background. In my peripheral vision, the river's movement pushed seaward, relentless and unbroken, its gentle turbulence at once soothing and ominous. But the murky brown water near my feet didn't seem to be moving at all.

I took the silver ID bracelet out of my pocket, raised my hand to throw it—and stopped. I stared at the engraving. Sunlight flashed off the ID tag, and I remembered the way I felt the day I bought it. How quickly my feelings had changed! My optimism and sweet infatuation were gone, replaced with bitterness and humiliation. I argued silently with myself, blaming Beverly one minute, myself the next, then John Johnson, then back around to Beverly, growing more frustrated with each pass. The ID bracelet had become a glaring and insistent reminder of how foolish I'd been. I hated the sight of it.

I got up and walked back to the kids I'd seen playing fisherman. When they saw me approaching, they smiled and held their hands out, hoping that the rich American had something for them. I should have thrown them the bracelet, but I walked by without a word, consumed by my own misery. The next day I went back to Tu Do Street and sold it back to the jeweler I'd bought it from.

As the wet season gave way to the dry, avoiding demonstrations and riots became part of our daily routine in Saigon. My family, friends, and I detoured and took precautions wherever we went, never quite certain when or where we were safe. I never sat at outdoor cafés for fear of grenades, and I carefully scrutinized my cabbies and motor-cyclo drivers for any evidence that might suggest foul intentions. Whenever I caught a cab or motor-cyclo, I never told the driver the destination; instead, I gave him specific directions and was always prepared to bail out if he didn't follow my instructions explicitly. Awareness was essential to survival.

After the theater bombing, ACS and its buses were placed under military guard twenty-four hours a day. Spike and I could no longer get away with smoking on the bus; to prevent grenades from being tossed in, its windows were fixed so that they couldn't be opened more than an inch. Cigarette smoke would be detected instantly. Every afternoon, we boarded our bus, now as hot as a sauna, for the trip home from school, ever aware of the possibility of a Viet Cong attack.

Just two months after Diem was removed from power, General Duong Van Minh's ruling junta was overthrown in a bloodless coup by the ambitious General Nguyen Khanh. General Khanh was careful to see to it that Nguyen Van Nhung, one of General Minh's toadies (and well-known as the officer who had murdered Diem and Nhu), was executed.

Rumors of political conspiracies flowed through the American community daily. According to Doc, most high-level Vietnamese Army officers were involved in several plots, often playing one side against the other just to be safe. During dinner time at home, he frequently provided simplified versions of what he'd been hearing at the station: "The generals, Minh and Khanh and Don and Kim and Major Nhung, overthrew Diem and Nhu, but then Khanh overthrew Minh and Don and Kim; but he had Nhung shot because he'd killed Diem and Nhu and was too dangerous to keep around. But Khanh felt guilty about Nhung's execution because Nhung worked for Minh, so he made Minh Head of State and put Don and Kim on trial for treason." It sounded like a Marx Brothers script, but with lots of blood and no harp.

After the coup, Saigon calmed down for a while. But when militant Buddhists and student activists discovered that many of the players in Diem's government had reappeared in new positions, they once again marched in protest, shutting down traffic and occasionally metastasizing into violent mobs. The chaos was almost as rampant as when Diem was president.

Because of massive corruption, bickering, and infighting, the new government failed to inspire or rally the country's people to its cause. President Lyndon Johnson had privately voiced concern about the wisdom of the U.S. efforts in Viet Nam (as had Kennedy), but in the spring of 1964 he reaffirmed his commitment to winning the war and appointed General Westmoreland to the role of Deputy Commander of the Military Assistance Command, Viet Nam (MACV). Westmoreland was slated to replace General Paul Harkins in June, 1964. The Viet Nam War was escalating.

Chapter Twenty-Nine

California Bound

F lirting with a strange girl at a party or asking one to dance can be a fear-inspiring ritual for a teenager, but trying to get cozy with a friend is much riskier. Getting dumped would've been easier to stomach if I never had to see Beverly again. I could turn my eyes and avoid her at school, but it was inevitable that we would eventually come face to face.

For a week after the party I dodged her, trying to forget our aborted "date." I even avoided Marie, knowing that she'd want to talk it over. But I didn't want to relive the whole stinking mess. One day I met up with Spike, and we rode over to the bowling alley. When we pulled up, Frankie was sitting on the steps to the building, leaning back on his elbows. Spike parked his moped and we sat down with Frankie, waiting to see who else might come by. I didn't want to talk about Beverly, but Frankie and Spike obviously thought that what I needed was some manly advice, culled from their extensive experience with women.

"Don't let her get you pissed off, man," Spike advised.

"Maybe she was on the rag," Frankie said. "My sister gets like that."

"Your sister's like that when she ain't on the rag, too," Spike said. He leaned over my shoulder and whispered, "There's plenty of other chicks around, man."

"Yeah, I know." Guys always say that kind of crap to each other, but they only believe it when it's someone else's broken heart. Besides, it's hard to sing a new song when you can't get the old one out of your head.

"Don't listen to that shit she's saying about you, man," Frankie said.

His comment stopped me cold. I hadn't heard any shit she was saying about me. "What are you talking about?"

Frankie chuckled a little, like the way Spike and I laughed when his sister was busting his balls. "I heard her tell Marie she thought you were a creep."

Spike gave him an angry look, punching him in the shoulder. "Shut the fuck up, Frankie."

Frankie rubbed his arm as he scooted away from Spike. "Well, you heard it too."

"Is that what she said?" I asked. Spike raised his hand again as if to slap Frankie, and I realized it was true.

"It was just girl talk, man," Spike said, turning his attention to me. "It doesn't mean shit."

I didn't know what it meant, but I didn't like it. Just when I thought I was getting over her, I felt anger flooding back. "Yeah, I was saying the same thing about her the other day," I lied. I was, but only to myself.

A cab pulled up and Bob got out and joined us. "Did you tell him what happened?" he asked Frankie and Spike.

"Oh, yeah," Spike said. "We snuck out of Bob's after the party."

Frankie pointed at Spike. "'Cause of this fucker we got caught by the white mice."

Spike's face lit up as he related their adventure. "We was over on Hai Ba Trung Street and I had these goose eggs, and a cop saw me throw one at a cab. We ditched down an alley and stayed there for about fifteen minutes. . ."

"And when we came out," Frankie interrupted, "these cops on motorbikes caught us and wanted to take us to the police station."

"Don't interrupt, shit-ass," Spike warned.

"And they wanted to know what we were doing, so we told 'em, 'We're going home. . .'"

"Don't *interrupt!*" Spike slapped Frankie in the back of the head, knocking his hair across his forehead. Frankie shot him an irritated scowl, retrieved a comb from his pants pocket, and set to straightening out his pompadour.

"They put us in a paddy wagon with a bunch of criminals," Bob continued, "and hauled us to the big precinct in Cho Lon."

"Like I was saying," Spike continued. "They was gonna throw us in jail, but we kept saying, 'we gotta go home, we gotta go home.'"

Frankie shifted away from him. "I was the one who kept saying it."

"You already shot your mouth off, so shut up, grease-ball," Spike warned.

"Well, I did! You just sat there."

"Bullshit."

"I finally convinced them we weren't throwing eggs at the cars," Bob explained. "Then they got a Vietnamese cop to take us to Hong Kong BEQ

(Bachelor Enlisted Quarters), and he told the MPs he wanted to throw us in jail."

"Don't look now, but guess who's here," Spike said.

Marie and Beverly had pulled up in a cab. Marie opened the door, then evidently changed her mind when she saw me. Beverly didn't move. She mumbled something to Marie and smiled nervously, looking embarrassed.

I stepped toward the cab, took hold of the side window of the open door and peered in. "Hey, Bev. What's with the big smile? You're grinning like a stuck pig."

Her smile vanished. "You're such a *jerk.*"

Marie tried to close the door, but I wasn't done. I tilted my head and faked a concerned look. "A *jerk*?" I said, sarcastically. I threw Spike and Bob a quizzical glance, then turned back toward the cab and Beverly. "Damn! I thought I was a *creep*!"

"Beverly and I are leaving, Les," Marie said. She frowned at me and slammed the door. "I hope you're happy, now."

I managed a nasty chuckle. "Close enough." As the cab pulled away, I welcomed the poison I saw in Beverly's eyes. I'd rather be hated than pitied.

As the cab sped off, I shed my phony smile and resumed feeling like crap. I thought I was getting over it, but one sight of her just stirred the cauldron of emotions I had been struggling to avoid, an ugly stew of loss and rejection. I didn't feel any better for it, but I had to say something.

Bob came up to me and rested his hand on my shoulder. "Come on, man. Let's go to the Thirty-Three."

The four of us strolled over to the Cafe' "33" and sat down for a smoke and a warm Ba Muoi Ba beer. I'd been so consumed with myself that I had forgotten to tell them the news. "My dad might be getting orders next week," I said.

A few days later, Doc confirmed to us that he was being transferred yet again. In Saigon, the constant violence and turmoil (and the prospect of more to come) had frayed Mother's nerves as thin as the fringe on an old rug. She'd been badgering Doc to request a transfer ever since Quang Duc's immolation, so she was naturally happy that we were getting out of Saigon. When she heard the news, she didn't get upset at all.

None of us boys wanted to leave, as usual, but this move was different. I knew that wherever we were going would never be as interesting as Saigon, nor was there any chance of our passing through Saigon on the way to another assignment. In the world as seen through the eyes of the U.S. military establishment, Saigon was the last stop on the way to nowhere. Wherever we ended up, I was sure I wouldn't know a single person there.

Lynn had been hanging out at AFRS with Doc when the orders came in. "We're going to Los Angeles as soon as school's out," he told me.

I knew we had to move sooner or later—I never expected to spend the rest of my life in Vietnam—but I'd figured we were good for another year or so. "It feels like we just got here," I said, annoyed. "I don't want to move *again*." In spite of my romantic split with Beverly and my run-ins with Mrs. Rehnquist, I felt comfortable in Saigon, as if I belonged there.

"They're talking about evacuating American dependents, anyway," Lynn added. "The MPs found a bike rigged with plastic explosives next to the bowling alley."

I never gave much thought to the dangers of living in a place as volatile as Saigon, although I'm sure my parents did. Terrorist attacks and riots had become commonplace, but I still wanted to be with my friends, not exiled to some crushingly boring suburb in America. The burdens of finding new friends, starting at a new school, and learning the ins and outs of a new neighborhood seemed more daunting as I grew older.

I called Spike to tell him about our new destination, but he wasn't home, so I took a cab to the bowling alley. He wasn't there either. I walked to the Cafe' "33" where I found Spike and Frankie at our usual table, smoking and trying to finish off some warm Beer LaRue ("Tiger Piss," as we called it). Spike's grin was smeared across his face, but he didn't need beer for that.

"Hey man. What's going on?"

"I just found out we're moving to Los Angeles." I knew Spike loved California because he talked about it all the time.

"Cool, man," he responded. "Maybe you can learn to surf."

"I don't know." Surfing didn't seem like much of a consolation for being uprooted again. "I'm tired of moving all the time."

"My dad says we're going to Oakland when we move back," Spike said. "You can come visit."

"How far is Oakland from Los Angeles?"

"It's up by San Francisco. What're you going to do with your dog?"

"Give him away. You want him?"

"Yeah, but my dad won't let us have another one." He took a big gulp of beer and thought for a moment.

"Whatever you do, don't give him to David Phu. He'll end up on the menu at Cheap Charlie's."

"Have you told Marie or Beverly yet?" Frankie asked.

"Beverly will probably be happy I'm gone. I haven't seen Marie yet."

After what happened at the party, I'd found it difficult to talk to Marie about the scene with Beverly, although she had gently brought it up a few times. I dodged the subject until she finally quit asking me about it. I did become a more careful listener, though, and had I adopted this habit sooner, I might have been able to pick up on Beverly's overwhelmingly platonic attitude toward me. The whole nasty affair could've been avoided.

Spike finished his beer and we walked to the bowling alley. We were sitting on the steps when Bob showed up. His perspective on my father's reassignment was different. "You're lucky," he told me. "I was so young when I left the States, I don't even remember what it's like there. I remember Karachi better than I do the U.S."

"Yeah, but all my friends are here. I don't know anybody in LA."

"What about Scott Pettigrew?" Spike said. "He'll be going back to Malibu soon."

"I don't even hang out with Scott here," I pointed out.

Spike got up and unchained his moped from a nearby tree. Frankie sat down on the rear and said, "How about a ride? I have to meet my dad at the *Cercle Sportif*."

"He still paying you to play tennis with him?" Spike asked.

"Yeah. Ever since I beat him."

"Must have thrown you a mercy win," Bob joked.

"Did not. I beat him fair and square."

Spike pedaled a little to start the moped. "Sure you did, man." He winked at us. "Sure you did."

"I did too!"

Bob was laughing now. "Hey, we believe you."

"Well, fuck all'a' y'all! Come and watch right now, then."

Bob looked at Spike and me. "I'll get you in if you want to go."

"All right," I said. "Let's go watch Frankie whip his dad's ass."

"I'll beat him good," Frankie bragged. "Y'all wait and see."

Bob and I took a cab to the *Cercle* and arrived about the same time as Frankie and Spike. The sentry was asleep in the guardhouse—it was siesta time—so Spike chained his bike to the inside of the gate, and we all strolled in like we owned the place.

Frankie's dad was waiting at the courts in white shorts and shirt, bouncing a ball against the wall, clearly irritated by his son's tardiness. When Frankie walked onto the court, his father pointed to a racket lying against the fence, then took his position on the other side of the net.

Spike, Bob, and I watched through the outer fence. Frankie grinned at us sheepishly as they started a warm-up volley, Mr. Hunter smashing shots over the net at a furious pace, as if he wanted to punish his son for being late. Frankie ran back and forth across the court, swinging wildly at the ball, lobbing it into the net on the rare occasions when he could hit it at all. He began sweating and his grin vanished.

When Frankie and his father started keeping score, we lost interest. Frankie didn't stand a chance. He must have been relieved when we left. Bob suggested we check the pool bar to see who was there, but Spike had other plans. "You guys go without me," he said. "I'm going to head home."

I knew Spike wasn't going back to the Gia Dinh neighborhood in the middle of the afternoon. He was probably going to Steve's to pull his pants down and earn a little spending money. I'd grown used to looking the other way as Spike continued his visits.

Bob and I went upstairs, sat down at the bar, and looked around the pool. A couple of the older kids from school were lounging around or swimming, while a dozen or so men and women members sipped drinks and gossiped. We hung out on the barstools for a few minutes, but none of our crowd seemed to be there.

"Let's get out of here," Bob said.

We walked out the way we had come in, and when we neared the entrance gate, I saw Spike sitting on his moped. Standing next to him was a security guard, waving his hands and shouting. Suddenly, the guard swung his arm at Spike, hitting him hard in the nose with his open hand.

"You see that?" I yelled. "Come on!"

In seconds, I was standing between the guard and Spike, screaming "Back off!" into the guard's face. I raised my fist as if to hit him.

The guard backed up and yelled, "You no come here!" He pulled out his nightstick.

Blood dribbled from Spike's nose down his chin and onto his shirt. His forearm was covered in red streaks from his attempts to wipe it away. "I'm okay, I'm okay." He looked at his arm. "I think."

I was still staring at Spike's nose when Bob began a heated conversation in Vietnamese with the guard. The guard shouted, pointing at Spike and then at the gate where his moped had been chained. Bob slid in front of Spike and blew smoke into the guard's face. Bob argued for a moment in Vietnamese, then switched to French, cursing fluently as the guard fumed and yelled, pointing first at Spike, then at me. Bob said a few more words in French followed by an epithet in Urdu I had heard him use before. The guard backed up.

"He thought I was stealing the bike," Spike explained, sniffing back the blood, "'cause he asked me for my *Cercle Sportif* ID and got mad when I didn't have one to show him."

"He oughta watch who he's hitting," I said. My anger was just beginning to wane, but Spike had already calmed down.

Another guard showed up and talked to Bob and the first guy. Finally, the bickering guards moved away from us, and Bob turned back to Spike to inspect his bloody nose.

"What'd you tell them?" I asked Bob.

"I said my dad was going to have their asses if they didn't leave us alone." He moved in for a close look at Spike's nose. "You all right?"

"Yeah. It looks worse than it is." He leaned his head back and pressed on his upper lip. "I thought you were going to clobber him there for a minute, Les."

"I thought I was too," I said.

"We should get out of here before they get any more bright ideas," Bob said.

Inside the gatehouse, the two guards continued arguing. I wondered if they were going to come back for a second round.

Spike revved his bike and sped off, the front of his shirt and his arms covered in blood. He looked like an accident searching for a place to happen. With Spike safely out of the way, Bob waved down a cab and we headed home.

It wasn't like me to get angry so quickly, but for days I had been feeling powerless and frustrated in the face of our upcoming move. That, and I was still feeling down over the fiasco with Beverly. Once again, it seemed like life was about to pass me by. When I saw Spike get slapped, I reacted as if it were my own nose that took the hit. I wanted to strike back against the unfairness around me, and the guard seemed like a convenient place to start.

But punching out the security guard, however justified it might have been, would have been a serious mistake. The management would have called the MPs, and I would have ended up trying to explain it all to Doc, who'd probably knock the hell out of me like he did on New Years Eve. The MPs would report the incident to Doc's CO, and the doghouse would become my permanent home. Fighting with Vietnamese kids was okay, but under no circumstances would Doc condone my hitting an employee of the most exclusive club in Saigon.

In the cab, Bob still seemed pissed off. "The *Cercle* isn't much fun anymore."

"You seemed to be having a good time cussin' out the guards," I reminded him. "I've never heard you speak so much French before. I think I even heard a little Urdu in there."

"I swear better in French," he said, apparently pleased that I had noticed. "It's like shitting ice cream."

Chapter Thirty

Leaving

T wo weeks after the incident at the *Cercle Sportif*, school let out for the summer. For most kids, summer is a time of freedom and sunshine, but for military and diplomatic Brats, June is moving season. The kids of ACS usually went out to Tan Son Nhut to say goodbye to those friends whose parents had been transferred, so sooner or later, everyone at ACS got a send-off. One day, half a dozen of us rode out to Tan Son Nhut to say farewell to Eileen and her family.

After a couple of choruses of "It's been nice knowing you," "I'll write every week," and "We're going to miss you," Eileen waved goodbye, walked out of the terminal onto the tarmac, and boarded the plane with her family. As the ground crew rolled the stairs away, I noticed Beverly standing alone in front of a window. I gathered my courage and walked over to stand next to her.

I fixed my gaze on Eileen's plane, taxiing slowly into position for takeoff. "I'm sorry about what I said," I told Beverly. "I didn't really mean it, you know."

Her reflection in the glass glanced at me with visible relief. "I didn't mean the stuff I said either."

I fumbled with the cigarette pack in my pocket, looking at Beverly and then at the floor. I was glad to be putting the experience behind me. "Let's forget about it then."

We stared out the window silently. Then Beverly spoke slowly, as if to make sure I heard her clearly. "Just so you know, when we got to my place, John asked me out and I told him no."

"So you don't like him?" Hearing this made me feel better. I may never have had a chance with her, but at least I wasn't passed over in favor of my worst enemy.

"No, I just needed a ride home."

Discovering this helped me understand that sometimes things aren't as they seem. She just needed a ride home—kind of like she needed a ride to the party in the first place.

But girls were still mysterious, mercurial creatures to me. Someday, I would figure out that the girls I should be dating were the ones I could have a conversation with, like Marie. It was a revelation that could have spared me a lot of trouble had it come sooner. Unfortunately, three years and five houses would pass before I even got to know another girl well enough to ask her out.

Eileen's plane accelerated quickly, rising in the unusually steep trajectory that pilots flying out of Ton Son Nhut airport used to avoid harassing gunfire from local Viet Cong. The VC liked to take potshots at any American airborne object, though I don't remember hearing any reports of damaged aircraft. The possibility of a goodbye fusillade from the VC always added a bit of extra excitement to any departure from Ton Son Nhut.

Our arms went up in a final farewell, a band of gypsies bidding goodbye to one of their own. I watched the silver aircraft climb into the hot afternoon sky and felt my spirit lighten. Beverly and I could be friends again, our soured relationship no longer hanging in the air between us like rotting fruit.

Our Farewell banquet on the My Kanh, June, 1964. From left to right: Mother, Unknown American, Lynn, David Phu, Lowell, the Author, Mr. Phu, Doc, Mrs. Phu, Unknown American

A couple of weeks later, I found myself standing in Ton Son Nhut airport waiting to leave, a day I had dreaded for months. I was once more being whisked into exile by the swirling currents of American politics and military expediency, phenomena completely out of my control. The past was a series of fond memories; my future was a black, unknowable slate.

Beverly, Spike, Marie, Mac, Frankie, and Bob came to see me off, standing in the terminal with my family. David Phu and his parents showed up to say goodbye. Thi Hai and Cuc made the trip too, Ti crying and hugging us over and over while Cuc looked on, her usual brassy smile gone.

I tried to keep the conversation light by joking around, but eventually the waiting ended. The steel ramp-stand had been rolled into place against the side of the plane. I shook hands and said goodbye, trying not to reveal the quaver that had gotten a strangle-hold on my voice. My family and I filed out of the terminal, climbed the stairs into the plane, and settled into our seats. Mother smiled at Doc, Lynn, Lowell, the stewardesses, me, the pilot—she was just glad to be leaving, I guessed. Even Doc was in a good mood for a change.

"I hope the VC are sleeping late today," Lynn quipped.

I ignored him and stared out the window, watching my friends inside the terminal goofing off, Spike teasing Frankie, Marie and Beverly laughing, Bob and Mac watching it all. Once we were airborne, they'd hop a cab to the bowling alley or to Brodard's. That weekend, they'd attend dances and parties and stay out all night. Their lives would go on without me.

I thought back to something Spike had said one day a few months before. We had been cruising through Cholon on his moped when we took a wrong turn and suddenly found ourselves in the middle of a riot. Protesters were lobbing rocks and bottles, burning cars, and flailing at police with picket signs. The white mice wielded what Spike later called "big ol' hairy clubs," chasing the rioters down the street, beating them to the ground, and hauling them away.

When Spike realized what we'd gotten into, he quickly turned around to backtrack. But a police van had pulled up behind us, inadvertently blocking our way out. As the angry mob turned their attention to the fresh crew of white mice, Spike gunned the engine, almost throwing me off the bike. I clawed madly for the back of the seat, the bike fishtailed for a moment, then we escaped through a narrow alley as the mob and police clashed.

Afterwards, we sat in the Cafe' "33" drinking warm Ba Muoi Ba beer and savoring the buzz of danger and adrenaline flitting through our veins. Spike took a drag on his cigarette and rocked back in his chair. He pursed his lips into a large O and blew smoke rings through the rays of light penetrating the round window near his head. Suddenly, he leaned forward through the cloud of smoke.

"Who else gets to do this kind of shit?" he asked.

"What do you mean?

"I mean, my friends in Oakland aren't going to believe me when I tell 'em all the stuff we saw here. They'll think I'm lying my ass off."

It was only now, as I sat slouched into my cramped airplane seat, sullenly staring at the terminal, that I realized how lucky I had been to live in Saigon. I'd discovered something special here, a sense of liberation from the dull daily routines that were anathema to me. Violence, poverty, war, disease, and the adventure of living amongst the gentle, good-natured South Vietnamese people had spared me the stultifying boredom of the middle-class suburban life I'd lived in the States. But I'd also gained friends who shared in the wonders of this unusual life, and within our group, a strong bond had formed.

Our common experiences overseas were part of the often confusing, zigzag path we traveled to adulthood, a path filled with the detours and side trips that characterized most of our lives as military, civilian or Foreign Service Brats. Perhaps it wasn't the best path to maturity—it certainly wasn't a life any of us would have chosen prior to moving overseas—but like any other childhood, our unique circumstances became a lens through which we could view and understand each other and the world, and finally, ourselves.

At certain times, some places mark the crossroads of history. They're imbued with an energy so strong it's palpable, like a lightning storm bearing down, mighty and inevitable. Destiny permeates such places, and everything that happens does so decisively, as if manipulated by an unknown mechanism or unseen hands. Viet Nam in the 1960's was such a place: a country of beauty and peril, and as brutal as life in Saigon could be, I wanted it no other way. Maybe it was just the idealism or foolishness of adolescence, but Saigon had gotten into my blood. The air would never again smell so sweet.

I had reluctantly begun to accept the fact that this period of my life was over, that the adventures of the previous eighteen months could not be reclaimed or repeated. But I felt as if I'd arrived just a few days ago! How could I possibly replace the friends and places I was leaving behind? I had no idea how to handle such a drastic change or the feeling of loss that overwhelmed me. Where was the Department of Defense manual that could wash away my blues with a few well-chosen clichés?

When the engines started up, a stewardess strolled down the aisle and asked me to buckle my seat belt. It was almost like she was telling me, "There is no turning back." Our jet taxied to the runway, accelerated, and lifted sharply. I gazed for the last time at the lush, green countryside below. In the distance, Saigon shrank away from us, an immense wilderness of humanity sprawled across the Mekong Delta, its collage of rooftops spread like a blanket beneath high, thin clouds. The delta's silvery rivers and tributaries shimmered in the hot morning sun as water buffalo lumbered through rice paddies in a slow dance as timeless as the land itself.

My experiences in Viet Nam transformed me in ways I would feel the moment my feet touched U.S. soil; a transformation I wouldn't understand for many years. The things I'd taken for granted before I arrived in Saigon—clean water, a stable government, the relative safety of a country at peace—I would come to view with a new appreciation, an understanding of what it means to live without them. But I'd developed a taste for the novelty and excitement of living in a strange new place, and without that exotic flavor, life in the U.S. often seemed bland.

In Saigon, I'd also become part of a unique community, a group of people who usually felt as alienated from the American culture they craved as they did from the Vietnamese culture in which they found themselves immersed. Like my fellow Brats, my childhood was one of privilege and pain, entitlement and anguish, as magical, complex and spellbinding as a fairy-tale one moment, then in the next, as demoralizing, puzzling and contradictory as the conflicts, environments, and cultures of the places I learned to call home. I didn't know it then, but we Brats were part of a third stream, a new tribe of transient Americans who'd grown up in the shadows of the Cold War: Third-Culture Kids.

Unlike soldiers, we Saigon Kids had no patches to wear on our shoulders, no ribbons for our chests. We would receive no proud salutes or award ceremonies for our service. Our stories would not be published, our tales would remain untold; there would be no commendations, movies, or other recognition of our unique yet unforgettable place in history.

When I left Saigon, the feeling of belonging to this group evaporated like a wisp of steam. Now, after many years of such moves, I am often beset by a feeling of isolation that lingers deep within me, a cloud that will, without warning or provocation, intrude on the sunniest of my days. It's not a feeling of loneliness, but *aloneness*, of being apart from the mainstream of America's people. No matter where I live, I feel as though I'm standing on the outer edge of the community, never quite knowing what it's like to be on the inside. There is no town, city, or state that I can truly call home, and I once felt like an outsider at my own birthday party.

I find it easy to make friends on a superficial level and generally feel comfortable with most people in a few minutes, but it's difficult for me to go beyond polite chit-chat with anyone except my family and closest friends. Because of my constant exposure to new social environments, I've gained the ability to size up a stranger in an instant, but I often fail to recognize those few people who are true friends. I am always devastated when I discover myself making this old mistake yet again. I know now that many of my friendships have been illusions I gladly indulged in, wanting only to once again experience a feeling of acceptance. It should come as no surprise that my best friend of the last forty years is also a former military Brat.

As I grew older, I became aware of a peculiar anxiety gnawing at me. I had no name for it, nor did I understand what it was exactly. But it grew as I did, always simmering just below the surface of my emotions. Only recently have I recognized this distress as a fear that grew out of my nomadic existence as a military Brat. It's a fear I'm certain I share with many other Brats: the fear of being forgotten.

Although the recollection of those turbulent times and the friends I made in Saigon resonates continually in my life, my dreams and memories have faded over the years, their essence distilled into a pleasant nostalgia that raises its head at the oddest moments. Film clips from the Viet Nam War on TV, a trip to Chinatown, passing a Vietnamese nail parlor, even certain mysterious, delicate odors, can all evoke the Saigon I knew long ago.

Epilogue

I wrote often after we left Saigon, penning a letter to Marie the next night during our layover at Clark Air Force Base in the Philippines. A month would pass before we had a mailing address, so my initial correspondence was a strictly one-way affair. Writing was the only outlet I had to vent my frustration at being uprooted and homeless again. In this respect, nomads and gypsies may be more fortunate: they get to take their friends with them.

Doc was assigned to the Armed Forces Radio Station in North Hollywood. We settled into a new ranch-style home in Reseda, just north of Los Angeles in the San Fernando Valley, a suburb as devoid of zip and zing as Saigon's antiseptic JDP compound. The neighborhood kids were nice enough, but it was incomprehensible to me that they often preferred to hang out in their living rooms watching television instead of being outside in the sun. Except for news reports about the rapidly escalating Viet Nam War, I found it difficult to watch TV for more than a few minutes at a time. I often wandered alone through the streets of Reseda, smoking and looking for somewhere to be, something to do, longing for the odd smells of Saigon's markets, streets dense with traffic, the cool feel of the bowling alley, the sweat of everyday life and the pace of history unfolding.

Reseda nights were so calm and quiet that for months I had trouble getting to sleep. A motor-cyclo chugging by or a cab backfiring: Those were the sounds that had put me to sleep every night for the previous eighteen months. Only the occasional chirp of a cricket broke the stark, cold nighttime silence surrounding my new home.

Getting around in a city the size of Los Angeles was impossible. My only source of transportation (other than begging Mother or Doc for a ride) was the local bus, which was as slow as riding an elephant. Even buying cigarettes was difficult: California had laws against selling smokes to minors, something I had never encountered before. Staying out all night was pointless; I had nowhere to go, no way to get anywhere, and no one to go with. I'd left Oz, but I wasn't back in Kansas. Our new home felt as alien to me as Saigon had when I arrived there from Pensacola in 1963.

In the two years we lived in the San Fernando Valley, I attended three schools and lived in three houses. I never understood why we moved so much. I suppose Doc just had the itch for a better neighborhood, a bigger house, or a more convenient commute. I no longer asked why we were moving, and my parents never offered an explanation.

At school, I met no military Brats, and I found myself consigned to the hated old role of outsider. At first, whenever a kid asked where I'd moved from, I would tell them, "Saigon," or "Vietnam." My reply would usually generate a blank stare at best, or at worst, a derisive "Where the hell is *that*?" After a while, I found it easier just to tell everyone I was from Florida. The few friends I made were neighborhood kids who had never been anywhere more exciting than Disneyland. I felt no regret when, two years after we arrived, Doc was reassigned (again) and we moved to Norfolk, Virginia.

In the States, the frequency and intensity of my battles with Doc lessened considerably. We never became chummy, but without the freedom of travel I had enjoyed in Saigon, and without Spike and Bob to generate fresh trouble-making schemes, I managed to avoid pissing him off most of the time.

Doc's world was organized around the rules and regulations of the military—a strict, no-nonsense society of discipline that demanded and received fealty and obedience without question. But I hadn't sworn an oath to a set of government regulations. I remained a sensitive and self-absorbed youth, reckless and moody, dismissive of adult authority and hell-bent on discovering for myself what made the world spin. In California, I continued to bend and twist the rules and conventions of family life as much as I dared, but the bland suburbs we lived in presented little in the way of excitement or opportunities for rebellion.

Had I been more mature, I might have noticed that Doc and I were alike in some ways (which might explain why his parents sent him to military school), both of us stubborn and determined to have his way. I might have appreciated how he submitted to military discipline without complaint while shouldering the burden of providing for a large family. I might even have come to view his nagging as the only way he felt comfortable expressing his love and concern for me. But is there a teenage boy anywhere who understands his parents better than they understand him?

Due to an increase in terrorist acts against American civilians and military personnel, all American dependents were evacuated from Saigon in January of 1965. Marie was sent to boarding school in Switzerland. Bob moved to Laos with his parents, Beverly to Santa Cruz, then Singapore, and Spike to Oakland, California. I never found out where Frankie ended up, but after high school, Mac finally settled in Switzerland.

In the summer of 1965, Mother dropped me off in South Central Los Angeles. Eileen had moved from Saigon to Whittier, California, and Beverly was visiting, so the three of us had lunch and hung out for the afternoon. The bus ride I took back to Reseda was four hours long.

Ironically, I hadn't missed Beverly in the intervening time. In spite of my clumsy attempts at romance, I had never achieved the friendly intimacy with her that I enjoyed with Marie, Spike, and Bob. Later that year, I spent a few days in Oakland with Spike, and one day I saw Scott Pettigrew on the beach at Malibu with his surfboard. We talked for a few minutes. Thanks to a friend whose mother had the time and inclination to sunbathe, I eventually learned to surf, by the pier at Santa Monica beach.

One year after my family left Saigon, the Viet Cong detonated a claymore mine on the banks of the Saigon River, aimed at the My Canh Restaurant. The explosion shattered the glass walls and windows of the crowded barge and sprayed diners and staff with lethal shrapnel and debris. Moments later, as help arrived, a bicycle-mounted bomb exploded next to the tobacco stand on shore. The bombs killed forty-two people and injured more than eighty. As the war began to make headlines in America, Mr. Phu moved his family to the United States. To avoid the draft, I joined the Army in 1968 and performed in the 50th Army Band at Fort Monroe, Virginia. Shortly after my discharge in 1971, I quit smoking. I eventually moved to Boston to attend Berklee College of Music.

My father died of cancer in Scottsdale, Arizona, in 1976, a couple of weeks after he turned fifty-two. In spite of my lifetime of conflicts with

Doc, I didn't hate him. I didn't understand him, nor did he understand me, but hate is too strong a term to describe my feelings. I always sought his approval and attention, but rarely got either, so ambivalence might be a better word to describe the way I felt toward him, even as he lay dying.

In recent years, I've met and talked with a few of his military pals. They all told me what a great guy he was. Had he lived longer, I might have gotten to know him as the man he was, not the father he wasn't.

In 1980, Mother died of cancer. She was only fifty-four years old. I've always believed that the stress of Doc's death was a major contributing factor in Mother's early demise. I was living in Boston during the last few years of her life and rarely saw her, but I spoke to her often by phone and could easily hear in her voice the terrible sadness that had settled on her soul. Mother was buried next to Doc at Fort Sam Houston Cemetery in San Antonio, Texas.

Lynn was diagnosed with cancer at the same time as Mother, but he didn't want her to worry, so he didn't tell any of us about his illness until shortly after she died. He survived his ordeal, and lives in Chandler, Arizona. Lowell became a dentist and lives in Mission, Texas, the only person in our family to ever move to Mother's hometown. Lee retired from the record business in 2004 and lived in Plano, Texas, until his death in 2013 at the age of sixty-nine. Sister Kenneth Regan is still alive and well and living in Indiana.

In 2011, I located Spike and was able to talk with my old friend for a few minutes. He seemed very sad as he told me about his life and struggles with addiction. He died in 2013, at the age of sixty-four.

Through the miracle of the Internet, I've managed to track down all the members of our old group. Rehashing our past adventures has revived memories I wouldn't trade for all the hometowns in the world.

It's been great talking to them again after all these years.

About the Author

In the years between his birth in 1949 and his nineteenth birthday, Les lived in Texas, North Carolina, Florida, New Mexico, California, New Jersey, Pennsylvania, Virginia, Hawaii and Viet Nam as a dependent of the U.S. Navy. His father, Bryant Joseph Arbuckle, was a Chief Journalist who managed the Armed Forces Radio Station in Saigon, Vietnam, from June, 1962 until June, 1964.

After a stint with the 50th Army Band at Fort Monroe, Virginia Les attended the Berklee College of Music (BA) and New England Conservatory (MM). He is a professional saxophonist living near Carlsbad, California with his wife, Joyce Lucia. He has performed with a variety of musical acts including The Brian Setzer Orchestra, Lou Rawls, Bernadette Peters, The San Diego Symphony Summer Pops Orchestra and The Artie Shaw Orchestra. His recordings for the Audioquest label feature well-known jazz musicians Kenny Barron, Cecil McBee, Victor Lewis, Mike Stern and John Abercrombie.

Printed in the USA
CPSIA information can be obtained
at www.ICGtesting.com
JSHW031457130324
59156JS00018B/572

9 781633 536333